The British Reggae Music Industry. A Windrush Legacy. My Story

The British Reggae Music Industry. A Windrush Legacy. My Story

Grantley Haynes

Elaine, my biggest fan, thank you so much for supporting not only me but also Kezia. A wonderful talk. Big love

Andrew xxx

12/01/2025

Copywrite © 2024 Grantley Haynes
www.wheelerstreetproducts.co.uk
Grantley.haynes@wheelerstreetproducts.co.uk

All rights reserved.

No part of this book can be reproduced in any form or by written, electronic, or mechanical means, including photocopying, recording, or any information retrieval system, without written permission from the author.

Published by Wheeler Steet Products

Printed in Great Britain

Although every precaution has been taken in preparing this book, the publisher and author assume no responsibility for errors or omissions and no liability for damages resulting from the use of information contained herein.
ISBN 978-1-0686835-0-3

Foreword

I have had the privilege of knowing Grantley Haynes for over 30 years. For years, my husband would speak fondly of his friend Grantley, sharing stories that painted a picture of an incredible man, though I had yet to meet him. Then, my closest friend also began speaking about a remarkable individual she'd known for years, someone who inspired everyone around him with his energy and warmth. When I finally met Grantley, I immediately understood what they had been trying to convey.

Our first conversation was unforgettable, stretching well over two hours. We spoke passionately about his lifelong love of music and his impactful work in the drug and alcohol support services. His passion, compassion, dedication, and boundless enthusiasm are traits that, if bottled, would indeed make him a millionaire.

Grantley's true gift lies in his love for people and his drive to see others grow and thrive. While this book tells the story of his journey through the reggae industry, it also reveals the depth of his resilience, unyielding determination, and refusal to ever give up. I am delighted, honoured, and humbled to call Grantley a friend and a cherished extended family member.

The Right Honourable Paulette Hamilton, MP for Birmingham Erdington

Contents

The Author.................................. 8

Acknowledgements......................... 18

Introduction............................... 20

| CHAPTER 1 |

The Windrush Legacy...................... 25

| CHAPTER 2 |

Influences................................ 49

| CHAPTER 3 |

The Arrival of Bob Marley and British Reggae ... 77

| CHAPTER 4 |

British Lovers Rock 122

| CHAPTER 5 |

The British Reggae Music Industry Gathers Momentum................................ 167

| CHAPTER 6 |

Radio 181

| CHAPTER 7 |

British MCs 197

| CHAPTER 8 |

Developing My Music Management Skills...... 227

CHAPTER 9

Record Companies and Contracts 262

CHAPTER 10

Pato Banton 276

CHAPTER 11

Tippa Irie 313

CHAPTER 12

Peter Spence 343

CHAPTER 13

Music Promotion 357

CHAPTER 14

GT's Records – The Early Years and The Releases 377

CHAPTER 15

My Boyz Beatz – GTs Records............... 382

CHAPTER 16

Social Media and the Music Industry 398

CHAPTER 17

Music Past, Present and Future 409

CHAPTER 18

Mirrors and Makeup – The Musical 424

The Author

Grantley Haynes explores the historical origins and Afro-centric evolutions of British Reggae Music as a genre, shedding light on the traditions embedded in British youth culture during the 1970s and 80s. With over forty years of experience, he explores the reggae music scene in the UK in the 1980s and beyond, examining the cultural impact and responses from both black and white youths. But perhaps most importantly, he highlights the development of Lovers Rock and British MCs, emphasising the profound influence of the Windrush migration and its lasting impact on UK culture, particularly in the realm of music.

Dive into the rich history of British reggae music with *"The British Reggae Music Industry, A Windrush Legacy: My Story"*. This powerful book uncovers the roots of a musical movement that shaped British culture, tracing its origins to the Windrush Generation and their lasting influence on the music scene.

Founder of GT's Records and My BoyzBeatz launched the careers of Grammy-nominated artists like Pato Banton and Tippa Irie and renowned lovers of rock vocalist Peter Spence. A local DJ turned music promoter, he organised the landmark Birmingham Maximilian MC clash in 1985, featuring Pato Banton, Macka B, Tippa Rie, and Papa Levi. As an insider, this personal account offers a behind-the-scenes look at the evolution of reggae music in Britain. From the early struggles to the vibrant success stories, the book explores how reggae became a defining voice for a generation, blending culture, identity, and resistance.

Whether you're a music enthusiast, historian, or someone seeking to understand the impact of migration on British culture, this book offers a unique perspective. Discover untold stories, personal insights, and the deep connection between reggae, community, and resilience.

Don't miss the chance to explore this compelling narrative. Order *"The British Reggae Music Industry, A Windrush Legacy: My Story"* today and experience the legacy of British reggae music like never before!

Money, Power and Fame, a double-edged situation

Grantley doesn't play a musical instrument. However, before the release of Hello Darling by Tippa Irie, he took saxophone lessons from Birmingham's legendary Andy Hamilton. Even though he ceased to continue his lessons, they taught him how to understand musical notation, chords and progressions, runs, colours and circular breathing. He coupled this with what he learned from listening to his dad, playing his records and listening to him explain the difference between a good and a great singer. However, his overarching learning outcome came when he found he could write music by communicating notes and melodies by humming, whistling or playing bass notes using my mouth (similar to James Brown, Michael Jackson and beatboxers). This enabled him to write compositions and songs for music he planned to record and produce. These key attributes assisted him in later years when he became a music producer in the 1980s and later for My Boyz Beatz.

No matter where he was or what Grantley was doing, he couldn't forget how much he found the mixing board from the moment he saw George Harrison behind those knobs and that board; he knew then that one day it would be him behind those knobs in some shape or form. Throughout his time in the music business, Grantley would find others before and after shows doing many things; you would almost certainly find Grantley with other engineers and muso's twisting knobs creating how he wanted the artists he worked with sound.

Grantley GT is waiting for the band to arrive for a soundcheck – A water-painted sketch

1, Grantley GT at the mixing board

2, Prince Fatty at work, with Tippa & I

Moments In Time

1, Photographer, Matt, Flint, Matt Paddy McGuinness, Will Mellor Grantley GT

3, Brian Lara & Grantley GT

1, Grantley GT & John Barns

2, Grantley GT & Josie Wales

3, Tippa Irie, Peter Metro & Grantley GT

1, The guys having fun with me on tour from left Ryan, Tippa, Peter and Steven

2, Grantley GT and Shabba Ranks Reggae Land 2024

3, Grantley GT, Jazzwad and Burning Spear AKA (Winston Rodney)

Acknowledgements

Writing ***The British Reggae Music Industry: A Windrush Legacy, My Story*** has been a deeply personal journey that would not have been possible without the contributions of many people. This book reflects my experiences within the reggae scene, the rich cultural history that emerged from the Windrush generation, and its profound impact on British music and identity.

I am deeply grateful to everyone who helped make this project a reality, from family members worldwide to the relationships that encouraged me to reflect, listen, and grow. Thank you also to all those who offered their expertise and support along the way. So many thanks to Dr Martin Glyn for his encouragement and Sue Brown for the many hours she spent interviewing me, petrified that she would get it wrong, but at the same time getting it right. Thank you

A special thanks to those who assisted in editing this manuscript: Mandy Gakhal, Shane Ward, Ernie Hendricks, Mark Wallace, Marcia Brown, Robin Giorno, Eva Oluban, Little Richie, Joanne Benjamin Lewis, and Terence Wallen, who spent countless hours with me, perfecting every detail.

To those who provided thoughtful testimonials, your contributions mean so much to me.

To my two sons and grandchildren, I want you to be bold and extraordinary; this is for you. I love you all so much.

Introduction

Reggae arrived in the UK before the Windrush migration. My mother and Father came to the UK from the island of Barbados and quickly became friends with other migrants from the West Indies to begin a new life in the UK, but with no real intention to stay. They planned to return to Barbados once they had earned enough money to purchase land to build a house, buy a car, and continue living the life they had left behind.

The decision to write this book made me think hard. I thought, should I write an autobiography or a story? Finally, I decided to write a novel because I see my life as a journey that began in childhood and has progressed into a role in the British reggae music industry.

Legacy means a great deal to me. The family in the UK and abroad equally. I didn't meet either of my grandfathers, but I was told about the people they were and the roles that employed them by my parents and family friends. I remember the day my mother told me that her father was murdered while cycling home. It hurt me so much; I was devastated that I never got the chance to speak to him and listen to his stories.

Writing this book enables me to share my story so that others can read it, map the roads I have taken as part of British reggae music, and share the love in its progress. I hope this story will assist them when they look back to find solace when I am no longer there for them.

For those of you who know little about this book's subject area, I hope this book becomes an introduction to the **British Reggae Music Industry** and encourages the reader to seek its contents in greater depth, i.e. the journey of second-generation Windrush migrants, those born in Britain and witness the contributions made to the music brought to the UK by their parents. If this is the case, this book is for you.

Looking back, I have worked with many reggae artists from the UK and worldwide. Committed to writing something that accounted for my years in the field and its many areas, I took to Google and carried out several searches; I searched libraries and bookshops, but still, I had no luck.

Failing to find anything that comprehensively concentrated predominantly on British reggae music, I decided to start writing. I began including British MCs, bands, sound systems, radio, and the media and how bringing these elements together formed an industry. No one book placed all of the elements in one place, capturing how the British reggae industry began, its development, its history, the hits, who some of the key individuals were, and where they came from. I felt that it was vital to write a book to help individuals like myself tell the story to future generations easier. It was my feeling that there would always be something missing from the history of the Windrush generation or those born of British, African Caribbean descent in the UK if the elements did not have inextricable links. This made writing this book more and more important as I went on.

I came across documentaries and literature focussing on the reggae sub-genre 'British Lover's Rock', which could be described as a blend of rhythm and blues rooted in two or three-chord progressions held together with one-drop rhythmic drum patterns.

I came across sound systems, a type of reggae public address system that featured a stack of 15" and 18" inch bass speakers mounted in wardrobe-styled cabinets with a set of smaller speakers on the top that enabled listeners to hear the treble or high notes. The power amplifiers are then connected to a preamplifier, and a turntable is placed on top of a four-inch sponge. This enables the reproduction of quality sound recordings for hundreds of people.

This book will give the reader in-depth and first-hand knowledge of **The British Reggae Music Industry. A Windrush Legacy, My Story**. I cover both aspects of the music business, highlighting the benefits and pitfalls when working with major record companies as well as the independent side of the music industry. I have added my experiences as a black British music manager and promoter from an insider's point of view. This British Reggae Music Industry publication offers a unique insight into the history of touring and performing the daily lives of various prominent UK Reggae artists.

This book offers a deep dive into the journey and story of those who contributed to British Reggae's evolution. Whether motivated by business interests, a passionate curiosity, or a love for the music itself, be it as a listener, artist, musician, or part of the production process, readers will find a step-by-step guide that sheds light on the various paradigms at play. From the moment someone pens a few lyrics or composes a few bars in the studio to the point where prominent performers bring the music to life before audiences of all sizes, this book captures the entire process, from the demo to the hit record, with all its triumphs and challenges.

Finally, I hope this book provides my loved ones with a snapshot of the sacrifices that kept me away from their hands and hearts, my pursuits and passions, and the course I took to provide for their futures.

Chapter 1

The Windrush Legacy

My Windrush legacy includes a tragic story about my grandfather, who was murdered while cycling home. As a fireside lawyer, he successfully defended a case for a poor local woman. The disgruntled plaintiff sought revenge by paying two men to kill him. One night, they ambushed him armed with a sledgehammer.

When many UK-born African Caribbean descendants were born (late 1950s -1960s), a typical African Caribbean household consisted of a mother, father, and several siblings. **Reggae Arrived in the UK before the Windrush Migration.**

The Windrush era refers to the period following World War II, when many people from the

Caribbean, particularly from British colonies, migrated to the United Kingdom. The term **"Windrush"** comes from the name of the ship **His Majesty's Troopship (HMT) Empire Windrush**, which arrived in the UK on June 22, 1948, carrying passengers from the Caribbean. This marked the beginning of significant post-war migration from the region.

These migrants were invited to Britain to help fill labour shortages and rebuild the country after the war. Many settled in the UK, contributing significantly to British society, culture, and economy. The era spanned from the late 1940s to the early 1970s, when thousands of people from the Caribbean settled in Britain.

However, the Windrush era has also come to symbolise the challenges and discrimination faced by these migrants. In recent years, it has been the subject of controversy due to the **"Windrush scandal,"** where it was revealed that many descendants of the Windrush generation were wrongly detained, denied legal rights, threatened with deportation, and, in some cases, wrongfully deported by the UK government, despite having lived in the UK for decades. This led to a public outcry and greater awareness of the contributions and struggles of the Windrush generation.

My mother and Father arrived in the UK from

the island of Barbados and quickly became friends with other migrants from the West Indies to begin a new life in the UK but with no real intention to stay. They planned to return to Barbados once they had earned enough money to purchase land to build a house, buy a car, and continue living the life they had left behind.

However, once in the UK, they found life more difficult and expensive than they initially imagined. One significant comfort was that the music they were accustomed to followed them, known at the time as Blue Beat, Ska and Rock Steady. As a little boy, I would hear a knock at the door, and a man with a large bag would sell records to my father, who had arrived from Jamaica days before. Later on, as the population of West Indians arrived, wholesalers began importing records from Jamaica and selling them to mobile distributors and into local shops in cities like London, Birmingham, and Manchester, to name a few.

My family consisted of my mom, dad and three sisters. We lived in Birmingham, UK. Like many others, life began with us sharing one room. We later moved into a back-alley house, followed by three or four years in St Martin flats, Highgate, Birmingham, before finally moving to the Balsall Heath area of Highgate, where my mother still lives. As a little boy with three sisters, I shared many fond moments with them, but I wanted to do boyhood things, so I remember always wanting to be with Dad.

1, Windrush Arrival 1948 -1971

2, St Martin's Flats - Estates, Birmingham

3, Highgate Close, Birmingham

I loved those times and remember listening to my dad and his friends debating various political topics back home in Barbados. My father began work in Barbados as a hotel waiter in the area parish of St James, and my mom came from St Micheal and worked as an administrative assistant to the government auctioneer. I liked politics and current affairs, mainly because it was our house's main discussion topic. I never met either of my grandfathers, but I heard much about them, especially my mom's father, who was what was known in Barbados as a fireside lawyer (a person who taught themselves the law through reading books and the experience of helping friends fight litigation).

I was privy to the dos and don'ts of living in a foreign country and found it fascinating. I remember my father and his friends discussing the Prime Ministers of Barbados: Grantley Adams, Errol Barrow, Tom Adams, and Owen Arthur. I would ask questions like who he was and what he did. These men assisted poor people in having running water, providing primary schooling, etc. However, no one spoke about slavery; I always believed that Barbados was a country steeped in history, similar to the UK. I had no concept that my family's origins were African. One of the most devastating facts about my family was that my mom's father was murdered as a result of winning a case for a community mother where the defendant was ordered to pay a cast of the equivalent of 60 pounds in 1955. Seeking retribution and harbouring feelings, she paid two men to kill my grandfather. As the story goes, they followed him many nights until one night, they met and knocked him dead with a sledgehammer. They were both found guilty of his murder and were sentenced to be hanged by the neck until they were dead.

My mother has always remembered that story. It scared me for life; what a loss. This is why my mom always trained me to be vigilant and careful with my life. This experience shaped my view of the world I was living in and somehow reminded me of the West Indian way of life, i.e. the talks about keeping my mouth shut and how to articulate my point of view only when necessary. I was to learn that this had its roots buried in the upbringing of my parents and historical slavery.

Christmas time was especially great mainly because we would usually have a visit from a family member, usually my favourite uncle who lived in London. Mom and Dad would stock up on food and drink, non-alcoholic for us, the children, and alcoholic beverages for friends who would visit. The debating would get going following Christmas dinner and snacks and not end until early the next day.

Having said that, when we didn't do that, as a family. We huddle around the television, watching a film like 'From Here to Eternity' starring Frank Sinatra or, my mom's favourite, any film starring Elvis Presley.

Entertainment back then came in the form of my sisters dancing in front of the black-and-white TV our family rented for half a crown per week.

1, Similar to the television my family used to rent

2, Old money, pounds, shillings and pennies

Mom and Dad would play the judges. This was fun; we would entertain ourselves like that until it was time to go to bed or the money time on the television ran out. I remember being so poor that we had to put half a crown in the back of the TV. The whole house would be devastated if we watched a good program and the money ran out. It would be Mom who ran frantically to a neighbour's house to borrow money.

Later, those dance battles took place in the community, at school, and at parties and dancehalls. It's funny how little things mean so much when you don't have much.

Yes, Christmas was usually lovely, even though we didn't have much but ourselves. Boxing Day was the heartbeat of us, our mom, dad, sisters and me. Dad would get up first, make breakfast, and draw out his record collection. He had an incredible collection that included bluebeat and ska records he brought and put away and some more up-to-date reggae records of that day. I remember vaguely a man knocking on our room door and selling Dad records on the doorstep. Dad later moved on to buying records from the local shop until he became a Christian, which took place some years later. Dad would pull out his record collection and play them on his Blaupunkt (Blue Spot). stereo radiogram purchased in 1963.

1, My dad's radiogram

2, 50s, 60s'and 70s Playlist

The sound was incredible, the bass was clear, and the midrange and tops made it more of a listening experience than Mom's transistor radio. Mom loved pop stars like Tom Jones, The Beatles, and Herman's Hermits.

I remember she would sing and dance to the hits of the 60s and 70s, which is why my tastes are so eclectic, but Dad would buy music. It meant more to him than to listen.

Apart from the memories I have of my dad and Music. I also really have to say that it was my eldest sister who introduced me to a lot of reggae songs, you know, that I still play to this very day, such as Margaret, Dennis Walks, Curly Locks, Junior Byles and Cherry Oh Baby, Eric Donaldson, No Jestering, Carl Malcolm, songs like that, and this was really because she used to have a lot of friends. She knew this Sound; she knew Sound systems, and she would borrow records from them and play them on the radiogram that my dad had so I used to listen to them, and she used to be chuffed with the fact that I liked them, so we listen to them together It was pretty cool, so thank God for my eldest sister.

I was 14 – 15 years old when my sister and I used to sneak out of the house and head for the local gigs, such as Saint Barnabas Church Hall, where the paster would allow young people to use the church hall, Ladypool Road, Balsall Heath, Birmingham. As we got older, we headed for the city centre to Locarno, on Hurst Street, Birmingham. I shouldn't have been near there on a Monday night because I had to go to work the following day. Nevertheless, if it weren't for a handful of pebbles thrown up against my sister's bedroom window on nights out at nearby Rebecca's, John Bright Street would never have happened.

I wasn't old enough, but I used to go anyway; I got experience from going to those clubs and sneaking out of the house and back after two o'clock in the morning. Sometimes, Mom or Dad caught on to the fact that I was out of the house, locked all the doors and stopped my sisters from letting me in. I slept on the bins those nights until my dad was heading out for work at 5 a.m. Worse still, until when he was off to church on a Sunday.

I remember a time in 1980 when two massive reggae bands live from Jamaica were playing at Bingley Hall, Broad Street, Birmingham. On the bill was Black Uhuru, supported by Dennis Brown. I couldn't afford to one get in and two miss it. It would be talked about for weeks after I had to go, so a few friends and I took our chances and planned to sneak into the concert. As a regular member of Rebbeca's back then, bouncers like 'Tex' got to know me and would give me special access because I worked for the club bosses.

Those days were fantastic; my friends and I will never forget them. Living the life, perfect times getting in and out of clubs, was great, but things changed; as life has it, I was attending Garretts Green College, Kitts Green, Birmingham, studying for my City and Guilds 706, 1 and 2 in catering and needed experience.

I spent many years working for Lucas, Great King Street, Newtown, in Birmingham, which no longer exists. I met some great friends who remain till today. I was part of the brigade system; one week, I would be placed in the main course section, and the next, I would be placed in the sweet section.

We would cater to thousands of people working there, from directors to factory workers. Even though it was hard work, it didn't seem like it because the other chefs and I were good friends. My skills as a chef came from my days as a commis (trainee) chef, and I began work at a club called Abigail's, owned by Eddie Fewtrell. As an employee, I had a complementary pass to Eddie's venues in Birmingham, Barbarella's, Rebecca's The Ceder Club, etc.

It seemed a long way from my longing to listen to Dad's records by myself and sneak a secret listening session to his records. However, my love, interest in music and desire to become a disk jockey (DJ) started here.

I grew up in the early 1960s, attending school and living in uncomfortable neighbourhoods with mum and dad always working. I remember feeling disillusioned until family members and friends would gather around and talk about the good times they had growing up in the West Indies. I remember the struggles I had while growing up in the UK and finding something good to work towards, and I thought about how to achieve better days. I came to the point where I was going out to enjoy myself and watching television. I always prayed that it would be me people were watching the day after or someone close to me.

I was learning that my decisions would always have consequences, so I began to think before I would act. Around this time, I started reading books about Martin Luther King, Malcolm X, and President JFK. Later on, I learned that Steve Biko fought for freedom in South Africa, even though black South Africans were legally free. Mohammed Ali was an icon, not just because of his boxing ability, but because he taught me that being black would not be easy; he taught me to get up and work hard to be something greater than I was yesterday. 'I felt I was good with music'; having said this, my dad always said that he didn't consider playing music a job.

Once, while walking through the kitchen, listening to him and his friends talking, I asked my dad why it seemed that all great black men had to face tragedy or die to become famous. My father and his friends looked around me in amazement; after a long pause, he looked at me and said that's why

I don't want you ever to miss a day from school; I want you to learn. I asked why Malcolm X wore his heart on his sleeve and if he was not scared. I questioned why Martin Luther King supported Rosa Parks, knowing he would eventually pay the price. My dad answered, saying, 'Jesus died for the sins of man'. He explained, stating that as my son, he would lay down his life for me to live on. These morals resonated with my faith as a child raised in a Christian family and stuck with me to some extent throughout my life.

Social Consciousness

Times were changing. In the USA, Berry Gordie's Motown used music to inform and educate people about the civil rights movement from 1954 to 1968. Marvin Gaye sang songs like 'What's Going On' in 1971 and 'Abraham, Marin, and John'. Berry recorded and released the speeches delivered by Martin Luther King, and it was the time when unfair treatment had to stop and met with resistance by any means necessary. By contrast, a similar story emerged on the other side of the Atlantic. The conservative minister Enoch Powell delivered a speech in 1968 noted now in history as the 'Rivers of Blood' speech; Enoch stated that if the UK did not handle the immigration situation at the time, the black man would have the whip hand of the white man leading to rivers of blood.

Reggae was used to paint a more subtle picture; songs like Bob Andy and Marcia Griffiths 'Black and White' had hit the National UK charts, The Wailers 'Get Up Stand Up' smouldering in the background, and there was an air of consciousness that encouraged the Windrush Generation to seek equal treatment. This was when I realised in my later years what West Indian political activist Darcus Howe was talking about.

It was a time when young black young people felt something was wrong. The feeling was that the cards were stacked against them no matter where they turned. There was a time when Mohamed Ali refused to list for the US Army, stating the Vietcong were not his enemy, further stating that his enemies were right there in America. It was a time when young West Indians began to see themselves as African descendants.

Before the arrival of Bob Marley, Winston Rodney of Burning Spear, Culture and Israel Vibration were in concert from Jamaica; consciousness and black awareness were all the talk and music with a message. Marcus Garvey became the subject matter for many songs by artists and bands about consciousness. Garvey, a Jamaican political activist, formed the Universal Negro Improvement Association and African Communities League (UNIA) in 1914, whose main aim was to bring unity between Africa; its diaspora to remove colonial rule to set about political unification. Garvey's legacy places him as a national hero in Jamaica, whose ideologies have influenced Rastafarians, black people across the world, the Nation of Islam and beyond before he died in 1952.

This connects with the music of this time because Haile Selassie was Emperor of Ethiopia until 1974 and is seen as the figurehead for Rastafari, a religious movement in Jamaica. Selassie visited Jamaica in 1966 to a hero's welcome by Rastafarians who considered him God and earth's rightful ruler. Understanding this alternative education requires time. Nowhere was more prime for this than Jamaica, especially after Selassie's visit in 1966. Music coming out of Jamaica reflected a search for the truth; hence, songs of that time characterised that narrative; this can be seen in the spirit of Bob Marley and his music.

This was not a subject that would be discussed across dinner tables in West Indian households or taught in schools; hence, many parents failed to grasp the relevance of Rastafari and discouraged their children from growing their hair and not combing it as unwelcome.

Popular TV programs were not questioned as to their misinformation or validity; they were accepted as fact, which didn't help the negative references to race that West Indians faced in society and schools. Programs like 'Till Death Us Do Part', Love Thy Neighbour' and the 'Black and White Minstrel Show' provided subtle backdrops for the day-to-day negative undertones. My parents were visibly embarrassed when watching films referencing Zulu tribes and Africa; they didn't understand what was being shown wasn't true.

The common thought of making drums, spears and clothing using animal skins was unthinkable. I remember my father saying, 'I don't want you to talk like that', "You were born here and English, speak English". I was to learn that he meant he didn't want my sisters or me to speak broken English (the Barbadian dialect).

The Trans-Atlantic slave trade wasn't something the British were proud of; hence, the historical events may never be taught in schools. Having said this, until that time comes, it would be helpful if an alternative learning environment could better inform people of African descent education, explaining how slavery came about, its relationship to the West Indies, and colonialism. I believe that this will assist African Caribbean West Indians in understanding why their lack of trust in each other continues to exist.

Slavery and The Trans-Atlantic Slave Trade

Slavery was a global institution that existed across continents for thousands of years. In Africa, it took on unique forms, with some enslaved people integrated into social kinship networks, contrasting with the plantation-based slavery seen in the Western Hemisphere. While plantation slavery was less common in sub-Saharan Africa, it existed on a large scale in places like Egypt, Sudan, and Zanzibar, often leading to high mortality rates among enslaved populations. African societies varied significantly in their reliance on slavery, from minority to majority slave populations, with some regions exporting large numbers of enslaved people annually, escalating from 10,000-20,000 per year in the 16th century to 100,000 per year by the 18th century.

The sources of enslaved people changed over time, initially drawn from the northern savanna and the Horn of Africa, later shifting to West Africa due to European demand. The slave trade severely impacted Africa's population, particularly in West Africa, where entire regions, such as Angola and the Congo, faced depopulation, and slave trade routes spread diseases like smallpox. Gender imbalances and social disruption followed, as men were often disproportionately taken, leaving a surplus of women and children.

European, Arab, and African participants all played significant roles in the slave trade. Muslim merchants dominated trade routes before European colonial expansion, while Islamic jihads in the 18th and 19th centuries fuelled slavery in West Africa. Europeans later engaged in the transatlantic trade, exporting over 11 million Africans, while the Arab slave trade sent an estimated 14 million to the Middle East. Abolition was gradual and met resistance, especially in the Middle East and parts of Africa, where slavery persisted into the 20th century. Bob Marley and other music icons remain vital to helping many West Indians understand something was wrong with what wasn't being taught and perhaps some of the reasons why; evidence of this always happens.

Wherever I go or have been in the world, when discussing black awareness and current affairs, I am asked the same question: Why can't black people unite?

In the song *'So Jah Seh,'* Bob Marley says, *'If puss and dog can get together, what's wrong with you, my brother? If Puss and Dog can get together, what's wrong with loving one another?'*

Whatever your viewpoint, I've realised as I've gotten older and with the benefit of education and my thirst to understand my blackness, is that the Trans-Atlantic slave trade produced something that I'm not sure will ever change in my lifetime, which is the lack of trust that seems to be present between us as a people. By this, I mean when I consider that we are people from the same continent (Africa) with similar skin tones find working together challenging. One theory that might explain this is somewhere between the time when Africans were kidnapped, falsely imprisoned, loaded onto slave ships and transported to many parts of the world: America, Europe, the West Indies and the UK; it is well-known that this process was aided by some indigenous Africans known to those captured.

Those left behind and who managed to avoid kidnap suffered considerable losses to families, segregating tribes, languages and families, forcing those captured into a state of dehumanisation, a lack of pride, etc. We all understand that moving house can be one of the most traumatic periods in a person's life; hence, undergoing this process as an enslaved person must have caused trauma close to death itself.

Getting to know someone who sleeps next to you and learning a new language takes time, especially when you have no introduction or never met them beforehand.

Considering the above paragraph, I have come to learn that this lack of trust began in West Africa when indigenous Africans were kidnapped and locked away by their counterparts before the arrival of merchant slave ships. The level of disbelief from one to another was difficult to fathom: "How could he or she sell me out?".

If you contemplate the route taken to the destination of enslavement, beginning with the kidnapping of someone who looks like you and talks like you, it's hard to understand if you are not used to this type of deception. This would be bad enough for most of us. However, it didn't stop there; it was followed by travelling in the belly of a ship for eight weeks, imprisoned miles away from home until the merchant slave ship you travelled on docked and was sold.

I pictured myself in this position, chained up with someone I didn't know beneath a boat, with males and females lying side by side, going to the toilet next to each other, unable to speak the same language for months, only to arrive in different parts of America and the West Indies to be sold again next to the sale of pigs, goats and cows. All the time, buried in the back of my mind, somewhere, this happened because I trusted someone who looked like me and talked like me. The question I would ask myself is, what advice would I give myself and my loved ones if I had the chance to turn back the hands of time six months prior?

Suppose we accept that for at least 400 years and 14 generations, African people were complicit in this process that led to the death and degradation of their people. In that case, it has to be said that habits and firmly held feelings take a long time to break. However, one can, therefore, understand the lack of trust in African Caribbeans and African Americans has played host in preparing the breeding ground for what has become post-tactical psychological factors that have transpired in West Indian families together with the upbringing and lack of trust between some people of BME origin.

Many of us are unaware that after the abolition of the Trans-Atlantic slave trade in 1807, slavery for children born (outside of Africa) of enslaved people taken from Africa remained enslaved into the 1870s across the world.

This is very significant if we are to understand why slavery continued for such a long time and where colonialism began. These factors enabled me to understand who I was and what my purpose would become. Colonialism is rooted in exploitation. Hence, it was easy to grasp that one intends to make money if one exploits another. Having said this, one's intention can also include cruelty and lack of kindness. Whichever one is employed, one must consider the context, the aim, and the desired outcome. I decided to learn all I could about black history. Consequently, I saw slavery as not one of hate but a product of business, profit and loss. The issues of race and class were to become something else, which is where the music came in, providing me with a different perspective and one that allowed me to gain a broader understanding of what I learned at school and Sunday school in church.

My parents would teach my sisters and me how to behave. In slavery, parents would teach their children not to question things and not look directly into my face with that look; for example, don't look the master in the eye. These traditions continued into the lives of West Indians; with the televised presentation of "Roots", I better understood the thoughts and emotions of enslaved people at that time, which helped me to understand simple traditions such as the opportunity to dance to music, the eating of cow or chicken feet rather than cold water cornmeal. On my first visit to Barbados, I was able to draw parallels between the food my mother used to cook and the importance of seasonings, for instance, the importance of how the marination of beef, pork, oxtail and chicken transformed the cheapest cuts of meat money could buy and became a main meal.

Caribbean people learned to cook using these cuts of meat and use seasonings to improve the taste, such as chicken foot soup and spices in cornmeal porridge; other parts of the Caribbean would mix cornmeal in a savoury way with fish and okra. Side dishes such as fried dumplings (bakes and johnny cakes) would accompany many meals because flour and water, being the main ingredients, were relatively inexpensive, where the cooking time was quick, and the method included kneading of flour and water. I learned that just like cheap cuts of meat my mother used in cooking, it tasted terrific with seasoning. I understood my talent came from how much effort I would put into things. I realised that I would stick to things until the job was complete. Music and me was like that. I understood that creative people loved to tell stories; I saw music as part of my education; hence, any part brought joy to those less fortunate around me.

I came to understand that the development of British reggae music was emerging from the experiences held by our parents from the West Indies. Those blessed with talent were learning to use these experiences similarly to find joy, educate, earn a living, and simultaneously provide others with entertainment.

Chapter 2

Influences

I began to understand the decisions I made carried weight. I had read about influential figures like Martin Luther King, Malcolm X, JFK, Mandela, Steve Biko, and Muhammad Ali. Ali, beyond boxing, taught me the challenges of being different and the importance of striving for greatness. "I felt I was good with music.

My journey and love of reggae music and British reggae started with highs and lows; disappointments hold a significant place in what, for me, started as a hobby and a love for something that became the career I love to this very day.

The development of British reggae music as an industry arose from a love for the music, followed by growth and demand. No Matter who I've spoken to, such as Roger Steffens (reggae historian),

Festus, Natty, Blacker Dread (Sir Coxsone), Mad Professor/Neil Fraser (Ariwa), David Rodigan, John Massourie (Black Echoes/Echoes), Chris Sedgwick, Chris Cracknell (Greensleeves), John MacGillivray, Chris Lane (Dub Vendor-Fashion) and Ali Campbell (UB40), to name a few, all have told me it began with their love for reggae music. This element drove the ideas that propelled them to entertain audiences and lovers of reggae to this very day.

Along the way, I learned that my desire was rooted in the ability to observe talent. From my experience, talent can be broken down in many ways, but for me, it starts the minute I see someone, listen to someone talk or watch someone working, irrespective of their vocation; I see something that causes me to think. Their thoughts, feelings, moods, beliefs and what drives them, you know, what would get them up in the morning, rain, snow or shine. The things I speak about lead me down a track where I might invest my time, money, skills and abilities.

One of the first UK reggae hits came from an American singer, Jonny Nash, with a song called 'Hold Me Tight' in 1968. Not long after, a band from Jamaica called 'Toots and the Maytals'. Toots Hibbert followed this closely with 'Do the Reggae', which, in my belief, gave the musical genre its name. With a constant stream of chart hits in the

UK and worldwide, the reggae genre grew from strength to strength.

Toots Hibbert and Grantley GT

In the 60s, with the growing reggae singles market, reggae was gaining momentum. Driven by its popularity with black and white urban young people, the music became a dominant market player. Record companies such as Island were propelling the industry at the time, founded by Chris Blackwell in 1962. Blackwell in Jamaica recognised the growing trend with reggae in the UK. Island set up the Island label with a loan from his parents when he was 21. Riding the wave, Blackwell was in the right place at the right time. He began releasing songs by Jamaican artists. His first hit came with Laurel Atkin's 'Boogie in My Bones'.

However, between 1962 and 1964, Blackwell recorded the smash hit 'My Boy Lollipop' by Millie Small and licensed it to Phillips Records. At the time, Chris regularly used his car to distribute the catalogue of Island records titles in his vehicle through London, Birmingham, and Manchester.

By contrast, some six years later, Trojan Records was founded by Duke Reid in 1968 out of Croydon, London. Alongside Lee Perry Bunny Lee, part of his production team, hits in the UK market flourished with songs from Jimmy Cliff, The Upsetters, The Pioneers, and Harry J's All Stars. Trojan had their first British number-one national chart hit in 1971 with 'Dave and Ansel Collins' **'Double Barrel'**. Followed by Desmond Dekker, Toots, Bob Andy, and Marcia Griffiths, all with gilt-edged chart hits at the time. Trojan did not stop there; armed with a strong production network and a host of talented singers and musicians, the hits kept coming: Dennis Brown, Gregory Isaacs, Bob Marley and The Wailers. There was Dandy Livingston, John Holt 'Help Me Make It Through the Night', and I remember Ken Booth's 'Every Thing I Own' and Judge Dread's series of hits cemented Duke Reid's Trojan Records legacy to partner Chris Blackwell's Island Records as the prominent market players.

British Sound Systems

It cannot be forgotten that had it not been for the arrival of the Windrush. The sound system would not have followed the new arrivals into the UK then. However, sound systems were essential for West Indians, providing young men and women with an opportunity to let their hair down and an escape from the nine to five, peace work and night shifts, but more importantly, a place where they could go to get a taste of back home in the West Indies.

Sound systems operating in Britain in the 60s and 70s were sounds like Duke Vin, Count Suckle, Count Steve, Duke Lee, Sir Frana B, Neville Musical Enchanter, Duke Reid, Duke Alloy, Quaker City, Studio City, Mafiatone, Zion, lord Koos, V Rocket, Baron, Sir Christopher, Mombasa, Lord Collie, Kaz (Manchester), Stereograph, Young Lion, Fatman and Sir Coxsone to name a few in England following Windrush.

Playing the latest recordings imported from Jamaica every week would send many West Indians out to the record shops in the week to purchase their personal favourites played by their favourite sound systems to relive the experiences and do it all over again the following week. Hence, the chart returns shops to highlight the selling singles, alerting DJs on 'Radio Caroline', 'Radio

Luxembourg', and later on, the BBC to the hits. These sounds provided a valuable service for the early reggae records coming out of Jamaica, and they still do to this very day.

Some of my friends who lived not far from me on Cannon Hill Road, Balsall Heath, had a youth sound system called Duke Wally. Vincent headed up the sound with other members such as Hopeton, Zephaniah, Mackey, Grey (The Bull), Dracula, Buff Bay, Timmy, Ratty, Michael and myself.

Around this time, I hung out with friends in the Balsall Heath area of Birmingham. At the time, they had formed a sound system called Duke Wally. It attracted many people from surrounding areas, such as Mosley, Kings Heath, Sparkhill, Sparkbrook, Five Ways, and even Ladywood and Handsworth. Somehow, I became a part of Duke Wally and participated in gigs and events we would attend.

Sound systems that progressed at that time and after that out of Birmingham featured the following:

Eternal Youth, Sound City, Ravers, Shelly, Jah Massigan, Siffa, Nyah, Jah Lion, Nyah- Esquire.

Party Sound Systems, in Birmingham, Turbo-Tronic, Stereo Classic, Master Blaster Skippy and Lippy, Rockers Roadshow, Jus-I, Baiders, Orthodox, Love-Line, Upfront, Lovein-ting, Mind Body and Soul, TC Connection, Siffa, Love Injection, Now Generation, New Sensation, Wassifa-Showcase and Observer.

1, Sound System stack featuring 8, 18"

2, From left – Benjie, Observer sound manager , sub-woofers 4 15" midrange drivers, 'Rumble Cup Winners' Solomon, Twinny Ranks, 8, 12" midrange and four horns, Valerie (V Rocket Sound), Sanction and Tyson

Observer Sound System, from Birmingham

Over the years, the sound has featured the following members:

Benjie - CEO
Gunzzy – Engineer - Deputy
Twinny Ranks - MC
Fat Head - Mixer
Percival - Selector
Bionic Steel - Selector
Mr Magic - Engineer
Siffa - Engineer
Supa D - MC
Major Popular - MC
Ringo Culture – MC

A sound system like Observer now carries a combined power source of approximately 25,000 watts.

What Is a Sound System?

Now, for those who don't know, a sound system comprises multiple layers. Most importantly, they include the team, who are as follows by role:

The Owner – Manager
The Operator – Selector
The MC, Mic Man or DJ
The Engineer
The Sound Box Builder
The Driver

The Road Crew
The Audience

You then would have the system or public address system (P.A.), which included speakers, usually double-fronted large wardrobe-style units that contain two 18" bass drivers; you would also need several single units containing 15" drivers, which would deliver the midrange sound (as illustrated above). This would be followed by what we used to call the top section. This would sit on top of the stack in a cabinet unit containing tweeters six or eight on each stack. Ideally, for a balanced sound, you would require a stack of speakers to the left and one to the right of the turntable or a stack in each corner. You would then require amplification. **Duke Wally** began with a **200-watt** valve amplifier, driven by **4 KT88 valves**, which could be wired in parallel or series, producing an output of 4 or 8 ohms. We had an old Gerard record deck, which we placed on a piece of four-inch square sponge to reduce unwanted rumble vibration. Finally, we had yards and yards of two core cables, which were necessary to connect each stack of speakers to the amplifier. These would be run from the amplifiers along the room's perimeter walls or on strategically placed nails slightly below the ceilings. This was all an education to me, and I learned a lot.

Between the ages of 11 – 16, I attended Lea Mason

C of E Secondary School, Lee Bank, Birmingham, until 1976, where I experienced good times and bad. You know, I don't remember my school days being unhappy at all, but they were tough, and the reason why they were tough is really because we had a lot of challenges. I remember lining up in our year groups after every break time. It was an orderly affair: first, second, third, fourth, and fourth years would follow each other into school and onto their next lesson. I was in my second year, and a friend who was a character would always jump in and out of line. However, Mr Walker, the metalwork teacher, saw him and called out, **"Harwood… Go to my room; you're going cry"** I mean, can you imagine the thoughts that ran through his head? To cut a long story short, he was crying the next time I saw him. That was our school; it was tough.

In those days, I was good at wood and metalwork; Mr Walker liked me. The woodwork teacher, Mr Roland, who stood about six feet four inches and was built like a brick house, walked around the school corridors, bumped into people at random with his broad shoulders, and knocked you halfway down the corridor. He was that tough.

My best memory of him is when Tony, Winston, and I participated in this cancer charity race in Sutton Park, near Birmingham.

Somehow, we had to ride simulated chariots (prams). I was pushed around a circuit for about two hours until the first chariot reached the winner's post. I don't know how, but we won and won the teacher's headmaster's and our mates' admiration. That was a good day.

At Lea Mason, there were two sets of stairs, one for the girls and a separate one for the boys. It kept us both apart until break time. I was a prefect in school back then and would be placed on stair duty now and then by rota. Sometimes, prefects would cover the tuck shop, which was ok on a good day. However, a day came when someone stole a bunch of tuck; in an attempt to retrieve the items, I held onto this guy, and he punched me in the face. I immediately felt the blood rushing to the area of my face that took the blow and went to the toilets. There was swelling and blood, so I removed my prefect badge and told my mate to give it to Mr Williams, the headmaster. I then went to see the kid who hit me and set about him as he did me. I didn't get detention or suspension as it was considered self-defence. However, the feud continued for about three years. Following this, we met and decided to bury the hatchet and became good friends. There was a fun side to being a prefect; I could punish pranksters by making them run up and down the stairs twice or thrice; it was fun, and I became known as a prefect and got respect.

I was introduced to sound systems back in the late 1970's. I was always interested in music as a young child. I had a small bedroom with a music system that I had pieced together from bits of broken radio grams and speakers roughly put into wooden cabinets. At 13 years old, I would use my pocket money to buy records. I also had a part-time job; as soon as I got paid, I would hit the shops, check out the latest tunes and buy crowd pleasers, those I liked.

I remember going to the (Diskery), a shop near my school, just off Bristol Road in Birmingham, with three of my friends, Dennis Hamilton, Tony Bailey and Winston Hayle (we were tight then and tight now), only that Winston is no longer with us (RIP). I remember buying three albums: John Holts – '1000 Vaults of Holt', Bob Marley's – 'Natty Dread' and Barry White's 'Your First My Last My Everything'. I couldn't wait to get them home to play them; I was so excited! That memory I would get a lot of joy from them. I waited until my dad left the house to play my music; it was the best thing in the world.

At school, as friends, we started a sound system called (Equator) that we were working on. This included Dennis Hamilton, owner of (HAT MAN), Winston Hayles, Tony Bailey and Walker, all Equator partners. We all got on as young teenagers, and it was fun within Unity with all sorts of shenanigans that you get up to as young people.

Tony Bailey, Grantley GT and Dennis Hamilton

We put our money together; a lot of money was needed to get together good equipment to sound right. But again, things stopped when members entered their separate ways, and Winston went to Germany. Dennis decided to go into making hats; still, in our teens, Tony Bailey went off to work for local government, and I went into a factory producing glass items. So, we all were destined to become who we needed to become.

Not long after, my friends introduced me to Duke Wally, a youth sound system based in the Balsall

Heath area of Birmingham. Wally began with a 200-watt valve amplifier (the general). Once we purchased the new 600-watt amplifier, driven by twelve KT88s, which would power the 18" bass drivers-woofers, the general's role was changed to power the midrange and tweeters (tops) section.

Understand me when I say sound systems would operate a single record player system. The single deck would usually be set on a four-inch piece of sponge placed on top of a three or four-foot valve amplifier case. You may wonder why we did that. Well, the most popular sound systems at the time were powered by bespoke valve amplifiers, driven by sometimes between 300 and 1,200 watts. The amplifiers would carry KT88 valves, and for argument's sake, each KT88 represented 50 watts of power delivered to the sound's bass, mid-range and top-section speakers. To cut a long story short, most sound systems would have what we call wardrobe stacks of speakers which contain two 18" bass woofer drivers; placed on top of those would be the midrange section, which would usually carry two 15" drivers or 12" drivers followed by a box which contained between four to twelve tweeters or a horn.

As you can imagine, sound systems would carry a lot of equipment, requiring a Luton-style van or larger for transportation, so costs would be a critical factor in getting a sound system to entertain an audience. Most of them would have a stack of speakers, as mentioned above, either to the left or the right of their amplifier or a stack placed in each corner of the room. Most sound systems in their teams would need someone who is electronically capable. This team member would ensure the speakers were wired correctly to the amplifier, depending on its impedance and phase.

Alongside this, as time passed, some sound systems incorporated a cross-over system separated by separate amplifiers connected to a pre-amplifier, which would then be wired to the record player. The purpose was to achieve musical separation between the bass woofers, the midrange speakers, and the tweeters, as well as between the amplifiers.

Remember, I mentioned the four-inch piece of sponge? Well, if you can imagine all that power passing through the speaker systems, a lot of what is known as rumble, wow, and flutter would be created that would be transferred to the stylus of the deck, which didn't sound good coming through 1,000 watts.

Vinyl Records and Dubplates

Over the years, members of Duke Wally had amassed thousands of records. There were loads in hefty wooden boxes; carrying those was a mission: the ample wardrobes, the record box and everything else. You had to be strong, up and down stairs, wow!

We lived well with others, allowing us to help each other out. We would share equipment and speaker boxes from sounds like Warrior and King Iwah. This lifestyle became tight because, on most Sundays, someone would have a ball and start playing football in Calthorpe Park, off Edward Road; we were supported by the local youth worker who went by the name of Pat.

As I said before, selecting music to entertain others is an art; you must be good. So, it was back to hitting the record shops and selecting good tunes. If you're going to be good, you must know how to choose the music to suit the people you play for, which I was schooled for during my time at Duke Wally.

At the same time, becoming the host or mic man was just as important because these individuals became the face of the sound system and the brand. We would play at parties, youth clubs and church halls, charging people a small fee to attend. This was all good fun; we would contribute weekly subscriptions to cover purchases and maintenance and purchase dubplates.

What Is a Slate or Dubplate

A dubplate is a song recorded as a special by the artist, usually over the original rhythm track for a particular sound system or individual. For instance, a song like 'Let It Be' by The Beatles rerecorded as a dubplate could contain the names of individuals, the company they work for, and so on; what makes it unique is that John Lennon and Paul McCartney's voices are on the dubplate and mention your sound system or the individual. It made it unique because other sound systems could not play it. We won the Silver Youth Cup! By playing a special of the Upsetters song 'Underground Roots'. Not long after this, Duke Wally broke up. It was primarily due to us leaving school and getting jobs.

Dubplates allowed us to battle against other sound systems in our league (youth sounds). We had many battles and were victorious.

However, Lloyd Blake and Eric, a side partner of Lloyd's, put on a competition, pulling together Vincent' of Duke Wally, George' of Lord Shirley, Junior' of Bismark, Doulfus' of Jah Massigan, and Pharaoh, Jungalist and Linval' of Jungle-Man. We always had to be prepared.

It is helpful to remember that the term dub could be ambiguous, one of which could be referred to with dubplates (songs remixed with or without vocals) and dub music, i.e. (Lee Scratch Perry, Jamaica, Mad Professor, London and King Earthquake from Birmingham have successfully carved their names in the market for driving forward dub out of roots and stepper's music mixed for lovers of reggae music of this type to worldwide multi-cultural audiences. On Saturday, 6th July 2019, in association with Irish and Chin at The Corah Suite Banquet Hall, St John Street, Leicester, Observer Super Power successfully won the road to the World Clash, UK Rumble Sound Clash against participants Empire Sound, Mello Tone, Mour Dan Infinity UK and Classique.

Slates, Dubplates, and specials are instrumental or vocal tracks sung by the original artist and featuring members of the sound system's name. Duke Wally would achieve this by travelling to London to meet up with Festus, the operator or selector of Sir Coxsone's sound system.

We would then head straight to the studio, which would cut the dubs we wanted, and Festus would deliver his unique mix (just for us, that no other sound could play). After paying for them, we would either stay overnight in London and watch Coxsone, Festus, and the teamplay, get some sleep in Wandsworth, London and head back to Birmingham.

Nowadays, dubplates cost between $100 US dollars and $2,600.00 or the equivalent for famous artists with big names.

Grantley and Blacka Dread

It was a fantastic experience heading to London; we met legends in the world of sound systems. I learnt a lot from legends such as Coxsone Dodd, Lloyd Coxsone, and Festus, (who I would watch operating the preamp, twisting the knobs left and right, which changed the frequency of the music as well as cutting the basslines and treble in the perfect time of the drum patterns).

Natty, who later left Sir Coxsone and became selector of Frontline International, and so on. We would sleep on the floors or just sofa surf, anything to have more money to spend on dubplates. It was usually only for one night, so ruffing it for one or two nights wasn't too bad.

As life would have it, and as time passed, transistor amplifiers replaced valve amplifiers. I remember I was at the forefront of the valve-to-transistor transition. My friends owned a shop selling electrical goods on Hurst Street, Birmingham, UK.

Matthews Electronics supplied me with two 500-watt transistor amplifiers to power my bass speakers and purchased the parts to make two hundred-watt amplifiers to power my top and mid-range speaker units, aided by a crossover unit which would separate the low and mid-range frequencies from interfering, which provided more clarity of separation. My uncle at the time was like a big brother who would always show me things I should be doing with my money. He would encourage me to save, 'You can't buy a house without a deposit.' He discouraged me from smoking by doing the math. It was my ambition, therefore, to buy my own house one day.

It came when I had enough money to buy a new system; now I could play my music with better sound quality, and the family would also enjoy it, so I was overjoyed.

My sisters and I have one of those loving, supportive moms. My first loan was from my mother, who gave me a loan of £200, and my uncle, at the same time, gave me a loan of £400 in 1981. In those days, that was a lot of money, and did I use that money well, even if I say so myself? I was good at woodwork and had learnt a bit of electronics from an evening college course I had started.

Life was so much fun back then. Groups of us would go out on Fridays or Saturday nights. I had to sneak out because my dad didn't want me to go out with a group unless he knew them. We would catch a taxi when we had the money, but most of the time, we would walk from our homes to the venue and back. Back then, the priority for some of us was weed, drinks, entrance fees, and taxi fare.

Saint Barnabas was a venue that was a must; most of the young people in that area would congregate at Barnabas; it was a meeting spot; we would catch up on the week's gossip, enjoy music and meet girls, as it was a church hall, there was no alcohol.

I've heard people say that cannabis is part of reggae culture. As a young person myself, I never had any experiences with cannabis or weed apart from trying it out one or two times. Friends of mine did, but it must be said my money was always spent on records. I would get pocket money and save half of it; I would even go without lunch money to have more to spend on music, whilst my mate would be passing around a spliff. They would have fun building three and five sheeters. You know, three-sheet or five-sheeter spliffs; it was part of youth culture at that time. It brought me back to my school days when we would assemble behind the school gates, out of sight.

Some of us would just be there laughing; some would be there smoking cigarettes, and some were there smoking weed. Somehow, weed didn't do anything for me; it didn't click. My father and uncle encouraged me to save my money for things I wanted in the future; one of these things became making things with wood and making amplifiers.

GT 600 was an idea that came out of my bedroom. I had a stereo that I had put together, made up of speakers I had picked up here and there. I was good at woodwork at school, so I used the skills learnt there to buy plywood and make the cabinets myself, saving a lot of money. I did a similar thing with the record turntable, making the plinth out of scrap wood.

Regarding the amplifier, I salvaged an old radiogram that had been thrown out, repaired it, and placed it in a lovely cabinet. I finished everything by sanding each piece down, painting, and varnishing them to completion.

I used to play my dad's record collection when he was out of the house, entertaining my mom, sisters, friends, and anyone else around. Even back then, people always commented on how I played music; they liked something about it. More importantly, I loved it; it gave me an escape!

What I didn't know then, that I know now, is that I was learning how to please people and entertain them. I never forgot that.

So, I carried on buying records and building up record collection. By this time, I decided to put together a disco roadshow where I would play various genres of music with the addition of a lighting system, strobe, sound-to-light and lasers. At the top end, my system would comprise left and right stacks, four 18" bass drivers, two 15" midrange drivers and two cabinets holding six tweeters on each side. My power constituted two 500-watt amplifiers for bass and two 200-watt amplifiers driving my midrange and tops. It sounded terrific when linked with a crossover connected to my DJ mixer.

I had a double-deck system that switched one record to the other. All I had to do now was generate the funds.

I borrowed £600 from my mom and uncle and

covered all the costs of building everything. I had £600 saved on my own, so I put all that money together, hired a workshop, and built GT 600, which became the transition from the sound system to becoming a DJ with my equipment.

I travelled anywhere and everywhere, going to different venues around Birmingham and London. I had a good school friend, Tony, who almost lived next door to me, to join me. I said come on, man, let's put a roadshow together.

I would play records at youth clubs to test the water. This was fantastic.

Tony would usually be the host on the microphone because I was good at setting things up and organising things; I realised that I shied away from using the microphone for fear of embarrassment, and I needed to improve. I could talk, but I needed to enhance my ability to use the microphone for the audience. We got along well, we got a lot of gigs, and slowly but surely, I got better; just as Tony began to move into more mainstream DJing, he met a DJ called Lionel who used to DJ at the nightclubs in Birmingham City centre, such as Rebecca's, Barbarella's and venues like that I think he was happy Tony wanted to become a Club DJ.

This meant I needed to move on. Tony left and placed my back against the wall; it wasn't bad, as that wasn't his intention. He wanted to do things he wanted to do, which was okay; I understood.

We have remained terrific friends to this day. Nevertheless, I learned to talk on the microphone, introduce records, host, and keep people on the dance floor. I played at birthday parties, youth club weddings, etc, gaining experience and knowledge.

Remember I mentioned my good friend, Timothy Lashley? Well, I have to thank his mother, Daphney Lashley, who showed me so much love and kindness that I will never forget her; I cried the day I heard she passed and flew home from a US tour to attend her funeral (RIP) Mrs Lashley. Another mentor who gave me a break was Hansel Jordan, a Barbadian and community leader who gave me a chance to DJ at West Indian dances. I learned about calypso and soca; they liked how I could mix traditional calypso for the elders and current reggae and soul, which appealed to a young audience.

Again, I could keep people on the floor. I used to play with another DJ, such as Count Nevis. He was awesome. I loved watching him play, especially for the older generation. It was a fantastic experience which I'll never forget. My mum would also attend those events with her friends and other family members. I felt proud of myself because I could repay the loan I got from my uncle and mom. I guess the audience's responses made her feel proud, too.

These experiences transported me from being a DJ to becoming a music manager and record producer.

I was a DJ in Birmingham at the same time, and one night, I was asked to play not far from my home at a church hall on the corner of Mary Street and Edward Road in Balsall Heath. This is where I made my name, and gosh, I was there playing against another sound that belonged to guys I knew from the area. They had a name; some knew me from Duke Wally's days. I was sceptical and didn't want to leave anything to chance; I had to play well, so we set out armed with a record box full of music. What helped was that GT 600 had a good team of loyal individuals. Roy (my right hand) could do anything and was so talented. The MC, Winston or Major (RIP), was a quiet, mild-mannered, technical, talented individual and brother to Pato Banton; having said that, you would never have known it if you met him for the first time. In his day, Mellow, or Andrew, was a brilliant, fast-talking MC; what a talent.

The team also included Brian, Peter, and Webster, not to forget our female counterparts, who played more of a part than they got the credit for. There was the singer, Patricia, her voice full and vocal range and perfect pitch. Life wouldn't have been the same if it hadn't been for Angela and Jackie Welcome (the sisters), Pam, Daphney, Thelma Anthony, and a group of fans who would follow us almost everywhere we played. That was young and eager to prove we were the best. I also had Pato up my sleeve. It was a big night, and we did well. Pato appeared, and I remember being surprised by a flood of friends and associates urging me to pass the microphone to a young singer named Peter Spence.

From then on, we didn't look back; birthday parties, hotels, and community events inside and outside Birmingham occupied us for almost three years until I started a new job in London.

Tony Bailey, or Tony Roots, was a friend not only at school but practically lived next door to me in Highgate Close, Birmingham, UK.

Attending the same school, Tony and I would play football and cricket together, sharing small talk and laughter. Our families shared the common denominator that many African Caribbean families shared at that time: Christianity.

Most days, we would call on the other and walk two miles to school. We were also placed in the same class and shared many experiences. We were both prefects, too, so leaving school and going our separate ways didn't divide us. We moved on to the next chapter of our teenage lives.

A few years later, I had built a roadshow and felt ready to put it on the road. At this time, Tony was DJing, so I asked him if he would like to participate, and he responded yes. Most of you who know me have asked at some point what the 'T' represents. When no part of my name resembles a 'T'. so, in need of a name for the outfit, it seemed simple enough to use the first letter of our Christian name, 'G' for Grantley and 'T' for Tony, hence 'GT'. The 600 elements of it came as a result of how much power we carried. It was at this stage my nickname was born. Tony and I continued for about six months until he became a DJ with a Barbarella and Rebecca DJ who went by the name of Lionel. I was alone for nine years, and the name GT just stuck.

Chapter 3

The Arrival of Bob Marley and British Reggae

The development of British reggae was influenced by bands like Burning Spear, Culture, Fred Locks, Dennis Brown, and Bob Marley. These artists helped the children of the Windrush generation, who faced prejudice and violence, connect with their West Indian and African roots—topics often avoided by their parents. The TV adaptation of Alex Haley's "Roots" was significant, revealing harsh realities and instilling a lasting sense of pride. This experience and a growing love for music and black history contributed to the rise of British reggae bands.

Looking for places to go, our parents would be forced to get together in a room and dance to let their hair down. It was the time of other record players and radios; blue beat and ska would be brought across the ocean from Jamaica and sold face-to-face by doorstep salesmen to individuals holding community parties, which became unlicensed blues parties which went onto the early hours of the morning. Some years later, the Windrush generation would attend night clubs that became a bridge between going out on a Friday and Saturday to a blues party, leading to reggae concerts over time.

Prior to the album 'Natty Dread', I hadn't realised that Bob Marley was as iconic as he later became. Listening to Natty Dread inspired me to look further, leading to the purchases of 'Burning', The Wailers, 'Catch Ah Fire' and, later, the body of work produced by Lee Scratch Perry. His music before his assassination attempt and exile from Jamaica did not resonate in the same way as it did with other acts at the time. Bob made London, UK, his home. In 1976, Bob wrote 'Rastaman Vibration' and produced the iconic 'Exodus'. Both albums show us both sides of Bob and tell a story of change, religion, politics and unconditional love.

A thoughtful Chris Blackwell considered how best to promote Bob Marley to the world outside Jamaica. He thought Bob about marketing; Bob quickly grasped how his natural charisma would assist the popularisation of music and the communication of his message from cold culture into the warm heart of people's consciousness. Bob Marley possessed a pleasant demeanour and was driven by a revolutionary concept. His music and what he was all about assisted Chris in marketing Bob and his musical message in a way that, most of the time, worked tirelessly to repeatedly promote the narrative within his lyrics. Marley's body of work continues to attract new fans, young and older, year after year. Tuff Gong/Island have reshaped strategies to market Bob's message into the hearts of listeners, which is one reason that supports his legendary status across the world today.

Bob Marley arrived in the UK in 1972 and toured venues up and down the country. The Wailers supported Johnny Nash following his string of UK hits, which included 'Cupid' in 1968, 'Hold Me Tight' and 'I Can See Clearly Now', both released in 1972. I remember owning the original 'Catch a Fire' album with the hinged sleeve, which opened like a cigarette lighter. I didn't know then, but I learned later that it was the first album released by Island Records in 1973, followed by 'Burning' by the Wailers.

It was a time of change in the UK. Growing up in the Windrush generation of the late 1950s and early 60s, my parent's priority was looking for work. Additionally, ska music made an impression on young British skinheads due to 'Black and

White' by Greyhound in 1971. A simple song with a clear message left an indelible mark on teenage Britain's musical tastes and changed how some people thought.

There was that period of unrest where the young generation, UK black people, were now in their teens and going through several different challenges. From you know, the teddy boys to the BMP and so on, it was pretty horrific, and some faced police brutality and otherwise. Hence, the house parties and blues parties continued until about the time of Bob Marley. At the same time, British bands began to emerge, including Matumbi, Aswad, Steel Pulse and Black Slate.

The Trojan label launched artists such as Desmond Decker, Bob, Marcia, and Jimmy Cliff, who were touring the UK. Bob Marley was touring the UK and other artists from Jamaica to promote their songs. This allowed British bands, musicians and singers to support these well-known live acts. The reggae circuit flourished from the blues parties to the dancehalls of Birmingham, Manchester and prominent cities in the UK. If you were a promoter in those days, the cost of touring an international band was significantly higher than touring a local reggae band. There are other considerations; at the time, British bands needed the pulling power to sell records or the tickets necessary to cover the gross potential and provide the promoter with profit.

Coming to the notice of the British public were bands like Aswad, Steel Pulse, Black Slate, Misty in Roots and The Reggae Regulars. They had learnt to play reggae music similar to Jamaica's music. We were inspired by what our parents played on their radiograms and listened to on the radio. Bob Marley had arrived in the UK, hits such as 'No Woman, No Cry' endorsed the release of his live album and the albums, 'Natty Dread' and 'Exodus' cemented him as a reggae icon, propelling reggae as a genre throughout the world.

Roots Music

At a time when immigration in the UK was reaching a peak, subjectively, I had little understanding of the word racism and its meaning. Historically, history lessons at school covered the transatlantic slave trade to some extent. However, I didn't understand its relationship to colonialism, current affairs and social justice. By contrast, I was learning something different from the narrative of the lyrics in reggae music. Then, it joined the dots for me and provided me with perspective. Song lyrics spoke of injustice and poverty and helped me understand why my parents grasped the courage to leave despite how beautiful the Caribbean was.

Reggae was becoming more akin to spiritual consciousness. This subject matter struck a chord with young British-born West Indians who had suffered tragic stories sometimes littered with unfair prejudices and the echoes of Enoch Powell's 'Rivers of Blood' speech delivered in the West Midlands since their arrival. By now, children born out of the Windrush generation were in their teens and were introduced to a level of awareness that, for some, was very painful, as they were now on the receiving end of the issues of race, class and gender. Faced with the reality of being told England was not their home, it was confusing; hence, many decided to resist.

Real-life struggles were beginning to make sense; it was bands like Burning Spear, Culture, Fred Locks, Dennis Brown, and Bob Marley provided children of the Windrush generation who were suffering prejudice and violence in the inner cities with an understanding of the history of not only the West Indies the origins of our parents, but Africa, our true origins as black African people. It was new and something most parents never wanted to discuss. It was a difficult concept to understand. My parents would always talk about the West Indies and its beauty. They talked about how they had little money but were happy, so it was challenging and not uncommon to understand that some families went hungry, toilets didn't have running water, etc. My most significant shock was 'Roots'; the televised version of Alex Hayley's book aired on TV. For the first time, there in front of us as African Caribbean was a historical graphic account of what it was truly like to be a slave. It made me think of the 1996 film 'A Time to Kill'; I almost wanted to get my own back, but the hurt was disappointing. Having said that, my new sense of pride was born, and my love for music and black history grew enormously.

Songs like 'My Boy Lollipop' provided West Indians with an escape from the harsh realities of their working lives and reminded them of the spirit of home, perhaps similar to the Church for some of us.

- **British Reggae Bands**
- **Critical Characteristics of a British Reggae Band**
- **Musical Style**

Reggae Influence A band's music features the core elements of their genre, reggae featuring an offbeat rhythm (skank), bass-heavy grooves, and often socially conscious lyrics.

Fusion with Other Genres: British reggae bands often blend reggae with other styles, including punk, ska, dub, rock, and more, creating unique subgenres like "reggae-punk" or "reggae-rock."

Cultural Background

Diverse Influences British reggae bands often reflect the multicultural makeup of the UK, with members from various ethnic backgrounds, including those with Caribbean, African, and European roots.

Themes and Lyrics Many British reggae bands address issues relevant to their experiences in the UK, such as social justice, racial inequality, immigration, and urban life.

Geographical Roots

UK-based Reggae Bands based in the United Kingdom tend to tour internationally regularly.

Linton Kwesi Johnson

Local Scenes Many British reggae bands are closely associated with specific local scenes, like the vibrant reggae scene in Birmingham (home to bands like UB40 and Steel Pulse) and London, such as Aswad.

Linton Kwesi Johnson is a Jamaican-British poet, musician, and activist known for his significant contributions to the genre of dub poetry. Born on August 24, 1952, in Chapelton, Jamaica, he moved to the UK in 1963. Johnson's work often addresses themes of social justice, racial inequality, and the experiences of the Black diaspora, reflecting his political activism and cultural heritage.

His poetry is characterised by its musicality and incorporation of Jamaican Patois, which he delivers in a powerful, rhythmic style. His most notable works include collections like *"Dread Beat an' Blood"* and *"Night Haunts."*

In addition to his poetry, Johnson has also released several albums that blend music and spoken word, further popularising dub poetry. He is regarded as one of the key figures in developing this art form and has influenced many artists and poets in the Caribbean and beyond.

Linton Kwesi Johnson (LKJ) is a seminal figure who not only developed British reggae but also served to pioneer his voice with political dub poetry. His legacy is multi-faceted, shaping British reggae and Black British cultural identity in several key ways:

Pioneering Dub Poetry:

Johnson is widely recognised as one of the originators of straightforward *dub poetry*, a genre that blends spoken-word poetry with reggae and dub music. His works are infused with social and political commentary, making them a powerful tool for expressing the struggles of Black Britons.

This form of expression resonated deeply with the British Caribbean diaspora, and he used it to address issues like racism, police brutality, and class oppression, bringing an intellectual and activist voice to reggae music.

Politicising Reggae Music:

While reggae is inherently rooted in resistance and Rastafarian ideology, LKJ's works amplified the political dimension of British reggae by addressing specific issues faced by Black Britons in the 1970s and 1980s. Songs and poems like *"Inglan is a Bitch"* and *"Sonny's Lettah"* articulate the frustration and anger of marginalised communities. His focus on political activism inspired other British reggae artists to incorporate themes of resistance and anti-establishment messages into their music.

Creating a Distinct British Sound:

LKJ's integration of reggae with distinctly British social issues helped create a sub-genre of reggae that differed from its Jamaican counterpart.

British reggae, influenced by Johnson, became more introspective and attuned to local experiences of urban poverty, racial injustice, and immigration, reflecting Caribbean heritage and British working-class reality.

Challenging Mainstream Narratives:

Through his poetry and music, Johnson challenged the mainstream narrative of what it meant to be British. He forced listeners to confront uncomfortable truths about racial inequality and the colonial legacy, bringing Black British culture into the national conversation. His work was significant in the face of the National Front and widespread racism in the 1970s, making him a voice for resistance and resilience, which resonated with young British disenfranchised black and minority ethnic groups.

International Influence:

Johnson's influence extends beyond the UK, as he became a global figure in reggae and the spoken word movement. His records, mainly through his label *LKJ Records*, were internationally successful, bringing British reggae and dub poetry to a broader audience. His unique delivery, blending Jamaican patois with British dialect, also helped to internationalise a distinctive form of British Black culture.

Archiving Black British Experiences:

His poetry and music serve as a historical archive of Black British experiences during a turbulent time in the UK's social history. LKJ captured the mood of post-Windrush generations, their struggles for equality, and the cultural contributions they made to British society. This gave future generations a way to connect with their heritage through music.

Legacy in British Reggae:

LKJ's work made reggae not just a vehicle for entertainment but a powerful medium for social change in Britain. He redefined the genre by combining it with political activism, and his works influenced a wide range of artists, poets, and musicians within the British reggae scene and beyond. Today, Linton Kwesi Johnson is celebrated as a musician, poet and cultural historian who transformed British reggae into a distinct, political, and culturally rich art form.

His influence continues to resonate, especially in the way British reggae serves as a platform for social justice. His unique voice helped ensure that the genre remains a key part of the UK's multicultural identity.

Benjamin Zephaniah

Benjamin Zephaniah is a British poet, writer, and activist known for his powerful spoken word performances and works addressing race, social justice, and inequality issues. Born on April 15, 1958, in Birmingham, England, Zephaniah grew up in a working-class Jamaican family and was heavily influenced by his heritage's reggae music and culture.

Zephaniah left school at 13, feeling that formal education did not suit him, and soon became known for his street poetry, which was inspired by the rhythms of Jamaican music and his experiences with racism. His poetry is characterised by its accessibility, blending traditional poetry with elements of dub, a form of reggae music. Some of his most famous works include *Pen Rhythm* (1980) and *The Dread Affair* (1985), but he is also known for his activism, campaigning against racism, police brutality, and other social injustices.

In addition to his poetry, Zephaniah has written novels, including *Face* (1999), a young adult novel dealing with issues of identity and appearance, and *Refugee Boy* (2001), which explores the experiences of a young refugee in England. He has also been a prominent voice in campaigns against animal cruelty and veganism, similar to the British MC Macka B.

Zephaniah was offered an Order of the British Empire (OBE) in 2003 but famously turned it down, citing his opposition to British colonialism and imperialism as reasons.

British Reggae Bands

Historical Context

Windrush Migration Influence The rise of British reggae is closely linked to the Windrush generation (Caribbean immigrants who came to the UK post-World War Two), who brought reggae and ska music with them and significantly influenced the UK music scene.

Political Context British reggae has often been tied to political and social movements, particularly in the 1970s and 1980s, when bands used their music to comment on issues like race relations, police brutality, and economic inequality.

Examples of British Reggae Bands

Steel Pulse emerged from Birmingham in the mid-1970s. They are known for their politically charged lyrics and deep reggae sound.

UB40 One of the most commercially successful British reggae bands, known for hits like "Red Red Wine" and "Kingston Town."

Aswad is a London-based band that combines reggae with elements of soul and funk, contributing to the popularisation of reggae in the UK.

These bands and others have shaped the British reggae scene, creating a distinct sound that reflects and influences the broader UK cultural landscape.

The Cimarons

The Cimarons are considered a British reggae band. They signed to Polydor Records in 1978 with the release of 'Maka' and embarked on a British tour with solo shows in the major UK cities and support for punk rock bands such as Sham 69. The band continued as a successful outfit for years but with changes in the line-up.

Winston (Reedy) Reid has been a successful lover rock singer, with hits like 'Paradise In Your Eyes', 'Moi Emma Oh' and 'Dim The Lights' in 1983.

The Cimarons and British reggae, it is more fitting to use the word transition. Transition because it could be said that the Cimarons were young people who were part of the Windrush generation. They had arrived in London, UK, and became part of the youth culture destined to fit into the music scene in the 60s. Like many bands at the time, as teenagers, they met at school in the neighbourhood or at the local youth club, as history would have it. The Cimarons band members included the following:

Franklyn Dunn
Carl Levy
Lloyd Donaldson
Locksley Gichie

Maurice Ellis
Carl Lewis
Winston Reid

As musicians and singers in their own right, and based in north London, the Cimarons also became session musicians for Duke Reid's Trojan Record label. They often came together as the backing band for well-known Jamaican artists who had hit the national UK charts, such as Jimmy Cliff, Nicky Thomas, Dennis Brown and Ken Booth. The Cimarons could be said to have emerged as a working band.

With a constant stream of work, both live, in the studio and on TV, the experience proved to be a valuable apprenticeship for what was to become of the band. The Cimarons released three popular singles, which included 'We Are Not the Same', 'Ethiopian Romance' and 'Morning Sun'. Armed with the connections and support they possessed, recording with reggae producer greats like 'Lee Perry' and 'Tommy Cowan's Record label, where they achieved a Jamaican chart number 1 for the cover of Bob Marley's 'Talking Blues' which provided the platform to continue recording songs in the UK and Jamaica at studios such as Black Ark, Channel One and Randy's.

Steel Pulse

Basil Gabbidon and David Hinds formed the

Band Steel Pulse. Driven by an innate inspiration to bring about a need to provide awareness of the unfairness experienced by African Caribbean black young people in Birmingham and other inner cities of the UK, Steel Pulse decided it was time to stand up and be counted. To this end, they did not hold back.

Steel Pulse's "Ku Klux Klan" release in 1978 marked a pivotal moment for the band and British reggae. Their debut album, "Handsworth Revolution," showcased a fusion of roots reggae with R&B harmonies and jazz inflexions, earning them acclaim and recognition. The album's success, including reaching 1 on the British reggae charts, solidified Steel Pulse's position as ground-breaking artists, not just imitators of Jamaican sounds. "Handsworth Revolution" remains a powerful testament to protest music, addressing social issues with soul and spirituality while giving voice to West Indian immigrant communities in England.

The Band consisted of the following members:

David Hinds
Basil Gabbdon
Steve Nisbiett
Alphonso Martin
Selwyn Brown
Mykaell Riley 00

David Hinds explained how Steel Pulse was influenced by Jamaican reggae artists Bob Marley and The Wailers and began rehearsing.

David continued by commenting that the band was propelled by the punk scene sweeping the UK at the time. David continued by stating, 'We were able to support bands like the Sex Pistols, The Undertones, Sham69, Blondie, and The Clash. Steel Pulse recorded several singles before coming up with a song called 'Nyah Luv' on Anchor Records before performing at famous city centre night clubs in Birmingham, UK, such as Barbarella's off Broad Street, Rebecca's, John Bright Street, Abigale's, Hurst Street, the Ceder Club, Constitution Hill, Hockley and the Elbow Room in Newtown.

From left: w/Steel Pulse's 1, David Hinds, Lead Singer

2, Amlak Tafari

3, Amlak & Selwyn

4, Grantley GT, Selwyn and Amlak Selwyn Brown

In the 1970s, I was lucky enough to work for Eddie at Abigail's in Birmingham. I was taken on by the head chef (Roger), who took me on as a commis chef while studying at college to complete my City and Guilds 706/1 and 706/2 qualifications. I say lucky because, on several occasions, Eddie would pop by and request Roger prepare a steak Diane or a Chateaubriand; he loved his steak cooked medium rare. However, Eddie didn't talk to me much, but one day, he said, 'I've got a few clubs in Birmingham. Have you ever been to any of them? I answered no. He told me that as I now worked for him, I could attend any of them free of charge. Just let the bouncers know you work as a chef at Abigail's.

Talking to staff members, I was told Eddie was a good boxer in a previous life. There were rumours that he had run the Kray twins out of the Elbow Room in Newtown and that they never returned. Eddie's clubs were the talk of the town, and at least one of them was the go-to venue for teenagers at that time. Rebbeca's was no exception. You would be entertained by a band or two on particular days of the week. This is where I first saw Steel Pulse. They were different to other local bands. They had an image that seemed to pull the band together. They played their instruments well and had outstanding vocalists and a good frontman easily identified by one big dreadlock that stood tall above his head.

It was no different in his other clubs. This 17-year-old got to see some well-known acts, such as Tom Jones, and go backstage, too. My mom was always delighted. It came to the time when Rebecca's was refurbished to Edwards No7 and Abigail's became Ladbrokes Casino, but I had left by then.

At this time, the musical tastes of British youth culture were changing. As David recalled, it was the punk rock era; Rastafarian was having a hard time in Caribbean clubs, which would not book them due to indigenous beliefs and didn't want to risk alienating other clubgoers to their clubs, which had started to spring up.

Not to be deterred, Steel Pulse took their brand of British reggae to other cities where teenagers could listen to different bands considered undesirable and driven by rebellion.

Burning Spear was booked to play the Rainbow, New Street, Birmingham, and Aswad, which had been confirmed as the backing band, which provided the opportunity for Steel Pulse to support Burning Spear. It was at this gig that Steel Pulse got spotted by Island Records. The first single from the album 'Handsworth Revolution', 'Ku Klux Klan,' achieved a top 40 chart hit in 1979.

Musical Youth

Musical Youth began their journey into British Reggae Music in Birmingham in 1979 through the fathers of Kelvin, Michael Grant and Freddie 'Junior' Waite. I met Fredrick Waite, also known as Little Freddie, at the Crompton Pub, Crompton Road, Handsworth, Birmingham, where I held a residency two nights a week as a DJ. I remember him listening to my set one night and telling me he could get me some gigs because he felt I was a good DJ. This encouragement gave me confidence and went a long way, especially when he commented when I played a song called 'Queen Majesty' by the Techniques and U Roy.

Grantley GT and Dennis Seaton

Kelvin Grant and Grantley GT

Freddie told me he had been one of the original members and was working with a young group I could see at the pub if I had time. I remember following him up on his invitation and thinking the group had something; they reminded me of the Jacksons. However, I felt they needed to use the 'youth' factor, and these guys had an infectious, charismatic flavour and could play their instruments. The Band consisted of the following members.

Dennis
Kelvin
Michael
Freddie 'Junior'

I lost touch with Freddie until I heard a remake of

the Mighty Diamonds song 'Pass The Kouchie' on Radio 1.

For a good reason, Musical Youth had changed the word Kouchie to Dutchie (an aluminium Caribbean pot used to cook). The group's lineup was slightly different and now included a new frontman. What was fantastic for me was that they had Kelvin MCing on selective bars of the song, which brought a youthful, up-to-date feel to the 'Mighty Diamonds' version. They had also strategically placed a steel pan melody, which added to the song's commercial appeal.

Managed by Tony Owens, the band was signed to MCA Records. In 1982, 'Pass the Dutchie' hit number one in the UK charts and achieved chart success worldwide. The band topped the Billboard Hot 100 at number 10, selling over four million. Musical Youth didn't stop there; they went on to have hits such as 'The Youth of Today', 'Never Gonna Give You Up', and the collaboration 'Unconditional Love' with Donna Summer.

Musical Youth Commendations

The first Black Band to have a video played on MTV. One of four British Reggae Artists/Bands to achieve Grammy Nominations, alongside UB40, Aswad, Maxi Priest, Steel Pulse, Pato Banton and Tippa Irie.

Micheal became a notable record producer. Fredrick Waite passed away on 20th July 2022, following a history of mental health problems. Dennis Seaton continues to perform as the frontman of Musical Youth to this day, trailblazing the legacy of one of the most successful British Reggae bands out of Birmingham, England.

Beshara

Elias Pharoah founded the Birmingham-based reggae group Beshara. The band traded under names such as 'Cool Dimension' and 'The Kushites' before settling on Beshara in 1979.

The band members consisted of:

Ray Watts
Dixie Pinnock
Errol Nanton
Michael Nanton
Anthony Garfield
Steven Morrison
Byron Baily
Paul Cunningham
David Carr
Forcett Gray

From my hometown, Birmingham, UK, members like Tony Garfield (a singer from schooldays) went to Percy Shurmer Infant and Junior School together and were friends; Byron Bailey and

I almost lived next door to each other; his brother (Tony mentioned earlier in this book) done a lot together.

I met and built up a friendship with their cousin Steve Morrison when he emigrated from Jamaica and came to live with them not too far from Cannon Hill Park, Birmingham. Finally, there is Dixie Pinnock, who I knew from the 'Church of the First Born', who was a talented guitarist and drummer.

Talented musicians in July 1980, John Peel played their single 'When You're Wrong' on BBC Radio 1. Beshara toured the UK at major colleges, universities, and nightclubs, attracting broad audiences. This led to a heavy schedule and new material, including the notable 'Men Cry Too', which reached number six in the British reggae charts, and 'Glory Glory'. Beshara sometime later released one of my all-time favourites from them, 'Shadow of Love, ' which also achieved a reggae chart top ten status, earning the band 'Best Sound Recording' award at the Hummingbird's Annual Black Music Awards in 1987. In the late 1980s, Beshara was chosen by Ijahman Levi to back him on his African and European tour.

Beshara has shared the stage with acts like UB40, The Abyssinians, Beres Hammond, and Simply

Red, to name a few, and appeared on television programs such as Rockers Roadshow, Black on Black, and Here & Now. Their song 'United' was used as the theme for the BBC documentary Ring in the Park and later covered by Pato Banton as 'United We Stand', featuring Ray Watts' vocals. Beshara was featured in the documentary Made in Birmingham: Reggae, Punk, Bhangra, and a band clip appeared in the 2011 BBC Four documentary Reggae Britannia. As a tribute to Ray Watts, Tony Garfield performed as Beshara at the "Giants of Lovers Rock Part 3" concert in London in 2011.

In 1992, the band headlined a concert in Handsworth, Birmingham, broadcast live by BBC WM. The band reunited in 1998 to work on their debut album. Unfortunately, Ray Watts, the band's vocalist, passed away in the year 2000, causing members to go their separate ways.

Ex-members reunited for a one-off performance in 2005 at the "32 Years of Lovers Rock" concert in London promoted by Orlando Gittens. Former members Steve Morrison and Michael Nanton became critical members of Pato Banton's Reggae Revolution band and toured with Pato, Sting and Gregory Isaacs. Consequently, they have contributed to Grammy-nominated albums by Pato and Steel Pulse.

Aswad

All members of Aswad were born in the UK and of the Windrush generation whose parents were from the West Indies and settled in areas such as Neasden, Willesden and Ladbrook Grove, London. Attending the same school and being musically minded, Brinsley put the word out for musicians who wanted to join a band, and a natural team emerged whose name was Aswad's; the members included:

Brinsley Forde
George Oban
Angus "Drummie' Gaye (RIP)
Tony Robinson
Donald Griffiths
Courtney Hemmings

When Donald Griffiths, Courtney Hemmings, and George Oban departed for one reason or another, Aswad became a three-piece outfit featuring Brinsley, Drummie, and Tony. Additional musicians played with Aswad as session musicians; I came to know brothers Patrick and Buttons when they joined UB40 as session musicians and Bubblers Tan Tan and Bammie at a later date.

In a conversation with ex-manager Bernie Dixon, he discussed viewing the young band as West Indian young people growing up in the UK. He didn't just see himself as a manager but a mentor;

he felt a sense of closeness to them as an educator. The name Aswad means (Black), but for some, it closely resembles Aswan, the Egyptian City.

Aswad became known as an influential outfit who possessed a fabulous presence. At the time, Brinsley Forde MBE was well known for his part in Aswad but, before this, for his parts in the Double-Deckers and Please Sir prime-time children's programmes in the 70s. Entertainment for young people would typically come on Saturday mornings, for me at the Alhambra Cinema, Moseley Road, Top Rank, Dale End, which became (The Hummingbird) Birmingham. Almost every young child would probably watch it back when there was only one channel, BBC 1. It aired over the weekend. I would be glued to the TV watching the double-deckers and watching Brinsley, who looked like a regular black kid, but his part was excellent in the program. Taking a break from acting and becoming a father, Brinsley contemplated turning to his passion, music. While working in Neasden, London, one day, he met Peter Tosh, part of the Wailers Band from Jamaica, featuring Bob Marley.

Through a friend, Brinsley struck up a friendship with the Wailers and regularly paid them a visit where they were currently staying nearby. Aswad learned a lot from the union, which led in some ways to their eventual signing with Island Records.

The next we would witness Brinsley's acting abilities would be in a film called Babylon in 1980, which was based around the brutality of black young people growing up in London, facing the brutal realities of being in a foreign country, which wasn't unfamiliar. The central thing for me is that it reflected precisely what was going on at the time: the brutality, the unrest, the issues relating to fitting in, and most importantly, the Dancehall. What was unique about the film Babylon featured Jah Shaka's sound system. As a lead actor, Brinsley played the part of a black youth facing prejudice where the escapism was reggae dub music. Dennis Bovell, who greatly influenced the musical score and produced much of the soundtrack, gave the film authenticity and featured marginalised young people.

This resonated at the time with young black men across the UK. This factor provides a kind of mentorship to the viewers as well as a break from the tensions of the issues of prejudice and unfair treatment at that time. Aswad's 'Warrior Charge' was vital in this respect.

Drummie Zeb, Tony Robinson, Sweetie Irie and I

The song has gone on to in-shrine the band into the history books, but the reggae charts and dancehalls, at the time which was the place where people met up to dance and skank to dub, which provided an escape from our 9 to 5s, free from the mundane realities of working in factories for the whole week and getting rid of it in the dance halls at that time you had sound systems like Sir Coxson, King Tubby, Mombasa, Stereograph, Small Axe, Sir Frana B, Frontline International, Dread Diamond and Jah Shaka. Sir Christopher and a lot of other sounds.

With Bernie at the helm, Aswad became the backing band for Burning Spear in 1977 and featured on the live album recorded at London's West End, Rainbow Theatre (also contracted to Island Records at the time). As with most British reggae bands at that time, the genre was root's reggae or message-based music that focussed on current affairs which directly related to black young people growing up in the inner cities of the UK, such as 'Three Babylon', 'It's Not Our Wish' and 'Warrior Charge'.

At the time, Brinsley was featured as the main frontman and songwriter. Following the release of Aswad, the album, Tony Robinson became the band's keyboard and bass player. Aswad followed up the self-titled Aswad with Hulet (meaning 2) in 1978. Seeking a wider audience, Aswad incorporated Michael Reuben Campbell as producer and manager, who later became manager, to release A New Chapter of Dub, which included 'Warrior Charge' a clever move in those days, because it provided a two-for-one, for example, The New Chapter album, with the removal of the vocals. In 1982, Aswad released their fourth studio album, 'Not Satisfied'. This album was to prove a landmark for Aswad because it was a particular year in the history of the famous Notting Hill Carnival, Notting Hill, London, in August 1983. Aswad played live and recorded 'Live and Direct' their fifth album to an animated audience with resounding success. A bonus that came with the album's success was collaborating with the incomparable Dennis Brown with the song 'Promise Land'. This placed Aswad in history books as one of the iconic British Reggae bands.

In 1988, Aswad's authenticity, creative musical ability, and audience took them to greater heights with the release of 'Don't Turn Around'; in conversation with Les Spine, their manager stated the band benefitted from having two lead vocalists. I always felt (Drummies) vocals were better suited to songs with a lighter tone alongside the band's infectious harmonies. 'Don't Turn Around' reached number one on the UK charts, followed by 'Give a Little Love', 'The Best of My Love', and 'Shine' in 1994, which benefited from Brinsley's delivery.

Aswad has toured extensively and graced venues such as Wembley Stadium, London Reggae Sunsplash, Montego Bay, Jamaica, and The Royal Albert Hall. As a producer, Aswad has produced for artists such as Cliff Richard, Maxi Priest, and

Pato Banton and collaborated with Sting and Greenpeace.

\Sadly, Brinsley left the band in 1996, and Angus (Drummie Zeb) Gaye died in 2009. He was well-loved and will be greatly missed.

Tradition

The British reggae band Tradition is known for blending classic reggae rhythms with influences from soul, funk, and other contemporary genres of the late 1970s and early 1980s. Their sound is heavily rooted in the cultural and political context of the UK during that time, where a fusion of Caribbean and British musical elements emerged within the reggae scene.

Band Members

Les McNeil
Paul Thompson
Chris Henry
Paul Dawkins
Tony Matthews
Michael Johnson
Shakeel Khan

Tradition formed in the mid-1970s and became a crucial part of the UK reggae movement, standing alongside other notable acts like Steel Pulse and Aswad. The band was known for its tight musicianship, socially conscious lyrics, and a distinctly polished sound that set it apart from the rawer styles of Jamaican reggae. Their music often addressed themes of unity, love (Lovers Rock), and social issues relevant to the Black British community, resonating with many during racial tension in the UK.

Musical Style

Tradition's music leaned heavily on smooth reggae rhythms characterised by skanking rhythm guitar patterns, deep bass lines, and steady, relaxed drumbeats.

However, what set them apart was their infusion of soulful elements, reflecting the influence of Motown and classic R&B. Their sound was described as (lovers rock), a subgenre of reggae that was more mellow and romantic and often featured sweet, harmonised vocals. Tradition also explored roots reggae, which is more politically and spiritually charged and rooted in Rastafarian culture and ideology.

Vocal Arrangements

One of Tradition's defining characteristics was its vocal arrangements. Their harmonies were lush and meticulously arranged, reminiscent of classic soul groups but with a distinct reggae flair. Lead vocals were often smooth and dynamic, delivering poignant lyrics that could alternate between socially aware messages and themes of love. The rich, multi-part harmonies gave their music a full, uplifting sound that worked with the laid-back instrumental backdrop.

In summary, Tradition blended reggae with British soul and lovers' rock, creating a distinctive and sophisticated sound musically and thematically. Their vocal arrangements, rich with harmonies, helped define their identity within the British reggae scene.

Tradition, a reggae band from North London, was formed in 1976, initially under Special Brew.

In 1977, the band signed with Venture Records and released singles such as 'Moving On', 'Rastafari', and 'Summertime'. They also headlined shows for the Anti-Nazi League's 'Rock Against Racism' tour, contributing to the fight against racism through their music.

In 1978, Tradition released a 12-inch single, 'Why Why', which helped solidify their reputation as an exciting live act. They backed prominent reggae singers, including Alton Ellis, Delroy Wilson, Honey Boy, and Culture, and also worked as a studio band for producer David Tyrone. That same year, their single "Breezin'" won the Best Single award from Echoes, and they briefly signed with RCA Records.

In 1979, Paul Dawkins left the band to pursue a solo career, with Shakeel Khan replacing him. As members gradually left, their 1982 album Spirit of Ecstasy heavily relied on Thompson's keyboard work. McNeil also pursued a solo career.

In the 2000s, Thompson and McNeil formed a new band called Reloaded. Later, in the late 2000s, Tradition reunited to perform once again.

Black Slate

Blake Slate, like many of the other UK bands at the time, came together in 1974 and featured the following members:

Anthony Brightly
Chris Hanson
Desmond Mahoney
Jesse Brade

As I mentioned, bands formed in the UK learned many original Jamaican songs well. This allowed promoters to remove visa complications and cut airfares and other associated costs. They allowed two or three individuals, including the vocal artist, to work with indigenous UK-based bands in rehearsals. Black Slate was no exception.

However, a difference was that two members were British-born, and the other two came from different islands in the Caribbean. Musicians would sing the praises of the band because they could play authentically.

Black Slate would also support Jamaican artists as a famous and backing band. The opportunity this presented meant they could sing their songs, which led to the release of their self-founded single, 'Sticks Man' in 1976. 'Sticks Man' focussed on the times of the day, which was becoming commonplace in the UK, which was mugging, which later became taxing and street robbery. This subject area spoke the urban street crime and therefore got the attention of young teenage people, which created the platform for their follow-up hit 'Amigo' released on Ensign records, a pleasant song with a vital reggae genre that closely related to their Jamaican counterparts and the African Caribbean community especially at a time when Top of the Pops was so influential in the UK.

'Amigo' also became a hit in Europe and forged a well-earned touring band career, where Ensign would continue to release several albums and singles, culminating with a US tour in 2016.

UB40

I learned of UB40 as a teenager going to blues parties and pubs in the Birmingham area of Balsall Heath, Moseley and Kings Heath, Birmingham, UK. Before getting to know them, I loved that their name Social Security Benefit card derived from the British social security benefit card (the DOLE) card, which was called UB40. I remember seeing UB40 play at two venues: the 'Hare and Hounds' Kings Heath and the Fighting Cox Moseley, Birmingham.

What was clear back then was that they had something unique. They were multicultural, had a strong sense of togetherness, some good chords, distinguished members, and great vocals that stood out, one that would have fitted right into a stage or studio in Kingston, Jamaica, but a Brummie. UB40 featured band members:

Ali Campbell
Robin Campbell
Jimmy Brown
Earl Falconer
Yomi Babayemi
Norman Hassan
Brian Travers
Jimmy Lynn

After Yomi and Jimmy's departure, Mickey Virtue and Astro joined the band. I was listening to bands from Birmingham, such as African Star (Crucial Music), Pato's original band. Eclipse, Salam Foundation, and others provided an excellent time for reggae music in Birmingham, the industry, and growth. However, a key factor was the release of a single or an album. This allowed bands to get heard when not playing live.

I'd been a DJ for a while, and I was learning the other side of the music industry, which was, as said before, about live music and the steps to rehearsing for live shows, writing songs, forming an image, production, studio recording, and hopefully, the charts. UB40 managed to do this, so like me, they gave most individuals entering the reggae music industry an inspiration, something to aim for, the first steps towards entering the madness of the music industry, and the doors towards chart success. For such a small place, at the time, Birmingham was a hotbed of talented bands who had emerged from the ground up to become top 10 in the National music charts. UB40 had done it on their terms.

The UB's would sell out pubs and music venues in the area solid, so you had to get in early if you wanted to see them. You have to buy your drinks and stack them high because there's probably no way you would get to the bar afterwards. I always left with a memory of UB40 and that unique voice; I later learned it was the voices of the Campbell brothers, Robin and Ali.

A number of their signature songs were original UB40 numbers. A popular thought by many was that the UB's were a reggae cover band to this very. However, nothing could be further from the truth. Great songs like 'King', 'Food for Thought', and 'Dream A Lie' were original and charted in the top ten, establishing the band as an authentic outfit and transforming the concept of British pop music. UB40 lyrics spoke of the times we lived in; they provided an alternative aspect to what was printed in the broadsheets and tabloids. Rooted in rebellion and a subtle eagerness to speak from the heart, their songs provided a narrative that told us that 'If it Happens Again' tells the story of Thatcher's Conservative Government. The UBs stated if she returned, they would be leaving.

The early '80s was a time, for some, marked by unemployment, signing on with your UB40 card, youth training schemes (YTS), the miner's strikes and the winter of discontent. The authentic lyrics in their music endeared youngsters like myself to the harsh realities of life. Many UB40's fans didn't know it then and wrongly believed they were a band that sang songs written by reggae legends. However, nothing could have been further from the truth UB40 wrote many of their original hits, such as those mentioned below:

1, **Present Arms**

2, **King**

3, **Food For Thought**

4, **If It Happens Again**

5, **Sing Our Own Song**

6, One in Ten

7, Rat In The Kitchen

UB40 covered songs by reggae greats, such as Lord Creator's 'Kingston Town', Honey Boy's 'Impossible Love' and Hopeton Lewis's 'Grooving'. By contrast, 'Red Red Wine' by Neil Diamond was a reggae hit in 1969 sung by Tony Tribe, and 'I Got You Babe' by Sonny and Cher wouldn't be classified as reggae artists.

Nevertheless, the production of Ray Pablo Faulkner and the band skilfully connected music and lyrics; UB40's infectious melodies provided the band with a unique blend in Ali and Robin's voices that embodied emotion, sincerity and commitment.

Similarly, the English Beat (Ranking Roger and Dave Wakling) recorded 'Stand Down Margaret. I guess Roots ethnic of unequal treatment, so I learned there was a more profound sense of where UB40 came from. They talked about things happening to young people, our parents, and generations before, and they gave us an understanding of the current affairs the popular media wasn't telling us. Ethnic mixing and a feeling that despite the general narrative, all ethnic groups did not possess the same views as the British National Party (BNP).

UB40's Jeffrey Morgan album cover clearly states Jeffrey Morgan Loves White Girls (written on a wall). At the heart of it was ethnicity and mix; I thought it was fantastic. These guys who lived in my area came from schools like mine, St Luke's and Moseley Art, within walking distance of my house. Talking with Brian, Astro, Ali, and Micki was no different to speaking with Pato or Tippa. It was like that. I remember giving Mikey some tracks to pass on to a radio DJ in California, which later led to negotiating an album deal in North America. The UBs were individuals who have always assisted us; they were well-grounded.

I remember leaving an interview at **KROQ**, and Ali and I were walking down Sunset Boulevard, Los Angeles, to his hotel for some drinks when he said to me, remember Grant, this is bigger than us; it's about our mates back in Birmingham; we got to do it for them, we represent them, that's where we come from, but were here remember, we're here in California! I'll never forget that conversation with Ali; he also told me who not to trust in the business. Ali never suffered fools gladly.

Grantley GT and Ali Campbell

They treated us the same from Birmingham to New York or anywhere else. I remember being on the cusp of the Baggariddim UK tour. UB invited most Birmingham MCs featured on the album onto their UK stadium dates. Pato being one, I had to fly him to Scotland to begin. We had just completed six shows over the weekend between Huddersfield and London.

I booked him onto a flight from Heathrow to Scotland without sleep. The main deal was that he met up with the band and completed the tour. Those days were crazy!!

UB40 was the only band at that time who invested in talent out of Birmingham, providing them with a platform not just a tokenistic platform but an absolute platform where you would record the song at the Abattoir, their Studio in Digbeth, Birmingham, invite them to a professional photoshoot, and provide them with a spot on their UK tour. You would have to pay to play with a band like Duran Duran, who lived around the corner from me.

Pato Banton was one of the MCs chosen to feature on the US American Album. 'Little Baggariddim' included Pato's songs such as 'hip-hop, lyrical, Robot', and 'King Step', providing us with another opportunity for media and ultimately contributing to Pato's debut performance at the ROXY on Sunset Boulevard, Los Angeles.

Chapter 4

British Lovers Rock

Lovers Rock, a British reggae genre that started in the 1970s and 1980s, brought together elements of traditional reggae that sat side by side with soul and R&B, reflecting a unique British sub-genre of its elder sibling reggae, a musical multi-cultural offshoot derived from the second generation Windrush decency.

Artists and musicians contributed to the development of the Lovers' Rock genre. However, its significant development began with young African-Caribbean female vocalists, such as Louisa Mark, Janet Kay, Caroll Thompson, and Jean Adebambo, who almost carved their names in the genre from its inception. British Sound Systems propelled them alongside record shops. The pirate radio stations' arrival inspired local radio DJs in the UK's significant cities. British MCs such as Papa Levi, Smiley Culture, Tippa Irie, Pato Banton and Macka B substantially brought a new flavour to reggae music, pushing this new musical genre into the dance halls and the whole community of youth culture. It can also be said that record companies, distributors, radio and the media were reinvigorated with the development of the British fast style, as was the world. It was a common thread that whilst on tour, people often asked what the difference was between British and Jamaican MCs, and I would always reply, 'the fast style'.

I've heard it often said that if music is the food of love, let it play on; that was certainly the case for me. My time in the British Reggae Music Industry started at eleven years old and spans over thirty-five years. Over this period, I have taken stock of the time spent in my working life and asked myself if it was worth it. Occasionally, I laughed and reflected; however, I decided to change things when all was said and done. Deciding to put pen to paper was difficult. I needed help finding the time and mind space, or I just needed more time to start. Nevertheless, my story in and outside the British reggae music industry will provide readers with an understanding of some of the mysteries within the industry, which some see as glamourous without ever really getting the opportunity to read about the disappointment between some of those beautiful moments.

Reggae singers typically have rich, soulful voices that embody smooth delivery and a relaxed voice with a powerful vocal style. They often infuse their singing with elements of Jamaican patois and incorporate melodic phrasing that complements the laid-back rhythms of reggae music. Additionally, reggae singers usually convey emotions ranging from joy and celebration to introspection and social commentary through their expressive vocal performances.

The British Lovers Rock reggae genre is known for its smooth, romantic and soulful sound. It emerged in the UK in the 1970s and 1980s, primarily among the African Caribbean diaspora. Lovers Rock incorporates traditional reggae, soul and R&B elements, creating a distinctively British take on the genre.

Musically, Lovers Rock is characterised by its laid-back rhythms, melodic basslines, and lush instrumental arrangements. The tempo is often slower than other reggae forms, allowing for a more relaxed and sensual vibe. Key instruments such as the guitar, keyboards, and horns create smooth, harmonious melodies that complement the romantic lyrics.

Lyrically, Lovers Rock focuses on themes of love,

romance, and relationships. The songs often feature heartfelt expressions of affection, longing, and desire, making them popular choices for slow dances and intimate moments. The lyrics may also touch on social issues and personal experiences within love and relationships.

British Lovers Rock is celebrated for its smooth grooves, soulful vocals, and heartfelt lyrics. It offers a distinctively British interpretation of reggae that has influenced artists and audiences worldwide.

Louisa Mark

Louisa Mark's voice is characterised by its unique blend of sweetness and depth. She possesses a captivating vocal tone that effortlessly glides over reggae rhythms with grace and soulfulness. Mark's singing style is marked by its dynamic power and sincerity, conveying a range of emotions from joy to heartache with authenticity. Her smooth delivery and melodic phrasing draw listeners in, making her voice instantly recognisable and unforgettable. Louisa Mark's voice leaves a lasting impression, showcasing her talent as a standout figure in the reggae music scene.

'Caught You In A Lie' and 'Six Street' Lovers Rock was an offshoot derived from rhythm, blues and Jamaican love songs. In Britain, reggae musicians learned how to play Jamaican music utilising two or three chords. At that time, 'Castro Brown and the Crown Prince of reggae, Dennis Brown, formed the DEB reggae label and began producing records with British-born groups and singers. They would draw together a set of session musicians, hire a studio and source the vocalists he felt would deliver the desired vocals for a final mix and release.

Dennis Bovell (Matumbi)

Dennis Bovell began his career in the music industry as a musician on the West Indian island of Barbados in 1965. Dennis told me that as part of the Windrush diaspora, Dennis was attracted to the music culture of Jamaica. Inspired by Reggae-Dub, Dennis and several talented friends at the time set up the sound system known as Jah Sufferer, which led shortly after, becoming a member of the reggae group Matumbi, which released a string of British reggae hits, including 'Man In Me', 'After Tonight', and 'Point of View'. Matumbi, fronted by Dennis Bovell, released 'After Tonight', which spoke of getting together with someone you had just met. 'The Man in Me' continued with a similar message, one of the relationships in 1976. Around this time, Dennis Brown came to the UK for the first time to support Black Uhuru. Grassroots reggae was now finding its way into the blues parties and dancehalls in the UK.

Dennis Bovell and Grantley GT

Dennis is an accomplished producer who has produced records to his credit, such as those of Janet Kay and Linton Kwesi Johnson, as well as his own 'Dub-Reggae' records using the name Blackbeard. On a typical day in the life of Dennis Bovell, you might find him cutting reggae dubplates as a passion. Because of his sound system links, Dennis was profoundly aware that generating dubplates in the studio was a great way to establish musical content for other sound systems and a potent tool necessary for promoting reggae records at that time in the UK.

Dennis is also an accomplished sound engineer who displayed his musical abilities by collaborating with Dip Records throughout the reggae Lovers Rock label, setting the vanguard and inception of the genre we now know as lovers rock, experimenting with the popular 80's New York sound of disco. Here, Dennis sought to raise the tempo of his brand of Lovers Rock with the chart sound at the time and with some success with a song that hit the British charts, reaching number two. 'Silly Games' sung by Janet Kay. Dennis told me he wrote the lyrics and composition for Janet, collaborating with Drummie Zeb of Aswad on live drums. He stated that he was looking for movement on the drums, and Drummie was able to deliver in abundance.

He has produced albums by a wide variety of artists, including Creation Rebel, the Thompson Twins, Alpha Blondy, Madness, Fela Kuti (the early pioneer of the famous African genre Afro Beat) today, along with Bananarama, Orange Juice, I-Roy and the iconic Linton Kwesi Johnson.

Bovell also co-wrote and co-produced the majority of material by British reggae singer Bobby Kray. In 1980, he wrote the score for Babylon, starring Brindsley Forde of Aswad and Jah Shaka sound system. Dennis also wrote music for the 1983 television drama The Boy Who Won the Pools and Global Revolution 2006.

To his credit, Dennis has been part of the production team for the BBC's series Reggae Britannia, Empire Road; he also produced the album Mek It Run, collaborated with dub producer

Gaudi, featured with Lee 'Scratch' Perry and The Orb, and again with the release of the film 'Lovers Rock, part of the BBC Small Axe production.

In recognition of his significant contributions to the music industry, Dennis Bovell was appointed the (MBE) Member of the Order of the British Empire in 2021. This prestigious honour underscores his immense impact and influence in the music world, a testament to his talent and dedication.

15, 16, and 17

15, 16, and 17, comprised of three girls, including Sonia Williams, Christine and Wraydene McNabb. Their first release encapsulated their ages and what was happening at that moment for black and ethnic minority young people. The girls spoke about their preferences and their love of black skin boys. 'Black Skin Boy' was released in 1977 and produced by Castro Brown on DB Music and Morpheus Records. Indeed, this trio can take credit for giving Gregory Isaacs the AKA 'The Cool Ruler'.

Brown Sugar

In the same year came Brown Sugar's release of 'I'm In Love With A Dreadlocks' on the 'Lovers Rock Record label, produced by Dennis Bovell, followed closely with 'Black Pride' Dreadlocks became an identifiable style of wearing one's hair for both men and women, who typically tie theirs back with an attractive cotton cloth wrap. It is related to one's cultural beliefs. Nevertheless, Brown Sugar followed up their local reggae hit with a flurry of songs: 'Our Reggae Music' and 'Black Pride'.

Investigators

The Investigators, a lovers' rock band formed in 1975, was based in Battersea, south London, England. The Band consisted of the following members:

Lorenzo Hall
Michael Gordon
Ian Austin
Reg Graham
Martin Christie

The remaining instrumentalists were session players. The group were no strangers to the UK reggae scene, having performed as the Private I's, working alongside Chris Lane of Fashion Records. As the Private I's they recorded at Otis Gayle's Studio One classic, 'I'll Be Around', although it was the b-side, 'Love Won't Let Me Wait', that secured a placing in the reggae chart, along with a version of Black Uhuru's 'Folk Song'. The band recorded numerous melodies, including 'Living In A World Of Magic', 'What Love Has Done' and 'Loving Feeling' on their Private Eye label, 'Love

Is What You Make It', and the seductive 'Turn Out The Lights'. For Inner City, they recorded their number 1 reggae hit, 'Baby I'm Yours', followed by 'Summertime Blues' and 'Close To You'.

The line-up also provided the foundation for Dee Sharp's debut, 'Let's Dub It Up', which topped the reggae chart in 1980, closely followed by 'It's Too Late Baby'. The releases did much to acquaint reggae followers with the newly formed Fashion label.

In 1981, the group toured the UK and USA supporting Black Uhuru, but to little acclaim. In 1984 the band gained recognition with 'Woman I Need Your Loving'. They continued to maintain a high profile, releasing lovers' hits, and in 1985, they performed as the opening act at the second Reggae Sunsplash festival in the UK. The showcase was a prelude to the European leg of the Sunsplash world tour, which has flourished, although not in the UK. Following the Investigators' ending, Lorenzo Hall and Michael Gordon pursued successful solo careers, with Gordon having a notable chart hit with 'Don't Want No More'. At the same time, Hall recorded the popular 'Don't Let Go'.

One Blood

Paul Robinson, along with his brothers Errol, Jerry, Ewan, and Trevor, was a reggae group One Blood member in the 1980s until the group broke up after Errol's death. One Blood released two albums in 1982: In Love and Super Showcase. The Band consisted of the following members:

Paul Robinson
Errol Robinson
Ewan Robinson
Jerry Robinson
Trevor Robinson

Barry Boom (born Paul Robinson) is a reggae singer and record producer from London, UK. Paul Robinson was a member of the reggae group One Blood in the 1980s along with his brothers Errol, Jerry, Ewan & Trevor until the group broke up after Errol's death. One Blood released two albums in 1982 - In Love and Super Showcase. He also worked as a producer and songwriter for other artists, including the debut album by Maxi Priest and Papa Levi's "Mi God Mi King" single (the first single by a UK-born artist to reach number one in Jamaica.

After One Blood, he worked with Robbie before pursuing a solo career under the name Barry Boom, which he had previously used as a pseudonym for his production work. He signed to Fashion Records, and his first solo releases in 1989 included reggae number ones with 'Making Love', 'Number One Girl', and 'Hurry Over'. His debut solo album, 'The Living Boom', followed in 1990, featuring his three big hits from the previous year. He followed this with Trust Me in 1993 and signed to MCA Records with a Taste of Things to Come in 1997. He later moved into Gospel Reggae, releasing the album His Love in 2018.

Carroll Thompson

Carroll Thompson's voice is characterised by warmth, clarity, and dynamic power.

She possesses a smooth and soulful vocal tone that effortlessly glides over reggae rhythms, captivating listeners with her expressive delivery. Caroll's singing often conveys a sense of intimacy and depth, drawing audiences into the emotional heart of her music. Her voice is captivating and soul-stirring, making her a beloved figure in the reggae music scene.

Born in the UK, Caroll became prominent in the early 1980s, when Reggae icons like Dennis Brown stuck a chord with young people. This opened the gates for homegrown Lovers Rock singers like Caroll, 15, 16, 17, Brown Sugar and Janet Kay to enter the market and carve out the genre better known to some as Lover's Rock. This provided a seamless pathway to the release of Caroll's smash album hit, 'I'm So Sorry,' in 1981. Her debut album, 'Hopelessly in Love', was released in 1981. The album included the hit singles "I'm So Sorry" and "Simply in Love," which became classics in the Lover's Rock scene.

Caroll's soulful voice and passionate delivery have earned her the nickname, like many other female British Lovers Rock vocalists, 'Queen of Lovers Rock'. She has been an influential figure in the UK reggae scene throughout her career, often collaborating with other artists and contributing to the genre's development.

In addition to her music career, Carroll Thompson has also worked as a session vocalist, contributing to various projects across different genres. She remains active in the music industry, performing and recording, and is celebrated as a pioneering figure in Lovers Rock.

Janet Kay

Janet Kay's voice is often described as smooth, soulful, and soothing, with a distinctive warmth and richness. Her unique timbre resonates with emotion and authenticity, capturing the essence of reggae music with her melodic delivery and heartfelt lyrics.

Janet Kay is a British reggae singer and actress best

known for her hit single 'Silly Games', released in 1979. Janet embodies the sentiment as a child of the Windrush generation, born to Jamaican parents; Janet became one of the leading female voices in the UK Lover's Rock British Reggae genre known for its romantic themes and smooth, soulful R&B sound.

'Silly Games', produced by Dennis Bovell, became a national hit, reaching number two in the UK singles chart and achieving iconic status within the Lover's Rock genre. The song is particularly noted for Kay's unbelievably high notes and the emotional delivery of its lyrics.

In addition to her singing career, Janet Kay has also worked as an actress, appearing in various British television shows, including the popular soap opera EastEnders. Like Victor Romero Evans, she starred in the television sitcom No Problem!

Janet Kay's influence extends beyond her recordings; she has inspired many other artists in the Lover's Rock and reggae scenes, and her music continues to be celebrated for its timeless appeal.

Jean Adebambo

Jean Adebambo's voice is characterised by its soulful timbre and compelling emotional resonance. Her rich, warm vocal tone effortlessly conveys strength and vulnerability. Adebambo's singing style is marked by its versatility, allowing her to transition between smooth melodies and powerful vocal runs seamlessly. Her expressive delivery captivates listeners, drawing them into the heartfelt stories and messages conveyed through her music. Overall, Adebambo's voice exudes a timeless quality that has solidified her place as a respected figure in the reggae music landscape. It was a fantastic time because it was a vibrant time; you could listen to Lover Rock for hours, Janet Kay's 'Silly Games', and Jean Adebambo's 'Paradise', arguably Jean's most famous recording until her untimely passing in January 2009.

Sandra Cross

Sandra Cross's voice is marked by its smooth, velvety texture and heartfelt delivery. She has a unique ability to infuse her singing with soulful emotion, effortlessly transitioning between melodic phrases and soulful runs. Cross's vocal style is captivating and evocative, drawing listeners in with depth and sincerity. Whether delivering uplifting melodies or poignant ballads, her voice resonates with authenticity and passion, solidifying her status as a revered figure in reggae music. Sandra Cross is the only girl among seven brothers (most musicians) from the inner city of Brixton, South London. Like many African Caribbean singers and musicians, she cut her teeth in church. Sandra sang and could play the piano at a very young age.

By fourteen, Sandra, with one of her friends, formed 'Love and Unity', entered a talent show, and won first prize with the song 'I Adore You', released by Studio 76 Records. It became number one in Britain's reggae charts in 1979. The following singles were 'I Just Don't Care', 'I Can't Let You Go', and 'Put It On'.

Sandra teamed up with 'The Mad Professor', who, as said previously, formed the 'The Wild Bunch' and released an album that reached the reggae album chart top in 1984. Sandra and the band toured Europe, where Sandra returned to release her first solo single, 'Country Living', a cover of the Stylistics hit but more fitting a song sung by the internationally renowned Mighty Diamonds from Jamaica.

Sandra entered the British reggae charts for ten straight weeks in 1985, finding its resting place at number one. Her second solo attempt, 'You're Lying', nested at the top spot for four weeks; Ariwa released her debut solo album, Country Living, in 1986. She won the British Reggae Awards for the Best Female Singer six consecutive years from 1985 to 1991. Other awards include the Radio London Entertainment Celebrity Award in 1986. 1989, she was celebrated in The Voice Newspaper Music Awards as Best Reggae Female Artist and won the Chicago Radio Awards for the biggest-selling record in 1990.

Ariwa released six albums on Sandra, including The Wild Bunch LP; in 1992, she recorded Lovers Interlude on Teichiku Records. In 1996, she recorded the first reggae/jazz album, Just A Dream, on Pioneer Records, a Japanese label like Teichiku. Sandra's latest recordings have appeared on SCM Records, an acronym for Sandra Cross Music.

Deborah Glasgow

I remember meeting Deborah Glasgow (RIP) in 1986 at the Mark Angelo studio in London. Deborah had accompanied Patrick Donagon for a meeting with me to discuss using the 'Hello Darling' track for lyrics she had written. I remember asking Debbie to sing the song acapella, which she did. What a voice, I thought, saying that. I loved her voice, one I would describe as having traces of Luther Vandross; her harmonies were something to be desired, reminiscent of Sandra Cross. Her spirit was extraordinary, bright, and loving, with a smile that beamed inside and out. In typical Deborah style, she said what do you think then? I responded that I'd talk with Tippa and Chris Cracknell. For those who know Debbie or the reggae business, the rest is history. This led to the remix and release of 'Your My Sugar', and a record deal with UK Bubblers, the Greensleeves Records, a subsidiary of and subsequent series of popular singles, including 'Knight in Shining

Armour,' 'When Somebody Loves You Back,' and 'Don't Stay Away.' Prior to this, Deborah released her first single, 'Fallin in Love', on the Ariwa label.

Following a brief break and talking to Chris one day, he commented sometime in 1989 that 'Gussie' Clarke, in Jamaica, liked Deborah's voice a lot and wanted to record some tracks with her in the new set-up he had in Jamaica. He stated that Steely & Cleevie had recorded some new riddims that would work well with Debbie's; hence, he was about to send her to Jamaica to record them. As things turned out, the recording sessions went well and very quickly.

The trip proved very successful for Deborah, and the highlight was that she became a household name in the UK and many parts of the world. The tracks, when compiled, became landmarks and led to Chris's release of the self-titled 'Deborah Glasgow album. An instant hit in the UK for sound systems, radio and personal collections alike, you could hear the bassline of her collaboration with Shabba Ranks, the release of 'Champion Lover' for Shabba as 'Mr Loverman' and 'Don't Test Me' in 1990. These vocal deliveries showed Deborah's incredible versatility when working with the local sound systems.

Years later, the re-release of 'Mr Loverman' proved you can't stop an excellent record with

Chevelle Franklin featured as the singer became a worldwide hit.

The album struck a chord in Jamaica with Debbie's collaboration with Beres Hammond on 'Perfect Situation'. Debbie continues on the album with favourites, showing off her vocal acrobatics alongside Dean Frazer on Saxophone with 'Fantasy Becomes Reality', 'Best Friend', and 'I Know Your Cheating'.

Fatefully, Debbie was diagnosed with cancer, which brought about her untimely passing in 1994 at twenty-eight.

Peter Hunnigale

A softly spoken, humble individual based out of Brixton, London, who is firmly present in the British reggae business. Peter Hunnigale (Honey Vibes), a British reggae lovers' rock singer best known for his melodically high vocal tones, has become one of England's favourite male vocalists.

Peter started his career as a bass guitarist with the Vibes Corner Collective and played the bass guitar for **The Pioneers** as a session musician. In 1983, LGR Records issued his debut release as a singer, 'Slipping Away', which he followed up with 'Got To Know You', written and produced for the Street Vibes label he set up with engineer Fitzroy Blake, a member of the Street Vibes Collective, which included Delroy (Fluty) and brother Paul Blake DJ Commander B.

Peter scored a reggae number one in the UK reggae chart in 1987 with the hit 'Be My Lady', followed by the release of his debut album 'In This Time'; featuring 'Let's Get It Together', 'Fool For You', 'Girl On The Side', 'Giving Myself Away' to name a few. What came next was the collaboration that solidified his name as not only a lover rock crooner but a dancehall vocalist with the number one hit 'Ragamuffin Girl' with Tippa Irie, produced by Paul Blake, voted best British Reggae Record by Echoes and eared them best record winning the Tony Williams award in 1987.

Gathering pace, Peter won the Best Newcomer award at the Celebrity Awards in 1987 and Best British Reggae Album at the British Reggae Industry Awards the same year. Continuing with his musical success, Peter's success, alongside his relationship with Tippa Irie, led me to negotiate the album 'The New Decade' on Island Records. 'Done Cook and Currie' followed on the Tribal Base label for rebel MC, which was produced and written by Irie and Hunnigale.

Peter has gone on to write with other prominent artists, such as The Mighty Diamonds with 'Absent From The Heart' for Mikey Koo's on Island Records, not to mention the famous Maxi Priest favourite 'Best of Me' for Virgin Records, which was subsequently covered by My Boyz Beatz featuring Lucy Tennyson. Peter has lent his talents as a writer and accomplished musician, recording in Jam

1, Tippa Irie, Grantley GT and Peter Hunnigale

2, Peter Hunnigale and Grantley GT

Peter followed his solo work with a second solo album, Mr. Vibes, in 1992. He rejoined Tippa in 1993 with 'Shouting For The Gunners' a single, celebrating their beloved football team, Arsenal football club in 1994.

Peter has gone on to record albums with Mad Professor Ariwa with Mr Government, 'Declaration of Rights' recorded for the 'Nah Give Up' which again featured Tippa Irie, notching up the Best Reggae Album MOBO award in 1996, as well as notable collaborations with Dennis Brown, Janet Lee Davis and Lloyd Brown before wrapping the year up with a performance at Jamaica's Reggae Sunsplash festival.

Not content with the offerings above, Peter has continued with collaborations with the late Nerious Joseph and Glamma Kid, furnishing another UK number one in the reggae charts with 'No Diggity'; music continues to know no bounds for Mr Hunnigale at this present time, nevertheless, watch this space.

Mike Anthony

Mike Anthony, a British reggae singer, is known for his smooth, soulful voice that blends elements of lover's rock, a subgenre of reggae that emphasises romantic themes. His singing style is characterised by:

Melodic Smoothness: His vocals are gentle and melodic, often flowing effortlessly over laid-back, rhythmic reggae beats.

Emotional Depth: Anthony's voice conveys warmth and vulnerability, especially in his love songs, a hallmark of the lover's rock style.

Clear Articulation: His diction is clear and precise, allowing the emotional content of his lyrics to come through effectively.

Laid-Back Delivery: His style is relaxed and soothing, matching the mellow, groove-centric production typical of lover's rock.

I heard about Mike Anthony through some business I had with Paul Robinson (Barry Boom) where. I was at his home listening to a demo he was working on for Tippa Irie when playing me something he was working on that he felt had tremendous potential; that person was Mike Antony. I commented that Mike's voice carried a delicate blend of reggae rhythms and a soulful, almost R&B-like smoothness, making his sound captivating and easy to listen to. Mike has just gone on and on and on.

Anthony was born in Lewisham, London, England. His early recordings, produced by Barry Boom, quickly gained attention in the reggae scene, leading to his first significant success with the top ten hit 'Crash Crash'. This was followed by popular tracks like 'Glide Gently',' 'Cruising in Love', and 'Open Your Heart'. He later signed with Fashion Records and released the hit single 'Still Your Number One', eventually dominating the reggae charts for several weeks with his cover of David Ruffin's 'Walk Away From Love'.

Throughout the 1990s and 2000s, Anthony continued to make an impact on the UK reggae charts with a string of successful songs, including 'No Halfway Love', 'Spread Love', 'Sexy Eyes', 'How Long', 'Don't Play Games', and 'Call Me'. His collaborations with Peter Hunnigale helped cement his superstar status within the lover's rock genre. He has also performed at notable events like Jamaica's iconic Reggae Sunsplash festival.

Don Campbell

Don Campbell, a British reggae singer known for his contributions to lover's rock, has a smooth, soulful voice often described as warm and melodic. His vocal style is expressive, bringing tenderness and depth to the romantic themes typical of lover's rock. His range is primarily in the tenor register, where he delivers clear, flowing melodies. Campbell's voice is not overly showy but is marked by its controlled, silky tone, and his ability to convey deep feelings with subtle vocal nuances makes his performances captivating.

His vocal range might not always cover extreme lows, but it is versatile enough to express vulnerability and strength, adding a rich, heartfelt quality to his music.

Don began his musical career in the early 1980s, playing with several influential reggae bands and artists. As a member of Carlton "Bubblers" Ogilvie and Tony "Ruff Cutt" Phillips' **Undivided Roots Band,** he participated in projects such as Creation Rebel, Singers and Players, and Style Scott's Dub Syndicate. Don also contributed drums to Vivian Jones' works, which were popular with Jah Shaka's cultural sound system sessions; as a session musician, he worked with Bim Sherman's Across the Red Sea album, which included Sherman's rendition of 'When The Roll Is Called Up Yonder' and a cover of Stranger Cole and Gladstone Anderson's 'Just Like a River'. Working with Prince Far, I laid the perfect foundation for him to begin his solo career in 1993, releasing his debut single, which quickly entered the British reggae charts.

His first three singles and debut album all topped the charts, earning him six awards at the 1994 British Reggae Industry Awards.

He later collaborated with General Saint on a series of records, including a cover of Neil Sedaka's "Oh! Carol," which reached number 54 on the UK Singles Chart. This was followed by "Save the

Last Dance for Me," which peaked at number 75, and "Stop That Train." These collaborations were compiled into the 1995 album Time on the Move.

Since then, Campbell has recorded several albums, including a version of the Bee Gees' "Islands in the Stream" with J.C. Lodge, and performed at the Bob Marley Day Festival in Long Beach, California 2003.

Winsome

Winsome came to the notice of the public and began her recording career in 1985 when she signed with John MacGillivray and Chris Lane's Fashion Record label. Her first release featured a cover of Barbara Acklin's 'Am I The Same Girl', a perfect moment to introduce Winsome to a busy reggae music industry growing daily. However, with its solid one-drop mid-tempo beat and melodic chord construction, the rhythm utilised Aswad's Brinsley Forde, Tony Robinson, Angus Gaye and Bigger Morrison as session musicians and Deborah Glasgow provided the backdrop for Winsome to carve a path for Burrell's vocal style. It is often described as a soulfully smooth yet powerful, warm melodic tone that blends well with reggae rhythms. Her voice is gentle, characterised by a clear diction and emotional depth. Winsome delivered her lyrics with calm confidence while still conveying the heartfelt messages and passion typical of reggae music.

Sparing no expense, the best of the best was called in to support this production. Indeed, it would have to be the case because Fashion was firing on all cylinders with this one track, 'Can't Take The Lies', 'Born Free', and 'Homebreaker'. With her string of hits, Winsome has toured throughout the UK and taken her brand of reggae outside to Europe. In 1987, she performed at the British reggae Sunsplash at Clapham Common, England. However, she didn't stop there; returning to the studio, Winsome recorded memorable collaborations with the following artists:

'Tonight's the Night w/ Gospel Fish
'Hold On' w/ General Levy
'Best Years Of My Life' w/ Sweetie Irie
'Lets Start Over' w/ Frankie Paul
'Rock With Me Baby w/ Nerious Joseph
'Superwoman' w/ Tippa Irie

From left: Jbeatz0121, Paulette Tajah, Tippa Irie Winsome Peter Spence and Grantley GT

In 1989, Tippa Irie and Winsome received a reggae award for the number-one hit, 'Superwoman'. Winsome has continued to record memorable songs that please fans near and far. Her contributions to the British reggae music industry will trigger memories for many years, ensuring that the name Winsome will never be forgotten anytime soon.

Paulette Tajah

Paulette Tajah came to the attention of British reggae radio, the charts, and the public in 1983 with a song called 'Move Up Close To Me' on LGR Records. However, the record that put her firmly on the lovers' rock map was her cover of Denice Williams' song' Cos You Love Me Baby' on the Raiders label in 1984.

I met Paulette shortly after this and would describe her vocal style and prowess as smooth and soulful. Her music lends itself perfectly to R&B and the lovers' rock subgenre, a romantic and softer reggae style. Her music typically blends heartfelt lyrics with mellow reggae rhythms, making her a standout in the lovers' rock scene. Tajah has often been celebrated for her ability to convey deep emotion through her vocal performances, with songs that explore themes of love, relationships, and personal reflection. Her interpretations of both original songs and reggae covers have earned her a dedicated fan base

In 1994, Paulette embarked on a project with Tex Johnson and produced an album of well-known lover's rock classics, "Happy Memories," which was well-received and is timeless in its nostalgic appeal.

'You Are The One' in 1985; in 1986, Paulette released 'You Are The One' and 'Glad Your Gone' on the Exclusive record label. Not one to remain quiet for too long, Paulette continued to work with several producers and record labels, including Anthony Brightlys' (Sir George) label with 'It Ain't Easy' and 'Miss You'.

In 1987 and 88, Paulette went into the studio with the Mad Professor at Ariwa and recorded the following tracks:

'Stop, Look Listen'
'Put A Little Love Away'
'Lonely'
'Last Night'
'Let's Make A Baby', the Billy Paul cover, further promoted Paulette as an artist to watch.

In 2001, Paulette released 'Back to the Old Skool', a compilation of rare groove classics in a lover's rock style, which was well-received by reggae fans and radio.

Tajah has been working on a new EP, "Journal of a Butterfly," where she has collaborated closely with the legendary Carlton 'Bubblers' Ogilvie and includes new original songs like "Giving You Up" on the "Big Frock Riddim" and beautifully executed covers like "Still in love." and "Smile" she also gained new inspiration for the album working with the artist, songwriter, composer, musician and producer Richie Davis, to create the song "African Woman," which has added another dimension to the body of work Paulette currently has. To this end, Paulette Tajah has continued to work with various producers and has been promoting herself for over three decades. There isn't no stopping her for now.

Vivian Jones

Vivian Jones is a British Jamaican reggae singer and songwriter known for his smooth vocal style and conscious lyrics. His music spans a range of reggae sub-genres, including lovers rock, roots reggae, and dub, making him a versatile artist in the reggae scene. Emerging in the late 1970s, Jones has released numerous albums and singles that often focus on love, spirituality, and social issues. His tracks like 'Sugar Love' and 'Jah See Dem a Come' highlight his ability to blend romantic themes with more profound, reflective messages. He remains a respected figure in reggae, known for his consistency and dedication to the genre.

Born in Trelawny Parish, Jamaica, in 1957, Vivian Jones moved to England at the age of ten to join his parents, who had emigrated a few years earlier. Settling in various parts of London, including Willesden, Alperton, and Harrow, Jones became increasingly involved in the local reggae scene. By the mid-1970s, he began performing with sound systems, initially as a deejay. During this period, he was a member of several bands, including The Spartans, The Doctor Birds, The Mighty Vibes, and The Pieces.

1980 saw Vivian launched his solo career with the hit single 'Good Morning', a remixed track from The Mighty Vibes that topped the UK reggae charts. His rising popularity led to him being voted 'Most Talented Singer' in a 1981 poll by Black Echoes magazine. A series of hits followed, gaining him recognition in the UK and Jamaica. However, disillusioned with the music industry, Jones returned to Jamaica in 1982, staying with his grandparents while recording new material.

After a brief hiatus, Jones returned to London and began working outside the music scene, but soon resumed recording in his spare time. In 1984, he released his debut album Bank Robbery, recorded with the London-based band Undivided Roots, featuring members like Carlton "Bubblers" Ogilvie, Tony 'Ruff Cut' Philips, and Eskimo Fox, an Alpha Boys' School alum. Dubplate versions of the track 'Flash It And Gwan' from the album gained popularity on Jah Shaka's sound system, leading to a collaboration on the Jah Works album in 1987. Jones's work with Jah Shaka is notably featured in Handsworth Songs, a 1986 documentary directed by John Akomfrah, filmed during the 1985 riots in Handsworth and London.

Throughout the 1990s, Jones continued recording, working with Jamaican producers such as Bobby Digital and Junior Reid and collaborating with artists like Sylvia Tella, Debbie Gordon, and Deborahe Glasgow. He also launched his label, Imperial House, becoming a prominent figure in the lover's rock genre with hits like 'Sugar Love' and 'Strong Love'. He also maintained a roots reggae presence with albums such as Iyaman (1994). In 1991, he was named 'Best Male Artist' at the British Reggae Industry Awards.

In the late 1990s, Jones scored an international hit with 'Jah See Dem a Come'. To celebrate his 50th birthday in 2007, he released the album 50th, featuring rhythms from legendary producers such as Bunny Lee. He followed up with Lovers Rocking in 2013 and recorded new material in Jamaica with Sly and Robbie and Bobby Digital, with plans for an album release in 2014.

Janet Lee Davis

Janet Lee Davis is a British reggae singer known for her smooth, soulful voice and contributions to the lover's rock genre, a romantic subgenre of reggae. Emerging in the late 1980s, Davis quickly became a beloved figure within the UK reggae scene. Her music blends elements of reggae with soul and R&B, creating a mellow, dynamic sound that resonates with themes of love and relationships.

As an artist, she is celebrated for her ability to deliver heartfelt performances with warmth and sincerity. Songs like "You're My Latest, My Greatest Inspiration" and "Baby, I've Been Missing

You" showcase her rich vocal range and emotional depth, solidifying her as one of the genre's leading female voices during her era. Davis style is timeless, appealing to reggae enthusiasts and smooth, romantic music fans.

Born in London in 1966, Janet-Lee Davis moved to Jamaica at the age of three, where she was raised. Years of singing in the local church choir led to starting her professional career in 1981, performing as a vocalist and DJ with the St. Catherine-based Ghetto Sound. After gaining recognition, she relocated to the UK, quickly becoming recognised with her solo hit for Flash, 'Never Gonna Let You Go'.

1987 marked the release of her number one in the reggae charts, 'Two Timing Lover' on the Fashion record label. Again, in 1990, she topped the reggae charts with C.J. Lewis, performing a cover of Keith and Enid's, 'Worried Over You'.

Janet's success led to her signing to Island Records via Mikey Koos, with the release of 'Spoilt By Your Love', produced by Koos and Bubblers Ogilvie, and 'Pleasure Seekers' produced by Bluey of Incognito.

Janet returned to Fashion with a flurry of UK Lovers Rock favourites, including hits like 'Ooh Baby Baby', 'Big Mistake' and 'Ready To Learn' and the collaboration with Tippa Irie's 'Baby I've Been Missing You', in 1994.

Janet has been awarded such accolades as Best Female Singer and Best UK Album by the British Reggae Industry and the Bob Marley Award for Best Female Singer by the Black Arts, Sports, and Enterprise Awards.

Kofi

Kofi, the British reggae singer, is known for her soulful, smooth, and expressive vocal style. As a vocalist, she blends the warmth of traditional reggae with influences from lover's rock, a subgenre emphasising romantic and mellow themes. Her voice is rich and velvety, often delivering heartfelt lyrics with clarity and grace, which connects deeply with her audience.

As a performer, Kofi exudes a calm yet commanding stage presence. She captivates listeners with her ability to convey vulnerability and strength, often allowing the emotion of her lyrics to shine through her performance. Her stage persona is approachable and elegant, drawing on the warmth and intimacy of lover's rock while staying true to the rhythmic roots of reggae. Overall, Kofi is celebrated for her ability to deliver powerful performances with genuine feeling and finesse.

Grantley GT and Kofi

Paulette Tajah Peter Sence Grantley GT & Kofi

Kofi first found success as a member of Brown Sugar, featuring Caron Wheeler and Pauline Catlin. Topping the charts in 1977, 'I'm in Love With a Dreadlocks' became the first release on the Lover's Rock record label formed by Dennis

Harris, John Kpiaye and the legendary Dennis Bovell. The label title came to become the definition for the genre of music known as Lover's rock.

Brown Sugar disbanded in 1983, and Carol became the artist known as Kofi and reinvented herself as a solo artist. Kofi signed with Mad Professor Ariwa, and they released three albums.

The hits came almost immediately with covers of the original Brown Sugar hits. Embraced by reggae lovers in the UK, the British reggae charts recorded them as such, with songs like:

'I Am So Proud'
'I'm in Love With a Dreadlocks'
'Black Pride'
'Didn't I' (on which Kofi also played bass guitar),
'Looking Over Love'
'I'm Still in Love with You'
'Proud of Mandela'

Kofi collaborated with MC Macka B on the British reggae charts in 1990 with their cover of the impressions hit 'I'm So Proud'. Kofi notched up British Reggae Industry Awards in 1988, 'Best Female Vocalist', for the songs 'Didn't I' and 'Black Pride'. Kofi went on to achieve further awards in 1989, establishing her status as one of the queens of Lovers Rock.

Kofi has gone on to work with Jazzie B of Soul II Soul, Motown Records, in 1992 on Soul II Soul Volume III album, 'Just Right' on 'Move Me No Mountain' and 'Future'. Throughout this period, Kofi released 'Step By Step' in 1992.

Kofi has participated in musical theatre commissioned by Disney-Buena Vista in Simply Mad About the Mouse: A Musical Celebration of Imagination, a project put together by Disney/Buena Vista, which includes LL Cool J, Michael Bolton, and Billy Joel, to name a few.

Kofi has gone on to work with producers and artists such as Mafia and Fluxy, Earl Sixteen, Luciano, Morgan Heritage and Freddie McGregor.

Victor Romero Evens

I choose to mention Victor in this book because although he was not born in the UK, the imprint of his contribution since his arrival on British shores has left its mark on British Reggae history, such as the likes of Dennis Bovell and particular members of reggae bands formed in the UK. Victor achieved his first reggae number 1 in 1981 with the song 'At The Club' on Epic Records.

Vocally, Victor delivered the British Reggae charts three of my favourites: 'At The Club', 'I Need A Girl Tonight' and 'Miss Attractive' in 1983.

Similar to Brinsley Ford (Aswad), Victor began his career on television, where he was featured on programs such as 'Black On Black' (as Moves) and 'No Problem' in 1983-1985 (as Bellamy) alongside Janet Kay (Angel) Judith Jacob, (Senisimilia) Chris Cummings (Toshiba) and Shope Shodeinde (Terri). He extended his abilities to the silver screen, where he was featured in the film 'Babylon' 1980 (as Lover) and Steven Seagal's film 'Marked For Death' 1990 as (Nesta) alongside my friend from Los Angeles, California, Prince Ital Joe (RIP).

Victor has starred in Performing Arts musicals such as 'The Big Life', 'Sugar Mummies', 'Moon On A Rainbow Shawl', 'Raggamuffin', 'One Love' and 'The Harder They Come' to name a few.

Recently, Victor performed and toured with Janet Kay and Carroll Thompson with the 'Lovers Rock Monologues', highlighting 'Lovers Rock' in its heyday. It chronicles the journey experienced by many UK Windrush descendants in the 70s and 80s.

John McLean

John McLean, a British reggae singer, is distinguished by his unique soulful voice and significant role in the Lover's Rock subgenre of reggae. His ascent to fame in the 1980s was marked by his hit single 'If I Gave My Heart to

You', released in 1985 and produced by Neil Frazer, CEO at Ariwa Records. This track topped the reggae charts for several weeks. Still, it solidified his position as a critical figure in the UK reggae scene, particularly within the lover's rock style. It perpetuated a fusion of reggae rhythms with romantic themes and soulful melodies. John followed the single with the album barring the same name, 'If I Gave My Heart to You' and singles 'Truly Bowled Over' and 'Starliner'.

John is a London-born reggae musician who has won over audiences with his deep and rhythmic sound. His music and collaborations with Ariwa fuse roots and modern reggae, creating an original and engaging listening experience. John recorded his second album 'Men Are Lovers Too' which features 'Even Though You're Gone', 'Dedication of Love', 'Can't Hold On', and a single for Fashion Records 'I'll Be Waiting', which utilises the Six Street rhythm and 'Black Is Our Colour', 'from Ariwa's 30th Anniversary Album. John's music often features smooth, heartfelt vocals that picture him caught in the raptures of relationships fraught with love and loss. It's hard not to imagine John sitting with a pen and pad beside a hands-free telephone, writing one song after another in tears (this is not to say I have never found myself in tears when losing a relationship). Still, John's talent and ability to do this hold no bounds. His vocal range with lyrics that focus on love and relationships, which is displayed in his album, making him a favourite among fans of this genre. While less widely known internationally than other reggae artists, John McLean remains respected in the UK reggae community.

If I Gave My Heart to You was such a favourite for My Boyz Beatz that I produced remixes for Peter Spence and Lucy Tennyson.

Lover's rock is a distinctive reggae music subgenre originating in the UK during the mid-1970s. Unlike the politically charged themes commonly associated with roots reggae from Jamaica, lovers rock is known for its romantic lyrics, smooth melodies, and softer sound, blending reggae rhythms with soulful elements. It provided a platform for British Caribbean youth to express their experiences and emotions and resonated with young Black women, often underrepresented in other reggae subgenres.

Lloyd Brown

Lloyd Brown is a British reggae singer known for his smooth, soulful voice and contributions to the UK reggae scene. He was born in London and began his music career in the late 1970s. His style blends traditional roots reggae, lovers rock, and modern influences, often delivering socially conscious messages or romantic themes.

Brown's music career took off in the 1980s when he began performing with various sound systems and reggae collectives. In the 1990s, he gained wider recognition with the release of his albums, particularly *Straight No Chaser* (1997) and *Against the Grain* (2003). His hits like «Main Squeeze,» «Bless Me,» and «Sharing the Night» established him as a prominent figure in lovers rock, a subgenre of reggae focused on romantic themes.

Throughout his career, Lloyd Brown has been praised for his consistency, longevity, and ability to adapt to changing musical trends while maintaining the essence of roots reggae and lovers rock.

Christopher Ellis

Christopher Ellis is a British reggae singer and the son of the legendary Jamaican reggae artist Alton Ellis, often referred to as the "Godfather of Rocksteady." Alton Ellis was a pioneering figure in the development of reggae and rocksteady music, known for classic hits like "I'm Still in Love," "Girl I've Got a Date," and "Ain't That Loving You."

Christopher Ellis has followed in his father's musical footsteps, blending reggae with modern sounds. He was born in London and grew up surrounded by reggae music. He gained recognition after working with the Ghetto Youths International label, which Stephen and Damian Marley founded. Some of his famous songs include "End of Time" and "Better Than Love," which showcase his soulful voice and modern reggae style while paying homage to his father's legacy.

Christopher has been keeping the family tradition alive by performing and recording in a genre closely tied to his roots, maintaining the spirit of reggae music across generations.

Lover's Rock Key artists in include:

Janet Kay
Carroll Thompson
Louisa
Brown Sugar
Maxi Priest

The Lover's rock movement was not just about the music; it became a cultural expression of the Black British experience, offering a sense of identity and community through its soothing sound and themes of love and tenderness.

As well as its many trailblazers, what cannot be forgotten are the artists who have also contributed to the rich sound of Lover's rock and those who have greatly assisted its longevity; these are as follows:

Arema, In Love
Bonito Star, Someone
SeSe Foster, Melanin Child of The Sun
Rose Capri, 'Passion'
Toyin Adekale, 'Smile', 'Here I Go Again' and Endlessly
Donna Roden, 'Be Kind To My Man', 'I've Fallen In Love' and 'It's True'
Sandra Reid, 'Ooh Boy', 'Feel So Good' and 'Don't Tell Her'
Private Collection, 'Direction', 'Slow Down', and 'Magic'
Phillip Leo, 'Why Do Fools Fall In Love', 'Second Chance' and 'Hypnotic Love'
CJ Lewis, 'Sweets For My Sweet', Everything Is Alright' and 'Best of My Love'
Charisma, 'Open The Door'
French Kiss, 'Missing You'
Wendy Walker, 'Make My Dream A Reality', 'Baby I'm For Real' and Gone He's Gone'
Frederica Tibbs, 'Angel', 'Here I Am' and 'Way I Feel'
The Blood Sisters, 'What About Me', 'Let Me Be Yours' and 'Ring My Bell'
Revelation, 'With You Boy'
The Administrators, 'This Is Reggae Music', 'She My Lady' and 'Emergency'
Trevor Hartley, 'Hooked On You', 'Call On Me' and 'Skip Away'

Intense, 'On my Mind, 'You Are The One' and 'The Very Best'
Taxman, 'Fatal Attraction'
Anthony Rich, 'Special Guest'
Nerious Joseph, 'I Need Your Loving', 'Love's Gotta Take It's Time' and 'No One Night Stand'

Chapter 5

The British Reggae Music Industry Gathers Momentum

British reggae music was rising, making waves in the UK charts; demand grew for reggae records licensed from Jamaica. The inception of the Lovers' Rock genre started with British singer Louisa Mark. Her cover of Robert Parker's Caught You In A Lie topped the reggae charts and continued with hits like 'All My Loving' in 1975, 'Even Though You're Gone' and 'Six Street' in 1978 on Safari Records.

British-born artists and bands began appearing in the reggae chart return shops throughout the UK as early as April 1974. This was due to the growing interest in people listening to the radio and T.V. and reading printed media such as Black Echoes, The Voice Newspaper, etc.

Recording studios in the UK were emerging with talented musicians, artists and producers producing British reggae music. Vinyl record-pressing factories had waiting lists due to the number of records that were being sold every week. The success of 'Pama' Records and Carl Palmer as CEO became a wholesale distribution hub for reggae 45 singles, 12" 45s and albums based on Craven Park Road, Willesden, London. Jet Star, as it was known, stocked imports from Jamaica and the rest of the world and became your first port of call if you had a record shop that stocked reggae.

I was introduced to Carl Palmar one Sunday morning when Don Christie who was one of the leading record shop owners in Birmingham, not to mention the man who loaned Pato and me the money to record and press 'Allo Tosh' by Pato Banton, asked if I would accompany him to London to replenish his stock, which he had run out of the week before. As Don entered the door, he was met by Carl, who had a very soft voice but spoke with an authority I noticed. He introduced me to Carl as GT, Pato's manager. Carl immediately recognised that I was new to the business and stated that if there was ever anything he could do to help, I was to call him. I liked Carl; he was good to me. Over the years, he assisted me with many decisions I came to make along the way.

It was great to see Jet Star grow and become the leading UK distributor years later.

This centralised point for Reggae allowed wholesale to take place, retail salespeople to assemble, and artists to pop in and meet DJs and other music business people. The best day for this is Sunday. It was a significant transformation from the days of the door-to-door salespeople knocking on doors and walking with records for sale. As private record labels emerged, wholesale record sales became centralised in London.

The majority of reggae artists flew into London airports and resided there. Picture this: If you owned a sound system in the 1960s, 1970s, and 80s, pre-release or import records would arrive in London, where the shops that sold the most records were based. You could add to this fact that recording studios were found to be more plentiful in London. Also crucial for sound systems were studios that produced test presses or dub plates (one of aluminium lased with black lacquer), better known as (Black Steel), which were plentiful in London. Finally, the majority of vinyl record pressing plants were based in London. This provided the opportunity for a one-stop wholesale shop that could supply record shops up and down the UK with the most popular selling records, including pre-releases; the platform was set for Jet Star to provide this service.

Reggae magazines and journals such as Black Echoes and the Voice provided up-to-date information on established artists and kept us updated with news about breakthrough artists on the rise.

What was great about the Echoes was the publication of their weekly reggae chart; it would contain underground hits that were played on British Sound systems in London, Saxon, Coxsone, Frontline, Fatman, Unity, Moambassa, I Spy, Small Axe, HiIthous, Stereograph, JAVA, Sovereign in Luton, Enforcer in Derby, Irration Steppers Leeds and Baron in Manchester.

Like other cities in the UK, Birmingham has always possessed a niche market for sound systems. Sir Christopher, Quaker City, Mafiatone, Studio City, Duke Alloy, Jungleman, Chuckie Hi-Fi, Lord Shirley, Bismark, Duke Wally, Jah Massigan, Nyah, Iron Sound, Meshack, Siffa, Wassifa Lovers Showcase, Now Generation, Stereo Classic, Radics, Orthodox, Lion, Rockers Roadshow, Observer, Upfront, Jus-I, to name a few, this is mainly due to reggae music's rising popularity and its growing availability.

In most inner cities of the UK, the BBC would have local reggae programs that would broadcast reggae shows on weekends in the afternoons and evenings. However, the BBC ran a nationwide reggae show and those found in regional areas hosted by the Ranking Miss P, which would serve fans of reggae music across the country. From a development prospect, popular songs from artists like Bitty McLean, Maxi Priest, Sandra Cross, John McLean, Janet Kay, Caroll Thompson, Peter Spence and Pato Banton came to the attention of Radio 1 and independent Radio Stations such as Capital, Kiss and other local radio stations across the UK. I remember the first Reggae DJ I got to know personally, The Ranking Miss P, who understood the audience; she could select the music for sale in the reggae records shops. The Ranking Miss P had an endearing personality that linked popular dancehall music and the playlists at Radio 1. As I said, if you were a reggae band, artist, or musician, you give your records to Miss P and get them heard, as well as by inner-city DJs and sound systems.

Steel Pulse and Aswad took a direction that transported the underground and crossed it over. Like any other genre at the time, it was taken up by independent local radio stations (ILR) that delivered music in Birmingham with a message to the mainstream.

Maxi Priest

Maxi Priest is a British reggae singer known for blending reggae and all genres of music. Born Max Alfred Elliott in Lewisham, London, to Jamaican Windrush generation parents, Priest is one of the most successful reggae fusion artists. He is best known for his hit songs, such as 'Close to You', which hit number one on the Billboard Hot 100 chart in 1990, remaining for three weeks (the Reggae worldwide artist from out of the UK) and 'Wild World', a cover of the Cat Stevens song that gained significant popularity in the R&B, Country and achieved top 5 on the American Billboard 100 charts.

Maxi's musical career began with him singing on the notorious Saxon Studio International sound system based in Lewisham, South East London. Maxi and Paul Robinson of One Blood released several hits on their independent label Bad Breed, soon to become Level Vibes, beginning with the Sensi and the phenomenal 'Mi God Mi King', featuring Saxon MC Papa Levi, as a double-sided 7" and 12" single.

If I were to describe him as a singer, I would have to say that he is an all-rounder, which is why although the majority of his musical singing style could be categorised as Lovers Rock with many of his earlier releases, songs like 'Throw Me Corn',

'Strolling On', 'In The Springtime', 'Pretty Little Girl', 'Let Me Know' and 'Best of Me'.

Maxi also penned titles such as 'Sensi', 'Love In The Getto', and together with Handel Tucker and the multi-genre 'Marcus' with Ray Simpson and 'Just A Little Bit Longer'. Priest's music often features a versatile presentation with a laid-back style, which helped him appeal to a broad audience beyond reggae fans. He has collaborated with artists such as Shaggy, Roberta Flack, and Shabba Ranks. Priest is considered a pioneer of the reggae Lovers Rock genre, which combines elements of reggae with other musical genres hailed as the king of Lovers Rock.

He is one of only two British reggae acts, as well as UB40, to achieve an American Billboard number one hit, such as 'Close To You' in 1990; a collaboration with Roberta Flack with a song called 'Set The Night To Music' reached a top ten position in American 1991; his cooperation with Shaggy in 1996 came top 10 in the UK.

While sitting down and chatting with Maxi and Smiley in his front room one evening, I remember Smiley had a (Studio One Instrumental Album) playing in the background when Maxi just started singing over the top of the tracks. It was something else; sitting in that chair, he went through about five or six songs that would later be released on the reggae chart-topping album 'Your Safe' Maxi Priest and 'Caution' released on Virgin Records. When he had done, he looked at me and said those are songs I'm planning to release on my album, 'What do you think?'. At the time, I had only ever heard reggae or dancehall MCs deliver lyrics in that way, but not singers. Maxi was faultless. I could have taken him to the studio right there and then. My response was that admiration that was up close and brilliant.

In 1996, Maxi released **'Intentions'** produced by the late (Drummie Zeb of Aswad); this was the first album on the Virgin 10 label and followed 'Your Safe'. Here, Maxi delivers lovers' rock favourites such as 'Pretty Little Girl', 'Must Be A Way' and a collaboration that included Trevor Walters singing Delroy Wilson's, 'Dancing Mood' Trevor Hartley singing John Holts 'Time Is The Master' as well as Drummie and Hartley delivering additional lines of quality, not forgetting those distinct Aswad harmonies that blend so well.

1, Grantley GT and Maxi Priest

2, Kevin Hinds, Maxi Priest and Grantley GT

Maxi's second album on Virgin 10 was significant because it featured a collaboration with Erskin Thompson, a friend who lived in a tower block just down the road from me in Birmingham. Erskin had gotten an advance from Virgins 10

Records, where he formed the Massive Reggae Various Artists series and the Maxi Priest project. Maxi was released in 1987 and contained the hit single 'Some Guys Have All The Luck' along with the cover of Cat Stevens 'Wild World', establishing him as a top British reggae singer.

This was one of the most exciting times in British Reggae Music. It was the same year and time that Synergy Reggae Sunsplash 1987 chose to invite and include British artists to perform in Montego Bay. Being around British bands like Aswad, Steel Pulse, Maxi Priest, Pato Banton, and Tippa Irie was good; meeting in Jamaica to represent the UK was surreal.

Speaking to Erskin, he told me he had planned to have Maxi record the album in Jamaica while he was there for Sunsplash. Sly, Robbie, David Rowe, Wiili Lindo, and others contributed to what became Maxi's breakthrough album 'Maxi' paving the way for Maxi's third studio album, 'Bonifide' which not only established him as a British Lovers Rock Icon and turned him international Reggae Artist. 'Close To You' took Maxi to the number one American Billboard Hot 100 position. There was no stopping him now. 'Peace Throughout The World' featured the Jazzie B (Soul 2 Soul) production and other favourites like 'Just a Little Bit Longer' and the lover's favourite 'Best of Me'.

Maxi Priest has successfully collaborated with producers and artists, both established and less well-known. He has worked with Sly and Robbie, Drummie Zeb of (Aswad), Shaggy, Beres Hammond, Jazzie B of (Soul 2 Soul), Roberta Flack, Lisa Fisher, Jimmy Jam & Terrie Lewis, Lee Ritnel and Apache Indian.

His collaborations with Shabba Ranks, such as 'Housecall', to his credit, have made Maxi into a worldwide household name and carved him out a place in reggae as a British Reggae phenomenon which continues to release album after album and a body of work to this very day.

Bitty Mclean

Bitty McLean is a British-Jamaican reggae, Lovers Rock, and ska singer, songwriter, and producer. Born in Birmingham, England, Delroy, as my friend Trevor Ranks, would always call him whenever we met. At the time, Trevor hosted a prime-time radio show on Birmingham's Birmingham's People's Community Radio Link (PCRL). He operated the sound system 'Love-In-Ting' and worked in one of Birmingham's most popular reggae record shops and Wolverhampton's 'Summit' Records alongside 'Don Christies'. Bitty had no better soundboard for him as an artist than Trevor; at the time, I wondered if he had a vested interest!! But seriously, Ali Campbell sang Bitty's praises, too. However, at this time, I hadn't heard the song. When I did, it was game over.

Bitty's unique sound, a reggae and pop emulsion, gained popularity in the 1990s. He started his career as an engineer at UB40's DEP International Studios and headquarters HQ, Fazeley Street, Digbeth, Birmingham and sang backing vocals on at least one of the band's albums.

'Just to Let You Know' released in 1993, including the hit single 'It Keeps Raining Tears From My Eyes', produced by Bitty, a Fat's Domino song covered by stretched 'Bitty's success beyond the shores of the UK where it achieved number two. His success continued into Europe, mainly due to him racking up a number-one record in the Netherlands pop charts and a number-one in New Zealand, down under.

The success, however, didn't stop there. Bitty cover of Hubert Lee's 1973 cover of The Shirelles, 'Dedicated to the One I Love', achieved number six in the UK charts, which firmly established him as a mainstream artist with global success. As can be imagined, with hits come tours. Bitty chose to build a relationship with his audience by supporting the likes of high-profile bands such as Wet Wet Wet, Simply Red and UB40, crooning the appetite of the audience with his smooth vocals and classic lovers rock style, a subgenre of reggae characterised by romantic themes and mellow beats, leaving the headlines with ready and waiting fans.

However, in 2004, Bitty produced Bitty McLean on Bond Street, KGN. JA and The Supersonics for Pecking's Records, what a record which, for me, titles like 'Tell Me', John Holts 'Never Let Me Go' found on his 'Songs For I' album, 'I've Got Love' and David Ruffins 'Walk Away From Love', have become classics in their own right. Here, Bitty displays his ability to transform the old with the new, utilising traditional reggae rhythms made in Jamaica by Duke Reid and Tommy McCook for the Treasure Isle Label and fusing them with a taste of Birmingham's British Windrush legacy.

Grantley GT and Bitty McLean

Despite this success, McLean continued to be an influential figure in British reggae worldwide. He often collaborated with other artists and produced music that blended traditional reggae with contemporary sounds. This led to his later collaborations with Sly Dunbar and Robbie Shakespear on their Taxi productions and label. The album 'Moving On' trailblazed this union, which led to six years, including 'The Taxi Sessions'. This included tours of Europe, North Africa, and Japan.

Bitty continues performing, lecturing, and producing records, spreading the word about British Reggae music worldwide. I'm sure he won't be stopping anytime soon.

Chapter 6

Radio

Pirate radio stations broadcast reggae from residential rooftops, celebrating African Caribbean culture and promoting grassroots British reggae music. London led this trend, similar to Radio Caroline and Radio Luxembourg in the 1960s. The 1980s saw a resurgence of pirate radio spawned by the Dread Broadcasting Corporation (DBC) and pirate radio across the UK.

In those days, it was almost impossible to get a hit without radio play. Without the internet and social media, radio was the national communicator alongside sound systems.

I remember Little Richie, a pirate DJ from (PCRL) days, telling me a story about the continual process of keeping a pirate radio station up and running in the 80s. He stated that transmitters capable of FM broadcasting were purchased cheaply, possessing the ability to transmit over a forty-mile radius from 15-storey Tower Blocks of apartments. He noted that a sound electronics engineer could make transmitters up on demand. At the height of the pirate radio revolution, stations up and down the UK would have spares on hand just in case the Department of Trade and Industry (DTI) raided their premises.

Broadcasting reggae music from the rooftops of residential tower blocks celebrated African Caribbean black culture. Pirate radio significantly promoted songs from a grassroots level, vital to developing British reggae music. London pioneered this trend, similar to Radio Caroline and Radio Luxembourg in the 1960s and (DBC) Dread Broadcasting Corporation in the early 1980s.

Birmingham's (PCRL) Peoples Community Radio Line featured a DJ playlist consisting of reggae, calypso, R&B, and many other genres of black music that the BBC and ILR stations failed to play. Before long, pirate stations were popping up regularly, some genre-specific focusing on soul, such as Invicta, Sunrise, and Solar. Sovereign became one of the first stations to play black music 24-7. This inspired Cecil Morrison, a local businessman, to develop PCRL to pioneer its market reach, which became the words on everyone's lips in the 80s. Boasting a roster of creative DJs, Cecil, alongside other black African Caribbean trailblazers, had grown tired and fed up with the empty promises of the BBC and local community radio stations to provide a more excellent representation for thousands of reggae music lovers and venues.

Following this movement, Soul Stations would become prolific in the early to mid-1980s, with Invicta joined by Horizon Radio and JFM in 1981. As stated earlier, Kiss 94.5 FM and London Weekend Radio (LWR) were among the first UK pirate radio stations dedicated to soul, funk, jazz, and hip hop. Reggae featured widely across UK stations such as Vibes, Station FM, RJR, Lightning, and Power Jam dominated London from reggae once-per-week segments to what listeners were now experiencing; they could listen to reggae 24 hours daily. It was a no-brainer; it transformed the reggae music business. Music of black origin created openings and new trends, steering pathways to cost-effective forms of advertising that drove crowds of young music ravers to the dancehalls, giving rise to the rave, jungle, garage and house scenes. Like the Shubin and Blues Party era of the 60s, pirate radio provided an escape for anyone suffering discrimination, economic frustration and unemployment.

The Telecommunications Act of 1984 granted what became the drive to investigate and enter properties and detain equipment deemed broadcasting without a license, found to be using equipment for illegal broadcasting.

The powers allowed the authorities to close them down. However, the Telecommunications Act failed to stem the growth of pirate stations, which led to the conservative government Broadcasting Act of 1990, which stopped the income generation through income in advertising revenue from which more well-known and organised stations were benefiting. These stations were offered the opportunity to apply for legal broadcasting licences. These Licenses produced radio stations such as Kiss FM and Choice, not to mention the careers of Tim Westwood, Jazzie B (Soul II Soul), Trevor Nelson and Norman Jay, who would regularly play reggae, soul, jazz funk, hip hop, and house music.

David Rodigan

London's Ladbrook Grove, at a club called Gossips, is where you would find David Rodigan on most Saturday nights after his show in the 80s. Although small, this club had a vibe; it grew enormously and couldn't hold the audiences Tony Williams and David were pulling in the numbers then. He partnered with Papa Face as the MC.

In London, I would always head to Gossips on a Saturday night.

I was thrilled by the contrast in Birmingham. You would find DJs like KK J, who would DJ at venues such as the Gilded Cage. KKJ was also the resident DJ at Tabasco, one of Birmingham's famous night spots (opposite Aston Villa's Villa Park), managed by Stead Wallen and Mr Virlie himself. Des Mitchell was the anchor DJ with his sparring partner G'man on the BBC then.

David Rodigan and I at the O2 in London 2019

My first live experience of David Rodigan was early morning at a club called Norwood Suite, Vauxhall, London. Alongside Smiley Culture and Asher Senator, Smiley stated he would chat lyrics as Saxon Studio International was headlining. I didn't know that David Rodigan would be on the bill. As luck would have it, I was right there, almost side by side with Rodigan, when he hit the microphone and stated, 'This is Rodigan on Saxon International' while at the same time selecting '54-46' by Toots and The Maytals, as you can imagine the place burst into a frenzy of excitement. If I remember correctly, he followed this up with Millie Small's 'My Boy Lollipop', but the intro was, again, on point.

Rodigan recounted that his love affair with reggae music began with that song and proceeded by putting the needle on the record; the rest is history. When it came to dancehall in those days, Saxon did not miss.

Trevor Sax of Saxon Studio International sound system thanked Rodigan and explained that Saxon was in session. Beginning with Marcia Griffiths 'Feel Like Jumping' followed by another Marcia Griffiths 'I Shall Sing' alongside the 'Answer Riddim' what took place next was an explosion of lyrical magnitude: Tippa, Levi, Daddy Colonel, Asher and Smiley, all from Saxon sound system delivered what the crowd wanted, which was the licence to 'Lick Wood' (make noise by stamping their feet and hitting the walls) to coin a phrase. Just as Squiddly Ranks coined the phrase 'Wicked' well, Saxon has to go down for the words 'Lick

Wood'. I had heard of his shows on Radio London, Capital and, of course, the battles between Barry G and Jamaica's RJR Radio, which at that time were epic; what an idea! He had become a popular figure in London. However, I hadn't heard much more until I began working in London and venturing out.

I suppose a crucial development in Rodigan's career stems from his time at Capital, where he hosted Roots Rockers. Also, using the same name, Rodigan promoted live shows at the Academy in Brixton, London. These shows would include several British performers and the occasional international reggae artist. Rodigan joined Kiss FM and gained a licence following the Broadcasting Act 1990. Rodigan's show aired on Sunday nights from 11 to 12 midnight. Concentrating on his love for reggae, he felt a calling to work among sound systems, battling with prominent sounds and selectors worldwide. His natural style and dialect worked well alongside the selection and presentation of specials and dubplates others could not play to his credit, helping him to secure winning positions.

Not just a master of the turntables, Rodigan also showcased his acting skills in the '70s and '80s. He made periodic returns to his early vocation, gracing popular TV shows such as Doctor Who, The Office Party, and Trial of The Time Lord with his presence. This versatility is a testament to his multifaceted talent and his ability to excel in various creative fields.

Rodigan's contributions to the music industry have not gone unnoticed. In 2012, he was awarded the prestigious Member of The Order of The British Empire (MBE), followed by the Jamaican Order of Distinction in 2020. His accolades include notable features in Grand Theft Auto and collaborations with renowned artists such as Shinehead, Chase and Status, Shy FX, Boy Better Know, and the ASAP team. These achievements and his legacy as a reggae DJ have endeared him to a younger audience, making him a popular choice at festivals and events. Not to be forgotten, Rodigan has travelled extensively with his sparring partner Papa Face from their meeting at Dub Vendor – Fashion Records until today.

Finally, in 2017, with Ian Burrell, David Rodigan penned 'My Life In Reggae, ' which tells the story of his love affair with reggae music.

Tony Williams,

I met Tony Williams just after I received a telephone call from him requesting an interview with Pato Banton a week after his performance in the West End of London's Lyceum Theatre. Pato had made a big impression in London that weekend and, as a result, was the new name on the British reggae music industry's lips. Tony wanted to be the first DJ in London to explore who this new guy was. Tony was so eager that he asked if Pato could pop into the studio that afternoon; given that it was a Sunday and we lived 130 miles away, I suggested we do it on the Radio live! Well, Tony was over the moon, and as a result, it was a great interview and a prelude for the single 'Hello Tosh'. (As the manager for Pato, I found things to be moving fast. I began getting calls from Island Records, Virgin, Greensleeves and Fashion. Pato and I felt an allegiance with John MacGillvary and Chris Lane because of their faith in Pato releasing 'The Boss' and 'It Ain't What You Do It's the Way That You Do It'. There were other considerations, which I will discuss later in the book.

Tony was a prominent reggae DJ who hosted his show on BBC Radio London between 1977 and 1987. It was called 'Reggae Time' on a Sunday; everyone who loved reggae would be tuned in that afternoon.

Tony was more than a DJ; he was also a record producer. Tony's career as a DJ began with soul and funk in the 70s. Like David Rodigan, Tony played in famous clubs like Gossips in London, Le Beat Route, and Samantha's. One early afternoon, Tony and I were chatting about how we got into the business, and Tony told me he had a friend called

Bo Kool. Tony explained that he was involved in a studio project some time ago. Tony and a few friends decided to produce a song, even though he had never been in a recording studio before, and pulled some excellent musicians together to make a song.

To his credit, Tony Williams's legacy includes the creation of The British Reggae Industry Awards, which celebrated and highlighted the vast talent of many UK reggae artists and how their transition led to success in the UK British national charts and the British Broadcasting Corporation (BBC) Top of The Pops at the time.

On the 27th of October 1982, Tony Williams hosted the first British Reggae Music Industry Awards at the prestigious Cafe Royal, Regent Street, London. The winners included:

Trevor Walters - Best Vocalist Male
Caroll Thompson - Best Vocalist Female
Victor Romao Evans - Best Newcomer Male
Donna Roden Best - Newcomer Female
Caroll Thompson - Best Single
Aswad - Best British Band
Dennis Brown - Best International Artist
Bob Marley - Lifetime Achievement Award
Sir Lloyd - Best Sound System

Tony can always take pride in the fact that the awards were held in prestigious venues such as the Café Royal, The Royal Albert Hall and the Indigo O2, where Orlando Gittens of Musical Therapy Entertainments Ltd currently hosts Giants of Lovers Rock in Greenwich, London. Tony can pride himself on being respected by the entire industry for putting it together for many years. From here, Aswad, Janet Kay, Maxi Priest, Tippa Irie, and Pato Banton went on to formulate international music careers to this very day.

Social Media and British Reggae

The introduction of radio in the early 20th century further revolutionised the music industry. Radio allowed music to be broadcast to a broader audience, making it more accessible. This led to the emergence of popular music genres, such as jazz, blues, and rock and roll.

The internet has become so advanced that users can share and download music online. Pirating music no longer requires dubbing tapes and burning CDs. People can download virtually any song they want through file-sharing platforms for free. This has caused revenue in the music industry to plummet.

In 1999, Napster provided straightforward peer-to-peer music-sharing systems that gave users free access to millions of records. As with other developments, pirates have driven the market for the revolution of MP3s and the birth of streaming sites such as Spotify, Apple Music, Deezer, etc.

The Decline of Vinyl and the Rise of Streaming

In the past, physical sales of vinyl and CDs were a significant driver for reggae artists, giving them a measurable footprint in the industry. The decline of vinyl, coupled with streaming platforms like YouTube, Spotify and Apple Music, has altered the music business. While streaming offers more accessibility, it can also dilute genre-specific markets.

The development of technology such as Creator and Notator, Logic Pro, Pro Tools, Cubase, Audacity and other digital audio workstations have transformed the music industry in many ways, including production, producing music from one's bedroom at home, cutting out the need for recording songs in expensive studios. **Distribution:** making it more accessible to distribute music online. **Consumption:** Making it possible to listen to music anywhere, at any time, and to create personalised playlists.

Social media in the music industry is assisting in its growth and evolution in many ways. From allowing access to international audiences at the touch of a button to giving direct engagement between artists and fans, social media's accessibility revolutionises marketing strategies.

Globally, music and the way people listen to music has changed. iPods and CDs are almost obsolete and are more about streaming music, singles and albums on Spotify, Apple, YouTube and other popular sites.

Once upon a time, music careers were driven by record labels, pluggers and traditional media outlets. Nowadays, individuals connect directly with producers, singers and musicians. Conversations occur in a minute-by-minute process, which has changed methods of providing feedback and promotion, providing new avenues for communicating news and influence. Social media has allowed news to be accessed in real-time, for instance, just seconds after a big event happens.

Instagram, TikTok, and Facebook algorithms often pick similar-sounding hooks and audio that inevitably go viral, allowing listeners to vary their musical tastes, from Rock or Pop to more eclectic listening tastes. However, this algorithm may restrict the diversity of music that becomes mainstream on the app and, consequently, into the broader music industry.

Television, radio, printed periodicals, and magazines are now distributed and accessed through digital channels, such as social media and search engines like Google, Yahoo, or email.

Social media has transformed the cost element associated with marketing and promotion. A typical story can reach millions of individuals in seconds and remain present for as long as the algorithm picks up on the number of shares and interests rather than a syndicated approach to printed media mechanisms.

The critical item within the spectrum of communication in our digital age is content, which could be what we do when, how we do it, and who we do it with. Anyone with a smartphone or access to the internet can consume news and information on multiple platforms immediately as it happens. The demand for content and what's happening in our day-to-day lives means that news outlets and social media sources may get news before mainstream sources in the past.

Social media platforms such as Instagram, TikTok, Twitter, and Facebook enable individuals to respond and offer feedback immediately after contributing to news, which, depending on an individual's profile and followers, can communicate the subject matter a lot faster and more comprehensively than many traditional news outlets have time to publish a story. If social media was as advanced at the time of the OJ Simpson, Los

Angeles car chase, can you imagine how fast that story might have spread? Sports, music concerts, disasters, and political events allow people access to the information they want when they want it on demand. This type of access, whilst having its positives, also has its negatives.

Platforms such as Twitter only allow short sound bites and word count content. Instagram restricts you to how many or where you might place hyperlinks to any post to audiences based on algorithms matching consumers' interests, ultimately restricting individuals and brands from reaching the desired audience. The most significant advantage social media has had over traditional media is that with one press of a button, one can inform the world with content and provide the world with an opportunity to give feedback and voice their opinion.

Nowhere has this opportunity presented itself more than in the music business.

Social media has also proved helpful for singers, songwriters, and musicians in releasing songs and distributing music digitally using online platforms such as CD Baby, Apple Music, Deezer, etc. With the aid of Shazam, Apple has made it possible for someone to stream music seconds after listening to it from any source. This process would have been previously done by music pluggers, publicists, and marketing and promotion professionals. To this end, I am unsure how much the British reggae industry has utilised this advantage in becoming a social media influencer, making the best use of competition and public engagement.

Irrespective of the crowded market, social media remains a cost-effective tool for advertising one's product to individuals known to the individual, boosting the reach of their product or service. Something as simple as posting a story, an individual can reach hundreds to thousands of new people depending on the number of people following their page. By nature of that single action, they are likely to encourage others to share posts and stories, utilising any particular platform's algorithms.

Chapter 7

British MCs

The growth of British reggae music accelerated globally, driven by creative talent and skilled musicians. Producers combined two and three-chord rhythms with one-drop beats, string quartets, and clever melodies. The magazine Black Echoes pioneered the movement, launching a weekly reggae chart. Journalists like John Missouri, Simon Buckland, and Anna Arnon highlighted Jamaican icons and emerging British reggae artists. DJs like Tony Williams, radio and David Rodigon supported the scene. Dancehalls and sound systems transformed British reggae by recording their shows on tape cassettes, made popular by sound systems in Jamaica, Coxsone and Saxon International. These tapes became so influential that even record shops sold sound clash tapes. The age of the British MC had begun.

Papa Face

Emerging from the vibrant South London music scene, Papa Face quickly established himself as one of the pioneering British reggae MCs. His unique brand of British dancehall, which was not a mere response to the MCs in Jamaica but a distinct alternative, began to resonate with audiences in the early 80s, predating the rise of Saxon Studio International.

Papa Face possessed a unique advantage regarding his placement in the market. Papa Face was an MC and an addition to his skill base and experience; Face was a music promoter. Generating the experience gathered from his sound system (Mafia Black), Face was able to use the knowledge gained from selecting music people loved to inform his craft in the studio and as a salesman in one of South London's well-known Dub Vendor Record shops, Clapham Junction, London. Papa Face was smart and soon attracted the attention of John MacGillivray, C.E.O. (Dub Vendor), who, with Chris Lane, put together the Record label (Fashion), which occupied a room at the rear of the record store. At that time, Keith (my music business partner) and I would collect the records I had produced and mastered directly from the pressing plant in Stratford, London or

John at Dub Vendor and deliver them directly to Mr Palmer at Jet Star, the distributor, Marcus and several shops across the UK, finally arriving in Birmingham where DJs would be waiting to get their copies of GT's Records new releases.

Papa Face was well placed that if I didn't speak directly with John, Face had no problem acting on John's behalf and getting the job done; he was good at it and always willing to provide advice here and there, which I found very helpful.

MacGillivray, Lane, and Face contributed to several reggae hits in the 80s, such as many that featured Papa Face as a solo artist and in particular two 'Dance Pon The Corner' and 'To The Bump', with female MC Bionic Rona on Fashion. These were so popular at the time that the BBC, catching the wave of the British genre, engaged Papa Face and Rona to their T.V. studios in London for a live session; something unique in the early 80s was that British reggae was coming of age. What followed next was a natural step forward for Fashion; Chris Lane began work with a young MC better known as Smiley Culture to produce a song called 'Cockney Translator', which brought about the number one hit and the media eager to capitalise on the growing wave of British based MCs ramming out venues up and down the UK dancehalls and clubs.

Working front of the house at Dub Vendor, Face met David Rodigan, who had a popular radio show at the time; where if you were ever in London, it was one of the shows you were best advised not to miss, mainly because it had so much in it, David would play the new songs on the street and in the clubs. Indeed, he didn't stop there. Rodigan provided the history and narrative of where the music was recorded and where you might get a copy. In a world with little information about reggae, Rodigan joined the dots. Soon enough, Papa Face elevated himself as a DJ, working alongside David MCing at venues such as Gossips, which would be rammed solid when Rodigan left his radio show and arrived at the venue.

Live at Dick Shepard Youth Club (D.S.Y.C) - Sir Lloyd

In 1982, following the release of the Greensleeves album **'LIVE with Aces International'** featuring Yellowman and Billy Boyo, Lloyd of Sir Lloyd Sound System had the idea to record something that presented what was happening in the UK's British reggae music scene.

Lloyd pulled together a few notable sound systems that represented past, present and future, such as Sir Coxson, Nasty Rockers, Saxon, Hitgtious, Jamdown Rockers, Sir Lloyd Frontline International and King Tubby. He chose the Dick

Shephard Youth Club, in Tulse Hill, South West London, in January of 1983. Lloyd placed himself at the vanguard of the local sound system culture, recording what was going on LIVE in the dance halls and with young people. LIVE at **D.S.Y.C.** released three (3) albums that featured singers and MCs like Tippa Irie, Maxi Priest, Papa Levi, Champion, Leslie Lyrics, Lorna G, Colonel Flux, Welton Irie, General T' Dirty Desi, General Slater, Dennis Pinnock and Sista Candy. Most of these performers were in their teenage years. It was a big thing for their names to be immortalised from tape cassettes onto vinyl.

The growth of British reggae music continued to gather pace worldwide due to its creative prowess, talented musicians and vocalists. Producers of the music possessed a style of imagery encompassing a deep knowledge of how two and three-chord rhythms could fuse with one-drop beats, string quartets and clever melodies. The music magazine Black Echoes trailblazed this movement, developing the weekly reggae chart. However, Echoes did not stop there; journalists such as John Missouri, Simon Buckland, and Anna Arnon penned the stories of prevalent Jamaican icons and up-and-coming British reggae artists and bands homegrown in the UK. They were dovetailed with radio station DJs like Tony Williams and Rodigan on Capital. LIVE at D.S.Y.C brought about a

'C' change in dancehall. Sound systems began to record their shows onto tape cassettes and distribute them around the UK and the world. Saxon International trailblazed this phenomenon; people would pay for copies of particular dances featuring the Saxon MCs. From this, the Saxon sound system became so well-known that I would turn up for a meeting with a record company artist and representative boss and see a Saxon tape on the desk; it was crazy!

The business was changing, new technology was emerging, and tape cassettes of Tony Williams, Rodigan, and Barry G. Sir Coxson were sold in record shops. Papa Levi's 'Mi God Mi King' had achieved number one in the UK reggae charts and sequentially number one in Jamaica, hailing the British MC fast-style era.

The Fast Style and British MCs

The British dancehall musical genre associated with MCs could be described as the **fast style**. The British reggae genre is associated with dancehall music and MCs and is characterised by its energetic beats, rapid-fire vocals, and lyrical prowess. Emerging in the 1980s within British Caribbean communities, this style draws heavily from the Jamaican dancehall tradition but incorporates elements of British urban music culture.

Musically, British dancehall reggae features heavy basslines, synthesised rhythms, and electronic instrumentation, creating a dynamic and pulsating sound. The tempo is often fast-paced, driving listeners to move and dance. Key elements such as drum machines, synthesisers, and digital effects enhance the rhythmic intensity and create an infectious groove.

Lyrically, MCs play a central role in British dancehall reggae, delivering rapid, rhythmic vocals known as "toasting" or "chatting" over the instrumental tracks. Their lyrics cover various topics, including social commentary, street life, partying and personal experiences. MCs showcase their verbal dexterity and lyrical skills through clever wordplay, sharp wit, and charismatic delivery, engaging audiences with their dynamic performances.

The rise of the British MCs contributed to the development of British reggae in its current form worldwide.

British reggae music is a genre associated with dancehall music and MCs. It embodies a fusion of Caribbean and British cultural influences, creating a vibrant and dynamic musical landscape that continues to evolve within the UK's multicultural communities.

As referred to previously, sound system tapes were one of the ways people shared music. They were trendy when most couldn't get to the record shop or the dance hall. I remember when my friends and I would listen to the radio and hope that the DJ wouldn't interrupt the songs so that we could record the whole track. We would press our cassette recorder microphones against the radio speakers to get the best recording possible. Saxon tapes were in high demand. People would press cassette recorder microphones against the radio speakers to get the best recording possible. My mate would carry his cassette player in his school bag and play music during school break times, and it was a good time.

Years later, technology improved. The quality of tape cassette players and cars' sound improved. Some Sony Walkman's sounded amazing, and some ghetto blasters were out of this world, some sounding like mini sound systems. What can't be forgotten were those stereo separate stack systems that were all the rage in our homes. With the cassette format, MCs were springing up nationwide: Pato, Leslie Lyrics, Champion, etc. There was a sound clash in every city with most sound systems.

Reggae music and the industry began to produce British reggae that made monetary sense. More independent reggae producers found that money could be earned from releasing reggae songs independently produced. It became possible to generate top 10 Reggae chart hits that could be sold directly to record shops around the UK. Sound systems and radio provided the promotion and publicity that enabled people to flood the stores weekly to buy music. Dub Vendor (Fashion), Greensleeves and Ariwa trailblazed this phenomenon, as did Jet Star and Hawkeye. The progress of these labels led to the mini-reggae industry's development based upon its Jamaican legacy years before.

Smiley Culture – The Cockney Translator

I got talking to Smiley Culture. We became good friends, and occasionally, I spent much time with Smiley in London. Smiley was a straightforward, well-known person; people liked him. He was very quick-witted and talented. Those who knew him would pass by his house to sit, drink, and chill out. Renowned musicians would always pass through and chill from time to time. As a promoter, Smiley and Asher would spend time at my house in the west midlands. always

Smiley came from Stockwell, south London, and attended Tulses Hill School, where he got his nickname. Before he began his recording career, he would travel around London MCing on various sound systems, most often with the Sir Coxsone, but settled with Saxon Studio International system, where he and Asher met and worked with reggae artists, including Maxi Priest, Papa Levi, Tippa Irie, Daddy Colonel and Steven Peterkin.

Signed to the London-based reggae record label Fashion Records, his first single, 'Cockney Translation' (1984), was a Jamaican guide to the East End dialect. The song mixed cockney dialect with London's version of Jamaican patois, translating between the two. The song's lyrics were later used in schools as an example of how immigration has affected the English language. Smiley Culture popularised the "fast chat" style of deejaying that had originated with Jamaican deejays such as Ranking Joe and was developed further by British toasters, particularly those on the Saxon sound system such as Peter King.

Smiley had achieved chart success with his next single, 'Police Officer', released towards the end of 1984. This was the supposedly autobiographical tale of how Emmanuel was arrested for possession of cannabis but then let off in return for an autograph when the policeman recognised him as a famous reggae artist. The record, although humorous, did have a serious aspect, highlighting the way the police unfairly treated black people.

Smiley appeared twice on the BBC flagship weekly music program, enabling him to be seen by the British record-buying public who loved the song, where it achieved a national chart position of number Twelve, selling over 160.000 copies.

In 1995, he became the first British MC to appear at Jamaica's world-renowned Reggae Sunsplash Festival. He then signed with Polydor Records, with the release of his album 'Tongue In Cheek', which featured the release of the single 'Schooltime Chronical'.

In 1986, Smiley, alongside Pato and Tippa Irie, auditioned for a TV show on Channel 4 television produced by Trevor Phillips called Club Mix. Although it was a very close call between the three, Smiley got the part of the host. Club Mix ran for one series and ended in 1987. He appeared in David Bowie's Absolute Beginners and was featured in many television adverts promoting online banking on behalf of the NatWest Bank.

Unfortunately, Smiley met his untimely death on 15th March 2011, and some would have it as suspicious circumstances.

He was a sincere friend and, along with his friend Ashar Senator, they assisted me in the early part of my career in the British Reggae Music Industry. I still miss him. Rest In Peace, Smiley.

Papa Levi

Of those MCs in the UK, Papa Face was one of the first to feature on the British scene. Stephen Peterkin's (Fast Style) birth changed the British dancehall landscape. Dennis Rowe and Lloyd (Muscle-head) Francis of Saxon International and its MC line-up placed the UK on the world map and British sound system arena. Tippa and Levi, in particular, became some of the most feared MCs to encounter in the dancehall, whether in the UK or beyond. As a result, Saxon became one of the most sought-after sound systems to grace any city in England.

Maxi Priest, a key part of Saxon's frontline, was not an MC but, at the time, a promising vocalist. In 1984 he teamed up with Paul Robinson of (One Blood) and with the band Caution, founding the record label 'Level Vibes' recoding two singles 'Love In The Ghetto' and 'Sensi' which both featured Phillip 'Papa Levi' Williams on the counteractions or (B sides). The story has it that Maxi recruited his Saxon stablemate Papa Levi because of the dub-infused focus of the compositions; Levi's 'In A Mi Yard' and 'Mi God Mi King's lyrical content provided the perfect backdrop and narrative for both songs.

Levi's social commentary featured a recount of the Brixton riots three years prior, 1981, provided a short story where Levi comments on the unfair treatment levelled at black young people in London at the hands of the Metropolitan Police and associated borough councils at the time. I remember this incident well, particularly because the riots in Brixton, Broad Water Farm, Birmingham and Toxteth became key reasons why, after graduating from Birmingham University Westhill College as an undergraduate, I immediately chose to continue my studies, enrolling for my Master's degree in Criminology, at the University of Leicester, (Scarman Centre for Public Order).

Those songs struck a chord in me, as did the streets, neighbourhoods, dance halls, and the reggae charts. As one of British reggae's most successful dancehall-dub-influenced recordings, Levi, at the time, was well known for his lyrics that featured both current affairs and social consciousness. Becoming well known for his take on Rasta and the fire which took so many lives in Brixton, London, 'In A Mi Yard' catapulted Levi and Saxon to the ears and eyes of the media and major record companies. 'Mi God Mi King' became a phenomenal hit on the UK reggae charts. Following its license to Sly and Robbie's (Taxi Label) in Jamaica, it also reached the number one spot in Jamaica, West Indies. It became the first UK British song to transcend the market, becoming a hit in Jamaica, the birthplace of Reggae. This turned Papa Levi into a worldwide British dancehall and sound system icon. You could find Papa Levi up and down the country, delivering his lyrics on Saxon International.

The queues to see Saxon were crazy; you would find celebrities in the dance halls all to coin a phrase (lick wood). DJs would shout If you love ah dem deh' style, ball forward. Saxon DJs would also shout lick wood, beckoning their audience to hit the walls and stomp their feet if they liked what they heard.

Many people missed Saxon shows; however, if you happened to miss Saxon live, something new would emerge.

Before the age of the internet and YouTube, sound systems had begun to record their shows onto tape cassettes. As time passed, copies of these cassettes were made and circulated widely throughout the UK, where fans could listen to dances a day or two later. The development of Saxon tapes created a demand for them, which became a type of guerrilla marketing technique that took root in two significant ways: local inner-city promoters and tape sales, which found their way into record shops for sale at the time.

Local inner-city promotion occurred in the dance hall, where young people met and discussed what was happening. The underground scene changed as the technological development of duplicate cassette recorders became how young people listened to and shared music. Remember, it was only ten years prior that radio, T.V. 2 track (reel 2 reel), or cartridges were the options for listening to music outside the family front living rooms in the 1970s—80s. Nevertheless, Papa Levi went on to sign with Island Records.

Lorna Gee

Also known as Sutara Gayle, she has made her mark in British reggae music and performing arts. Pato and I met Lorna, who encouraged us to check out Mad Professor, based in Gautrey Road, Peckham, London. I remember leaving my car and thinking I was back in Birmingham.

Born and raised in Brixton, South London, after meeting with producer Mad Professor, releasing her first single, 'Three Weeks Gone - Mi Giro', which kept Lorna working towards what became the track that made her name as a singer in 1985, called 'Gotta Find a Way', this earned Lorna her first of two BBC Radio London Reggae Awards for Best Female Artist in 1985 and 1986, with her distinct, soulful voice and commanding stage presence. Her music often blends lover's rock with roots reggae, giving her songs both a romantic and conscious edge. Lorna's ability to convey deep emotions, from love to social commentary, helped her stand out among female reggae artists.

As one of Britain's female MCs, Lorna came across to me as very street bright as you could imagine one would have to be living in a man's world filled with the trappings of 'battling with other MCs and sound systems) such as Saxon, Coxsone, and Nasty Rockers. Lorna's lyrical versatility and vocal delivery further enabled her to explore her talent by engaging audiences and driving her unique personal touch to her performances.

As a staunch community activist, Lorna has performed alongside mainstream artists such as Paul Weller, Madness, Sade, Boy George, Gil Scott-Heron, Sting, and Maxi Priest.

In 1985, Lorna and her family were hit with personal trauma when, as a result of the Brixton riots, the Police shooting of her sister, Cherry, in a raid. Tragically, Cherry was left paralysed by the shooting in later years and passed away in 2011 from complications directly tied to her injuries.

Like her male counterparts, Lorna received credibility and was awarded.

She entered the Lover's Rock, as I would call it, the Queen Hall of Fame in 2008 and received the Rock Gala Award for her contributions to the genre. In the early 1990s, she moved to the US, releasing hits like 'Lef Him, Nice', and 'Oh No Not My Baby' by the Gold Disc label. In 1992, Lorna won the New York Tamika Reggae Award for Best Female Deejay.

As an actress, Lorna Gee, Sutara Gayle has significantly contributed to music and film. Sutara extended her talents to the stage and screen, where her charisma and natural ability to embody diverse roles made her an asset to productions. Her acting work showcased her versatility and ability to transition from music to drama, seamlessly blending her artistic expressions. After graduating from the Webber Douglas Academy of Dramatic Art in 2003, there was no stopping in 2006, she toured with the Royal Shakespeare Company in their production of 'The Crucible', which won two Laurence Olivier Awards for Best Director (Dominic Cooke) and Best Revival. She also starred as Madame Arcati in Noël Coward's Blithe Spirit at the Holders Festival in Barbados, West Indies.

Sutara has performed notably in screenings such as BBC's 'Eastenders', (ITV's) The Bill, Ashes to Ashes, the film 'Fallout' and 'Batman': The Dark Knight 2008, and BBC Radio Four drama 'Blood Sweat and Tears'.

Macka B

I first heard about Macka B in the early 80s at an Oaklands Youth, Sports, and Social Centre venue in Birmingham, UK. I was there with Pato Banton, who was there to MC on the Jah Wassifa sound system. Macka was incredible; he was a lyrical dictionary. He seemed to effortlessly deliver his flow in a way no one else did, but the crowd loved all 6" 2' of him.

As I got to know him better as a promoter, I would include him on the bill at the Rising Star Night Club, Henry's, both of Mount Pleasant Bilston, West Midlands, and Maximillian Night Club, Broad Street, Birmingham, UK, in which Macka B and Pato stood toe to toe against Tippa Irie and Papa Levi.

As previously said, Macka B was known in the West Midlands dancehall circuit mainly because of his lyrics. However, this alone was not the defining factor for Macka B; he was more than that - he was a gentleman with manners; 'Gentleman with manners' is one of Macka B' iconic lyrics alongside 'Bible Reader' was the first time the subject of the Bible homogenised with the dancehall directly, this was a critical factor that made Macka B the MC stand out, along with the fact that he practised the faith of Rasta and made no apologies for educating the dancehall with political, spiritual, and sometimes tongue-in-cheek humorous lyrics that had the dancehalls enthralled. Macka B was a perfect candidate for Mad Professor's Ariwa record label's dub-induced beats.

Macka B and Grantley GT

Macka B has continued to carve his name in dancehall and is recognised as a credible artist worldwide today. He remains a gentleman with manners.

Sweetie Irie

Aswad's Angus (Drummie Zeb) Gaye featured Sweetie to MC on the dancehall mix of their 1989 12" single 'On and On'. From the success and subsequent sales figures, it made sense for Island Records to sign Sweetie, which led to him releasing the debut album 'DJ of The Future' in 1991. He appeared on 'Smile,' which achieved a gold classification in the British Phonographic

Industry (BPI), and featured on the ragga remix of their song 'Smile'.

Following Aswad's 1991 tour of Japan, it was followed in June of the same year by the 'Original Raggamuffin' British tour, which included Tippa Irie, Sweetie Irie and Peter Spence, backed by the Rough House Crew, produced by Parco Tachyon Co. Ltd. What a tour across eight days as a unit we played three venues Tokyo, Osaka and Nagoya. It was a culture shock from beginning to end. Everything on the contract rider was in place. As the front-of-house mix engineer, I was aware of Tippa and Peter's set list; I had only communicated via phone with Sweetie and General, his father, and the manager. Nevertheless, I was able to provide my band members with the song list to which they learnt the songs to the T. It was also agreed that we would double up and use extended soundchecks as rehearsals. The shows were incredible. I realised that Sweetie was excellent with a band and brought something unique each night. What a performer, and all credit to Tippa, Peter, Myki Tuff as opener, and the band.

It was no surprise that Sweetie went on to collaborate with GT's Records, Peter Spence and Tippa Irie on the Japanise 'Original Raggamuffin Tour'

The remix of the Gorillaz hit single 'Clint Eastwood' achieved a British chart number four and secured platinum BPI certification in the UK. Sweetie has shown no signs of stopping, continuing his collaborations, year after year, with artists like Kideko and George Kwali, 'Crank It' Ministry of Sound.

1, Sweetie on stage in Japan,

2, Legend and Sweetie Irie

3, Promotion for Original Raggamuffin

Sweetie performed at the BBC proms for a 'Top of the Pops' special, a first for British reggae, where he displayed his versatility. As you can imagine, he did not let the audience down at Glastonbury and Wireless festivals.

Sweetie has earned his place as a premier league British MC and will continue to grace us with his talent and performance abilities for many years.

General Levy

I first listened to General Levy at an event in London where he was MCing on the sound system Tippa-tone, and to put it mildly, both General and Sweetie Irie blew the place apart. I was on a break from an American tour and, with some friends, decided to go out of town.

Some years later, while talking to General, he explained that he was musically influenced by listening to Saxon cassette tapes featuring Papa Levi and Tippa Irie. He stated that as well as Saxon tapes, he also possessed a collection of dancehall tapes of many MCs connected to the world of sound systems at the time. General continued by telling me that he explained in detail the position he stood at the live recording of Saxon International: 'Coughing Up Fire' on the 9th of November at the Factory, Paddington, London. Realising his ability, General became more serious and set out his stall to become an MC, but more importantly, to present the audience with something different in what was known as the fast style.

The first UK label to recognise General Levy's ability to take his talent far and wide were Lloydy Crucial and Robbo Ranx, later releasing songs with Fashion Records, producer Chris Lane (producer of Smiley Cultures, 'Police Officer'), as with General's dancehall prowess; these songs paved the way for what was to become the genre General is best known. The UK music scene had begun to change; instead of all-nighters, emerging were day events that played a range of music, which included Jungle. DJs such as Micky Finn, Randel, Ron, and Dextrous pioneered this genre, benefitting from the underground dancehall scene and the pirate radio revolution.

In 1994, 'Incredible' with M-Beat General crossed over, gained a top 10 hit in the British pop charts, and performed on the BBC's Top of Pops. This solidified General Levy as one of the most influential MCs in the British music industry.

Since collaborating with M-Beat General, he has consistently performed in clubs, dance halls, on and off sound systems, main stages, and festivals.

General's current collaborations with Joe Ariwa include 'In the Ghetto' and 'Be Conscious and Wise' Dub Showcase, with My Boyz Beatz and Jbeats0121 'Put The Guns Down' and 'Time Fi Di Come Up' for GTs Records, which also includes the remix ft Tippa Irie.

General Levy and Grantley GT

Apache Indian

Apache Indian, born of Indian origin, unlike Pato and Peter, who were brought up in the Balsall Heath area of Birmingham, Apache was brought up in Handsworth, Birmingham, UK, which back then was known to us as the heart of the black community. Even up until the 1990s, it was predominantly Black and Asian who accommodated most of the housing and shops.

I remember first meeting Apache; he did not have locks then. He had a high top with partings down the sides, which was the hairstyle at the time. It was at a small nightclub between Handsworth and West Bromwich in the West Midlands. It was a typical West Indian venue where Apache was performing. What caught my attention was that he had a significant fan base that was Asian, equal in numbers, male and female. This was not a regular thing. Sure, you would find males in reggae clubs, but it was a rarity then and even now to find Asian females in reggae venues. His performance was good; I remember him working the small stage well, and he left an impression on me. As I was leaving the venue, someone who knew us introduced us and told me he would be big and I should sign him now. As the story progressed, it wasn't to be.

The next time I heard about Apache, he was working with Wooligan, a local music producer based in Handsworth who previously owned a popular sound system called Orthodox, who was known for their cultural roots and, of course, their sound quality. As I was primarily out of the country then, part of the conversations would focus on people breaking through. Apache's name would always come up, and he could be found in the dance halls generating a name on sound systems.

Wooligan and Apache collaborated on several tracks; I met up with a DJ contact, Mambo, who told me that he had moved on from DJing and was now managing Apache, who was about to embark on a tour of India. I was so happy for Mambo because Apache had cracked up the hits 'Chok

There' and 'Don Raja', and as Mambo stated, he had signed with Island Records, which was known to have the distribution network to generate sales worldwide. Another reason why Mambo and Apache would work was due to his relationship with Erskin Thompson, a DJ on BRMB radio, who went on to work with Loose Ends and Maxi Priest. My Introduction to Erskin Thompson through a friend of mine, Sid, from Matthews Electronics, Hurst Street, Birmingham, when I was an up-and-coming DJ; he went on to mentor me even though he had moved to London and was working with some great bands.

Apache moved on in collaboration with producers Simon and Diamond, who came up with a sound that slotted right into a market made for them. At that time, bhangra was sweeping all over the West Midlands, with names like Bali Sagoo and the Sahota's causing a storm wherever they went: concerts, weddings, and parties. Bhangra was what you heard. Bhangra was a fusion of reggae drum and basslines, two and three-chord drops merged with Tabla and dole Dhol drums, essential for percussion and authentic Indian sound.

The team utilised this sound on Apache's first album 'No Reservations', recorded in Jamaica and produced by Simon & Diamond, Phil Chill, Robert Livingston, Bobby Digital, and Sly Dunbar in 1993, utilising the patois he embodied from the streets of Handsworth Birmingham. Apache followed this with songs like 'Boom Shack-A-Lak'.

By now, and with his growing popularity, Apache began to write more light-hearted songs such as 'Girls Dem Fiyah' but didn't forget about songs that had more authentic issue-based subjects closer to home with songs like 'Arranged Marriage', 'Aids Warning', and 'Election Crisis'.

Apache Indian has collaborated with British reggae icons such as Maxi Priest, General Levy, Shaggy, Boy George, and Tippa Irie and received awards for his contributions to the music, culminating with his British Empire Medal (BEM) at the 2022 Commonwealth Games in Birmingham, UK.

While reggae's roots lie in Jamaica, the origins of Lovers Rock, The British MCs, Dancehall, Ragga, and Dub are firmly rooted in the UK, consequently a legacy of Windrush.

British reggae music MCs have played a pivotal role in shaping the sound and culture of reggae in the UK. Emerging from the dynamic and diverse urban environments of cities like London, Birmingham, and Bristol, these MCs brought their unique voices and lyrical styles to the forefront of the genre. Influenced by the roots of Jamaican reggae and dub, British MCs infused their performances with local experiences, addressing themes like social justice, identity, and migration while celebrating life and community.

The UK's reggae scene flourished in the 1970s and 1980s, propelled by the Caribbean diaspora, with sound system culture as its backbone.

Often performing at local sound system parties, MCs became essential figures who entertained and conveyed powerful messages over heavy basslines and rhythm. Unlike traditional Jamaican "toasters" (early MCs), British reggae MCs often incorporated elements from other genres such as punk, dub, and later hip-hop and jungle, creating a distinct fusion that resonated with British audiences.

Notable MCs like Smiley Culture, Papa Levi, Macka B, Pato Banton and Tippa Irie contributed significantly by blending Jamaican patois with British slang, creating a unique linguistic style that helped reggae reach a broader UK audience. Their performances were often characterised by sharp wit, political commentary, and a deep connection to their communities. MCs like:

Top Cat, 'Love Me ses', 'Stamina' and 'Girlz Dem'
Asher Senator, Asher In Court', 'Abbreviation' and 'Fast Style Origination'
Tenor Fly, 'Roughneck Fashion', 'Born Again' and 'Loyal To The Game'

Crucial Robbie, 'Proud To Be Black', 'Dem No Bad' and 'Love Jamaica'

Frighty & Colonel Mite, 'Life (Is What You Make It), 'Do The Ragga' and 'High Grade'

The MCs, who contributed to the British MC phenomenon, assisted the reggae genre and laid the groundwork for later developments in UK rap, grime, and dancehall.

Chapter 8

Developing My Music Management Skills

My career as an international music manager began with giving advice; it was something I used to do. I recall advising Pato in 1982 before he challenged Judah, an MC from Birmingham, for a significant (battle). Pato shared that he had only one new lyric and was worried about losing. The growth of British reggae music accelerated globally, driven by creative talent and skilled musicians. The magazine Black Echoes

pioneered the movement, launching a weekly reggae chart. Journalists wrote about icons and emerging British reggae artists. Radio DJs and sound systems transformed British reggae by recording their shows on tape cassettes, a trend that became so popular that record shops sold sound clash tapes. The age of the British MC had begun.

As an international music manager, I travelled by ferry to Belgium and drove by van to Holland in 1979. Since then, I have been lucky enough to travel to every corner of the world as a DJ, roadie, driver, live sound engineer, producer, promoter, record label, photographer, performing arts musical director, and music CEO. However, it all started from humble beginnings, very hard, consistent work, and my love for music.

Following successful promotions, including one I remember well at Steptoe's in Birmingham, I became friends with Pato Banton, Tippa Irie, Smiley Culture, and Asher Senator. Steptoe's was a prominent nightclub (originally La Dolce Vita) located on Smallbrook Ring Way, Birmingham, with a capacity of two thousand people.

Smiley and I had met previously when we talked about the music business, and I ended up advising him at times. It wasn't on a contractual level, but I was somebody with whom Smiley felt comfortable. Consequently, he and I would connect whenever Smiley came to Birmingham. I got to know Asher well because he and Smiley usually rode together.

As previously referred, advising was something I just used to do back then. Back in the day, I remember giving Pato a tip when he was about to challenge a popular MC from Handsworth who went by the name of Judah in Birmingham in 1982; I had picked him up to give him a lift to a venue, Oaklands in Handsworth. On the way, Pato stated he had only written one new lyric and was expecting to get buried (lose the competition). I remember Pato spitting the lyrics to me; they were fantastic. Having listened, I asked, at what point in the competition are you thinking of delivering this? Pato replied, stating, I'll drop it about lyric number 4 or 5. My response to Pato was to start the battle with the first song he had written! Pato replied,' Are you mad? My response was that Judah would think you had lots more in store.

From that point, I began to see myself as an advisor to artists and read as many books as possible on the subject. In a relatively short time, with the aid of some good people who encouraged me, a few supervisory and management courses, and the books I had read, I was ready to take things more seriously. The life experience gained until then gave me the initial confidence.

My Mentors

I am so grateful; throughout my journey in the music industry, there have been many individuals who have taken me under their wings, and in times of both struggle and success, these individuals have greatly assisted my development in the following ways as outlined below:

Mrs Haynes - Mom
Mr Haynes - Dad
Uncle Ossie
Uncle Lesley
Keith Brown
Erskin Thompson
Carl Palmer
Miles Copeland
Tarquin Gotch
Andy Bowen
Bernie Dixon
Tony Owens
Lloyd Blake

Experience and Expertise: They provided their knowledge, experience, and specialisation when I needed it most. This enabled me to find solutions to complex situations, avoiding the common pitfalls in the music industry's cutthroat theatre and assisting me with organisational and negotiation skills, a track record of success in artist development and promotion, and a good understanding of contracts and legal matters related to the music industry. Find someone who shares your vision and values and who you can trust to represent your interests effectively. They provided encouragement, help, confidence, building and frequently offered constructive feedback, which assisted me in developing self-awareness and emotional intelligence.

Goal Setting and Accountability: I was aware of setting goals; however, my mentors assisted me with framing my goals in ways that made me hold myself accountable to the aims and objectives I had set for myself, helping me recognise the importance of structure, focus, motivation, and consistency.

Perspective and Insight: As a new boy, my mentors introduced me to the wide-ranging music industry. They offered their perspective on trends, directions, and strategic thinking, helping me to understand the bigger picture, explore alternative solutions, learn to approach problems methodically using my creative vision and develop my goals as I saw them at that point.

Developing My Style as a Manager in The Music Industry

The more I read about management and applied the principles of what I had read, including the practical experiences I was undertaking at the time, the better I felt I became. Most managers in the music industry start with either experience, education or both. This is essential because the industry is full of highs and lows. The pitfalls can leave one with devastating ramifications. However, with the ability to spot talent, building a solid network of contacts who can assist you with organisation, negotiation, marketing, and the best ways of developing promotional skills will give you a good start.

Developing a track record of success as a promotor is also a good starting point. This will give you a good understanding of contracts and legal matters related to the music industry. However, you should seek assistance from a professional music business lawyer before signing contracts or carrying out agreements.

Finding someone who shares your vision and values and someone you can trust to represent your interests effectively is also essential for an artist. My professional management career began with Pato Banton. I gained much practical experience as a DJ and promoter in the British reggae industry whilst working with Smiley Culture; it improved my confidence and belief in what I could offer to someone talented in music. Following the success of 'Allo Tosh', three to four record companies showed a serious interest in signing Pato, Island, and Virgin, to mention two. I talk and discuss Pato Banton in greater detail in Chapter 10.

Becoming An Artist in The Music Industry

Over the last forty years of working with many artists, young and older, one piece of advice I would offer would be to:

1. Follow the keyboard; I mean to match each note of your voice with the piano.

2. Decide why you want to do music. Is it for the money or because you love it?

3. Be true to yourself and your team

4. Remind them that the blueprints already exist. Use them and place the you that is you into them. We are all different, be different.

Coaching and developing artists are things I love doing. I look at it similarly to what builders do when they build houses, what authors do when they write books, and what football managers do when they develop teams to some respect. What is critical is getting to know the individual personalities within the team and, more importantly, what they want for themselves and need from others they work with. What comes next for me is the development of clear aims and objectives. These need to be as easy to understand as possible. The difficulty and skill from here on are to be found in executing the plan and modifying it to the specifications of individual personalities from time to time.

British reggae music has benefitted from talented musicians, artists and bands since its inception. Many might describe themselves as trendsetters while at the same time being considered performers by their fans; in today's music industry, social media and the development of artificial intelligence, it has become imperative that to become a successful artist, you will have to possess some online channel, a website, YouTube, Instagram, Tic Tok, Snapchat or Facebook. This is because methods of marketing and promotion have changed. The tools used in the 70s and 80s would have been printed material, music magazines, and analogue recordings utilising 2" 24 track tape and 2 track quarter inch master tape, which would then have to be mastered onto acetate to press vinyl albums or singles. The above can be done in a bedroom with a laptop digital audio workstation (DAW).

By the same measure, printing and the basics of journalism can all be achieved digitally by most individuals with the know-how using a smartphone, an email address, WhatsApp and a range of appropriate apps. It's now more about knowledge and how we manage it.

igital media is used to promote singles and albums. More importantly, it is used to communicate directly with fans and to determine where people can go to listen to what's new with the artist or project.

Vocalist, performer, or both: The artist's ability to deliver and talent level must be considered concerning the desired entertainment factor.

Impact and visionary: Are they one or the other or more of one than the other? However, the key consideration here is artistic purpose. We all can agree that an artist's vocal performance can lead to more incredible popularity on the radio for most songs; however, if the legacy is also something that an artist wants to achieve, such as Bob Marley or Bob Dylan, this calls for vision, which can take years of hard work, depending on the artist's initial aim.

A great performer may include dancing and choreography, and the overall vision and storytelling ability on and off stage, using cute long and short videos, displayed their confidence at performances. Whether or not nerves are at play, they appear to be at home and in their comfort zone.

How Much Do You Want It?

The idea here is about desire; ask yourself, as an artist, 'What do I want, and why do I want it?' Here, the question for the artist is, what does my audience want, and what would I like people to invest in and why?

Image and outfits play an additional aspect alongside choreography, consistently producing iconic moves in multiple songs and displaying potential.

The performers choose the area of setting trends, and visual identity will generally appeal to a younger audience, focusing on an excellent visual aesthetic that is great for developing good branding, mainly because you can look at them and instantly understand what they are about.

People may love the sound of a great singer's voice. There might be something about their tone that is so beautiful it grabs you. It may sound comforting, energetic, and empathic. At the same time, that's the magic that becomes their unique selling point. Great songwriters write songs that have something you can, or that resonates with something in your past or that you might be experiencing in the here and now; spoken word, poetry, inspiring the storylines become the source of great memories that keep listeners engaged, creating a need for individuals to repeat the listening experience for hours where they end up learning the words. This is why many people love songs; they can provide great vibes while bringing laughter when times are tough.

For singers and performers who reach this stage and generate a reputation for delivering, managers tend to seek them out. If I took you on, I would calculate that your career would improve to the extent that in exchange for my ability to guide you and your path in the music business to a point where you, as an artist, could make a living from what you were doing.

In return, as the artist, I would be expected to be paid a percentage of the money I assisted you to make, usually around twenty per cent. In addition, my role would include putting in place connections with agents, promotors, and record companies, allowing you, the artist, to concentrate on the business of developing your craft, making music and writing songs.

I saw it as my job to assist an artist in developing a buzz, playing open mics, supporting shows, and showcasing afternoons and evenings. Here, you will get feedback from people in the audience who may also like what they see and follow your progress. At this stage, remember the aim of what you do and why you do it.

Road Management

A road manager in the music business is responsible for coordinating and overseeing the logistical aspects of a touring musician or band's performances. This includes managing transportation, lodging, scheduling, and ensuring that all technical and stage requirements are met at each venue. They often travel with the artists and act as a point of contact between the performers, venue staff, and other crew members. Additionally, they may handle aspects of finance and merchandise sales and resolve issues of all descriptions whilst on the road. It is a demanding role that requires strong organisational skills, problem-solving abilities, and working well under pressure.

The road manager will possess strong organisational skills, practical communication abilities, and a thorough understanding of logistics. They must be adaptable and have a keen eye for detail to ensure the smooth running of the artist and their teams, allocating resources where they will make the best impact in line with the delivery of the project from beginning to end.

Interest in Pato's live shows grew. As a DJ, Roberto understood the market to some extent; hence, I explored the opportunities of playing venues further north with him. Pato's songs were regularly played in the Bay Area; therefore, we gathered shows between Los Angeles and San Francisco.

Pato and I had travelled to the USA three times. We built up a good following supported by Pato's performances and interviews, and we passed around imported versions of 'Mad Professor

Captures Pato Banton' and 'Never Give In'. We had covered a lot of ground, travelled thousands of miles and were happy with our achievements. However, there was more work; I felt we needed three things to improve: a record deal, Pato's British band of musicians and a booking agent in the USA who could take responsibility for booking shows in North America and Canada.

Roberto had a natural affinity for presenting Pato, and due to his skills and abilities as a publicist, we increased Pato's penetration in southern California's club and university market. However, I set about developing a strategy that would get Pato signed to an American record company and go on to achieve a distribution level crucial to utilising what we were achieving by touring and local radio.

Having discussed this with Pato, the priority was to get a deal and bring the British band to the US. I advised him that there was no doubt I would get him signed; the tricky part was finding the right team needed, a road manager who could drive and at least one good roadie.

Don Kilbury

Don is a good friend who is supportive, trustworthy, loyal, and understanding. Don can listen without judgment and offer encouragement in both good and bad. To this day, Don remains a good friend who respects personal boundaries whilst communicating openly with genuine care for my well-being. Apart from his excellent road management attributes, he became my American personal assistant and business partner, proving time and again himself as someone who shared the values of the team, complementing its strengths and weaknesses whilst communicating effectively as one who is reliable, trustworthy and is committed to the success of the venture and channelling his expertise, resources, and networks to enhance the business.

I met Don Kilbury shortly after Pato performed at California State University, Long Beach. Aki, the student musical director, did a sterling job enabling Pato to perform to a sold-out audience. Don occupied an identical role to Aki, where he was the student musical director at California State University, Northridge. Don had heard about the show at California State University, Long Beach, so he was there at the show to watch the show and hopefully book a date.

Between 1986 and 1987, I could have recruited a road manager and P.A. in a vast territory like the USA. However, I ultimately decided to train and grow with an individual who possessed the aptitude to work directly with teams, each project taking place at the time, and its long-term goals.

There would be occasions when the recording of albums, tours, personal appearances or engagements had to occur on the other side of the world, such as in the UK. Because of this, at the back of my mind, I knew the project would not be a one or two-year thing. I believed that I would go further. With this in mind, I sought to develop an international management team that would respond to the projected vision, be flexible, and have a membership with the skills and abilities to deputise in the absence of others, as and when required. Consequently, the management team's growth grew in line with Its long-term vision, which was no mean feat.

To summarise, the shows at California State University Long Beach and California State University Northridge went down a storm and completed both shows successfully. Don was especially interested in reggae music; I'll never forget Don having a personalised number plate with reggae on it. Don was also a musician; he formed his band while attending college. With the experience he gathered gigging, he put it into practice. He owned three guitars then and knew quite a bit about the California music scene. He was young and very eager to prove himself in the music industry. Hence, our conversation was during his intern weekend in the Bay area.

Don and I negotiated a pay rate suitable for the job description and person specification. In addition, I covered responsibilities and expectations in line with the agreed work plan. I clarified that he would be accountable to me and that his remuneration would be my responsibility. Don and I worked together for nearly 25 years and have remained good friends. He was an excellent road manager, and communication was never an issue. We extensively discussed strategic plans, including logistics, cost-effectiveness, and different approaches to prioritise the artist's interests.

In 1990, I flew to Chicago to work with our agents and fine-tune the logistical dates for the forthcoming 98-date US tour. Considering we would be away from our families and homes for three months, I needed to ensure the team would spend as little time travelling on the road and increase the opportunity for us to rest well and sleep in a bed as often as possible. I then flew to California to finalise the H1 visa applications with the record company, along with the launch of Pato's album 'Wise Up'. The album needed to be accessible for purchase in local record stores and major chains like Tower Records, particularly for the California leg, where supporting Ziggy Marley was on the agenda, with an expected combined audience exceeding 130,000.

Don Kilbury and I

A contract I had signed months before was for Pato Banton to play Reggae on the River, which I considered an anchor date for a 98-date Pato Banton tour I had planned three months prior. However, the opportunity for Pato to be the opening act, supporting Ziggy Marley on his 'One Bright Day' US Californian tour dates presented itself. What caused me frustration was in the process of confirming six dates with Ziggy, which amounted to the entire California leg of the 'One Bright Day American Tour', in which the first date was to begin at Irvine Meadows Amphitheatre. However, Reggae on The River, which fell on the same date, in Irvine in southern California and 'Reggae On The River', Humboldt County, located in Northern California, is an hour's drive between both locations.

Don and I spent hours discussing the tour's pros and cons, its aims and objectives, projected costs, and the likelihood of making a profit at its end. I am proud to say that we have never lost money on a tour in my history as a music business manager.

A Career-Defining Decision

There was a decision to be made. I still had to work out how to play two significant dates on the same day. Having slept on it and discussing it with Don, we decided to look at flights. Coming up with nothing, the decision was made to private hire a seven-seater jet from a small airport a few miles from Reggae On The River Humboldt County that would transport us to John Wayne Airport, Orange County, in America. The road crew consisted of eleven, which meant four members could not travel to Humbolt and head back to Irvine after the show the night before. Don and I met with Pato and the band to explain the situation. Thankfully, they were all happy. I was still worried even though the pilot and seven-seater aeroplane were covered by insurance. Despite my internal concerns, all went smoothly; I didn't have the pleasure of feeling okay until the tour bus picked us up at Orange County.

We went on to meet Rita Marley, Ziggy Marley, and the Melody Makers, and we successfully supported the Grammy-winning album and tour 'The One Bright Day.' Other things could have ended my music career, but I'm pleased to say I managed to sidestep that.

I will always be grateful to Rita and Ziggy's team for allowing me to change the sound and record Pato's live performance. This is a big deal, a no-no with most headline artists. Almost thirty-five years later, fans can listen to these shows on the album I remastered at London's Abbey Road Studio by My Boyz Beatz' calling it, Pato Banton and The Reggae Revolution live in the USA and Canada.

Keith Brown

A good friend who is supportive, trustworthy, loyal, and understanding, listens without judgment, offers encouragement, and is there in good and challenging times. Keith shares the organisation's values and complements the strengths and weaknesses of what it delivers and stands for. Keith has played a role in the success of GT's Records and My Boyz Beatz. He has also chaired Wheeler Street Young Entertainers and Entrepreneurs in Action since its inception.

Since the 1980s, Keith has been there. Unlike others, Keith recognised I needed help spinning several plates at the time, promotion in the early days, GT's management company, and deputising when I was out of the country on international business and tours. I think the best way to describe his contributions was that he grew with all aspects of the company, so it could not be said that his role would be described as a road manager because he had invested his time and money too, which is why I say with great appreciation, that his role constituted more than that of a road manager.

I remember one of the many times Keith deputised for me was when he travelled to Europe with Tippa Irie, supporting Gregory Isaacs. Keith not only saw the tour through but also handled aspects of bookkeeping and logistics whilst communicating with our administration officer in the UK and myself in America. I learned the best way to guide someone with Keith's skills and abilities was to present them with the task and ask them to identify what they need from you to facilitate it.

As a management team, to save on the costs an artist would pay for an agent, our capacity as a management team would act as the agent, providing the artist with a 10 -15% saving. Keith and I would seamlessly cover this role end to end. This role increased with marketing, promotion and distribution of GT's record releases, taking particular responsibility for drafting album and single release biographies for DJ postal mailouts, imperative for providing up-to-date information for periodical music magazines before the internet revolution.

Grantley GT and Keith Brown

All the artists I managed toured internationally. The costs associated with flight tickets, transfers from their home to airports, day-to-day hotel accommodation, food, and per diems can sometimes be enormous, an area for which record companies usually provide tour support. Tour support can become a double-edged sword for bands because every dollar or pound of tour support is often recuperable. However, if you're an artist or band that has sold millions of albums, the record company may have recouped the tour support budget provided. It's a loan, and as we know, all loans have to be paid back; it all adds up and is displayed when the artist gets their statement.

I was so fortunate or I would research events I planned to do time and time again, which meant that I almost never lost money on shows or certainly not overseas tours. Over five years, I would invest in purchasing the tour bus and merchandising, allowing us consistency, cash flow and day-to-day profit. The money was borrowed from my bank in the UK and gradually paid back over a four-year term, secured by my house in England. Pato, Keith, and I covered flight tickets, transfers, and merchandising.

Hence, I decided to hold onto the record company's offer of tour support. This method of self-funding, food, accommodation, transport, and merchandise allowed us to work as a unit that benefited, where possible, from the profits as an integral team.

Sometime in the summer of 1993, our friends needed help managing the accounting systems of their record shop based at Unit 3 Brookfield Shopping Precinct, Springhill (off Dudley Road), Birmingham, UK. We found that the experience Keith and I gained from GT's records, artists, and promotion could be transferable in retail, i.e., weekly sales, stock control, rotation, and accounts. We could break down the roles between us to a point where we could run the shop based on our skill base.

We began with a staff training program. We established this to update existing staff members who were:

Mikey Biggs
Too Sweet
Gee

The training program provided them with information on how they could better use the till system to improve the stock rotation system. We introduced job descriptions and person specifications that appropriated the critical functions of a record store. Keith took responsibility for this development area. Within six months, we were thinking about another shop, which led to opening a shop (in our backyard), Mosley Road, Balsall Heath, Birmingham. For a while, things worked well. However, with a combination of market forces, location, issues concerning staff recruitment and lease-related problems, we decided to cut our losses, conceding that we had some memorable moments and gained experiences money couldn't buy.

Love and Belief

Engage with any fan of Reggae music; you will hear the word love. Ask any artist who has worked in the field for years; you will come across the word love. However, love is not a word you might often hear in the Reggae music industry, maybe because it might be confused with profit or loss. By contrast, you may listen to the word belief, and perhaps belief accounts for what you need when you embark upon something that usually you have little idea of the outcome; however, because there is something about it that grabs you or resonates with something from your past, such as a fond experience we are drawn in, and we generate belief.

Working in reggae music has come either out of my love for it or because I believe in it. Also, when people love and believe in something or someone, they are willing to contribute to the cause or pay for the privilege of participating or the entertainment factors that bring it about. I became a DJ out of my love for the music I purchased and the joy I got from watching people enjoy themselves while listening to my records and dancing with friends.

My love affair with music was taken to another level when I signed my first management contract in the British Reggae music industry. My decision to become a manager resulted from my belief in what I could achieve with my skills and abilities. For the first time, I asked myself what constitutes a manager in the music industry. It may sound funny, but in short, the answers were contained within each contract schedule; it was no different to a 9 – 5 contract. The terms could be viewed as a job description and person specification. For me, this made my role easier to understand and made it easier for me to measure myself on whether I was delivering or not. The music business differs slightly in its construction input and outputs from most traditional counterpart organisations. However, I will describe below some of the key factors I focussed on when I began my tenure, to which I sought to focus the method of my delivery around and go on to explain in greater detail in this chapter:

The 3 Es

Efficiency

Effectiveness

Economy

Planning

Organisation

Leadership

Staffing

Evaluation

I found it difficult to understand at the time, but it is simple to understand why I received little support from some of those who knew me. This left me feeling the need to prove myself at every management stage in my first two years of managing two high-profile artists. Nevertheless, I continued by delivering on the contract, taking advice from mentors and reading books that covered making records, how the money was made, and the correct procedure to employ when seeking to develop artists and success in the music business, not just the Reggae business.

With my head down and getting on with the job, I didn't even realise that the issue of my competency was no longer a factor. I was now beginning to get artists seeking my services. I had to become somebody who had delivered and someone good at getting the job done, who could handle pressure, gaining a reputation for knowing what to do in really difficult situations.

The fundamental difference for me was that I understood what artists wanted. Apart from earning a living, they wanted to earn money from a job they loved doing. I saw one of my roles as guiding them in a direction that would achieve longevity. I remember responding to a question from an artist: if I knew how much income I forecasted would be earned the following year? How many hits do you think we will have? Consequently, my ambition was to encourage artists and musicians to focus on believing in what they did, where they wanted to go, and their ideas for how we could get there, starting with their belief in themselves.

Whilst this has its exceptions, the artists I have managed have always delivered what they do from a place in their hearts; therefore, using my skills, experiences, and abilities has allowed me to be part of their art.

Growth

There are some fundamental rules about growth, and some pros can be considered cons. For the above to become possible, the following needs to take place:

Songs and Song Writing
Hit Singles and Albums
Concert Ticket Sales

Song choice and the correct release structures are all key factors in generating hits. For instance, Pato Banton's 'Allo Tosh spent four weeks at number two in the British Reggae charts; having said that, keeping it from the number one spot was Wayne Smith and a song called 'Under Me Sleng Teng', followed by several remixes. Although 'Allo Tosh' provided Pato with a big hit, and the song did provide us with numerous licencing opportunities and shows, the fact remains that people tend to remember hits and, for that matter, hits that enter number one and stay there.

Considering songs and songwriting, most artists tend to have some emotional connection or, like poetry, write stories that recite the narrative of a personal experience in their lives. Others may pen that which relate to the listing audience in one shape or form, such as the Beatles or Bob Marley, cover many subjects that focus on love, or the love of someone unavailable, breaking up, loss, pain, Freedom, injustice, rebellion and freedom to name a few. The thing that ties lyrics and composition (melodies and music) together is where the talent for writing good songs begins. Songs can come quickly, and others may take time. Whichever comes first, the next stage is more technical and more about the skills found in effective and efficient vocal arrangements.

From this point on, the task is to navigate one's career through what sometimes can feel like a river or ocean and try to get through it. At the same time, to grow, you have to swim. If you keep swimming, you will reach a point when you forget how difficult it was to break through. Sometimes, I wonder what would have happened if I hadn't faced the uphill hike head-on; I guess I would have just kept going. People ask me all the time how I did it. It started when I was young; I just wanted to work hard. I felt something would come of it in time, and it did. I learned from family and friends to ask for help and learn from others. Through my experiences, I have been fortunate to realise that as people, 'we learn best when we are faced with difficulty or experience pain or some type of suffering'.

For most of us, this indicates that we didn't get something right or that something needs changing. If you look at some of the wealthiest people in this world, their outlook differs from that of someone who has struggled from the bottom up and become rich.

Of course, there are exceptions, but generally speaking, these individuals usually come from a place inside of themselves of moral authority, one of service and sacrifice, even sometimes at significant cost to themselves, the unsung heroes. Everyone knows someone like this; their path may be difficult, but they find reasons and the spirit to assist the path of change and are sometimes willing to die for it.

Ask anyone; the path toward success is fraught with disappointments and setbacks. However, with these lessons, would success feel so rewarding? Or would the reward feel like entitlement? Through it all, it is when we find others we can love and trust that our lives have more meaning, where setbacks and disappointments are shared, providing a brighter light at the end of that tunnel.

Lonely Days

I remember touring being the absolute worst time of my life when it came to missing Family, close friends, and such. At that time, the cost of a one-minute telephone call would run at one pound a minute. Later, you could buy calling cards, reducing the price by about two-thirds, which was still very expensive. I tended to settle my hotel telephone bills straight after calling, allowing me to monitor my finances. The costs would sometimes run into hundreds, and by the time I spoke to my children, girlfriend and parents, the challenging emotions set in where sometimes they were too much to manage, but the job still had to be done. On top of all that, as a leader, the feelings I experienced assisted me in managing the feelings of others. I cast my mind back to times when I thought success was glamorous. From experience, most of the time, it is; however, sometimes, if not managed effectively, things can go wrong, and life for those who entertain can end in a dark place.

I remember being at the height of success but feeling alone and reduced to tears. You're talking about normal individuals here. Friends back home see one side, the positives of travelling to different countries, while people at home would never understand how lonely the journey was. One comfort I could turn to was Pato, Tippa, and the band. The team I travelled with became family; we were often like brothers.

Learning From Failure and Using It as A Springboard for Success

Failure was one of the most valuable learning outcomes during my time in management. For most people, the fear associated with not doing something well, such as passing an exam, being dismissed from employment or even being dumped by a partner, gives rise to personal setbacks and stumbling blocks that might prevent us from achieving our goals. However, I learnt from reading that most successful individuals and organisations had one thing in common: they had learned to master the art of learning from failure.

Changing My Mindset

My first step in learning from failure was changing how I saw it and not taking it personally. Instead of seeing it as the end of the road, it was challenging, but I looked at it as a method for close friends and colleagues to provide me with feedback. My mentors were good at this once I had approved them to be ruthless with their feedback. I further instructed them to discuss what didn't work with me and enquire about what did work. This always helps me learn and, more importantly, grow.

The Growth Mindset

My belief came from the likes of my dad and uncle, who encouraged me to be brave and not to worry about what people thought about me; they would always say, let people judge you by what you say and what you do; if you get it wrong put it right, whatever it takes, where there is a will, there's a way. I have never forgotten that statement. Intelligence can be developed through dedication and hard work. This is the mindset that I believe got me through my early days of growing up in the inner city of Birmingham and, indeed, fostered my resilience to face the setbacks I encountered. This allowed me to understand that failure was a natural learning process and that the most innovative ideas often arise from numerous failed attempts.

Those reading this book and who know me personally will know that, more often than not, I reward myself with the effort I have put into a task, regardless of the outcome. This reinforces the idea that nothing beats trying, but failing to try and learning is more important to me than immediate success.

The Lessons Learnt from Honest Reflection of Self

Once I looked at failure differently, I could repeat the process, transferring perspective. This process always involves examining what went wrong and why, allowing me to draw lessons for the future. I often take a step back and assess the situation objectively. Identify the factors that contributed to the failure without self-blame or making excuses.

Aims and Objectives

1. What was my initial aim, and why did I choose it?

2. What were my expectations for the project?

3. What specific actions or decisions led to things not going to plan?

4. What external factors or unforeseen circumstances led to changes that may have taken place?

5. How did I respond to early signs of diversion?

Feedback: I seek input from others involved or people with different perspectives. They may notice factors I may have overlooked and provide me with valuable insights.

Patterns: When I need to improve, I consistently look for recurring themes or patterns. These highlight underlying issues or blind spots that I need to address.

Turning Learning into Action

I have learnt that failure is only valuable if I use the insights to make meaningful changes. This involves creating and implementing strategies to avoid repeating the same mistakes repeatedly.

S.M.A.R.T

Specific: Outline specific steps to improve based on your knowledge of yourself. These could include acquiring new skills, changing processes, or adjusting your approach.

Measurable: Review your progress towards your goals regularly. Be willing to adjust your plan as needed based on new insights and changing circumstances.

Achievable and Realistic: Establish clear, attainable objectives considering lessons learned. Break these goals into manageable tasks with defined timelines.

Time is Limited with Support. Surround yourself with individuals who encourage growth and learning. Share your experiences and lessons learned to create a culture of continuous improvement.

Remember

Failure is an inevitable part of any journey toward success. You can turn setbacks into stepping stones by changing your mindset, systematically analysing your failures, and implementing the lessons learned. Remember, the road to success is often paved with failures, and each one brings you closer to your ultimate goal. Embrace failure, learn from it, and let it drive you to greater heights.

Chapter 9

Record Companies and Contracts

In the 1980s, if the album sold 50,000 copies at £15.00 per album, it would likely generate £750.000. The record company would look to recoup the recording advance, any additional costs over and above those paid out in the initial recording advance, tour support, a percentage of any costs of shooting a video, and a percentage of the promotion costs. It is helpful to remember that a recording contract is similar to a lone; it has to be paid back.

A typical recording contract for a British reggae band in the 1970s - 80s would include an advance payment to be spent on the recording of an album, with the option for three or four more albums.

In the 80s, if the album sold 50 thousand copies

at £15.00 per album, it would likely generate £750.000. The record company would look to recoup the recording advance, any additional costs over and above those paid out in the initial recording advance, tour support, a percentage of any costs of shooting a video and a percentage of the promotion costs.

The figure or percentage the band or artist would receive somewhere within the recording contract after the above advances and costs had been recouped or paid back. At this point, bands or artists would begin receiving royalty checks on a six-month basis of whatever percentage was agreed in the recording contract.

Should any queries or discrepancies arise, they would be calculated based on what was written in the recording contract and the associated numbers. This agreement would detail what items the company could recoup from the sales and earnings of singles, albums, or CDs and any costs from royalties due for payment to the artist or band. When calculated, this would result in a profit or loss for the artist, either positively or negatively.

Publishing music is critical for individuals who write lyrics and compose music. In the UK, artists, songwriters, and composers without representation are best advised to join the musicians' union and sign up with the Performing Rights Society (PRS), which will manage the collection of royalties derived from songs released for commercial sale or listened to by members of the public. The legal terms used in the music industry for this business area are exploitation and protection.

Additional functions include copyright administration, which, in effect, consists of managing copyrights and works. They register compositions with worldwide copyright offices such as the Performing Rights Society (PRS), Broadcasting Music Inc. (BMI), the American Society of Composers and Publishers (ASCAP), and other collection organisations worldwide, principally protecting their rights. The publisher's role is to provide a license for the compositions belonging to composers for use in films, TV shows, commercials, video games, and public performances, including mechanical permits for recordings and synchronisation licenses for audiovisual media, such as royalty payments derived from the sale of recordings, live performances and radio plays, by promoting compositions to other recording artists, producers, and media outlets increasing the use and monitorisation of those songs. As expected, your publisher is responsible for providing contracts for using your work, maintaining the legal reference, and keeping it secure.

PRS, PPL and MCPS

Similar to the role of music publishers, the British Performing Rights Society (PRS), the Public Performance License Ltd. (PPL) and the Music Copyright Performance Society (MCPS) carry out additional functions on behalf of songwriters, composers, and music publishers, which include:

The above organisations monitor when music is played, where it is played and who plays the songs following their professional release. For instance, PPL's role is to ensure that venues that provide live and recorded music have the correct license, enabling them to calculate and collect royalties from across several different platforms for distribution. These include businesses that use music publicly, such as radio stations, TV channels, social media platforms, restaurants, bars, clubs, retail stores, offices, live venues, shopping malls and public houses.

These societies distribute collected royalties to their members, including songwriters, composers, and publishers, based on data regarding how often and where the music is used. Having said this, becoming a member usually incurs a cost, ensuring that its members' intellectual property and rights are protected and enforced, preventing the unauthorised and infringements use of their member's music.

PRS and MCPS, in particular, provide additional services such as training, educational workshops, and adversarial support to continue fair music industry practices and policies for its members and help with claims and compensation where intellectual property has been breached. Examples of organisations mentioned above include ASCAP (American Society of Composers, Authors, and Publishers), BMI (Broadcast Music, Inc.) in the United States, and other affiliate licence and collection organisations outside the United Kingdom.

Licenses

The need for the correct licenses is crucial in the music business. Having learnt and understood this, I included it in the book. Here are some of the primary considerations:

Sync License: This license is crucial for film, TV, advertisements, and video games. It allows the use of music alongside visual content to enhance storytelling or evoke specific emotions. It covers the synchronisation of music with video or audiovisual works.

Mechanical License: When an artist or producer wants to record and distribute a cover version of a song, they need a mechanical license. It gives them the legal right to reproduce and distribute copyrighted musical compositions in a recorded format, such as CDs, vinyl, or digital downloads.

Master License: While a mechanical license covers the composition, a master license grants permission to use a specific song recording.

This means the licensee can use a particular version or performance of a track in their project, whether a commercial, film, TV show or other media.

Public Performance: This license is necessary for playing music in public spaces, including live performances, concerts, radio broadcasts, and even background music in businesses. It ensures that composers, songwriters, and publishers receive royalties when their music is performed publicly.

Print Rights License: When someone wants to print and distribute sheet music, songbooks, or other printed materials containing musical compositions, they need a license. This license grants permission to reproduce and distribute a song's musical notation and lyrics in print form.

Theatrical License: Theatrical performances, including stage plays, musicals, and other live productions, often require permission to use copyrighted music. A theatrical license allows musical compositions to be performed within these productions, ensuring compliance with copyright laws and proper compensation for rights holders.

Effectiveness, Efficiency, and Economy In the music industry, management involves overseeing an artist's career, handling business affairs, negotiating contracts, and coordinating promotional activities. Managers often guide strategic decisions, support artists' development, and liaise between artists and industry professionals.

Managing artists and bands in the music industry can be extremely rewarding but also challenging. The pros can include the opportunity to work with creative talents, potential financial success, and building lasting relationships. Managers are usually paid 15 - 20% net of an artist's income. Agents generally request between 10% of the gross artist fee for a tour or 15% of an individual one-off show, plus VAT.

However, the role of a manager may become challenging, especially when dealing with unpredictable industry trends, achieving commercial success in one of the world's most competitive markets, or resolving conflicts among band members and rival artists, which requires a high degree of administrative work.

Administration

A reasonable administration manager typically possesses strong organisational skills, excellent communication abilities, attention to detail, leadership qualities, problem-solving capabilities, and proficiency in managing resources effectively. They should also have a solid understanding of administrative processes, prioritise tasks, handle multiple responsibilities efficiently, and adapt to changing situations. Additionally, being tech-savvy and having a customer-focused mindset are valuable traits for success in this role.

Throughout my tenure in the business between the eighties and nineties I was fortunate enough to have had two assistants, which began with Ranking Bev. Beverly set up the administration system while I resided in Birmingham.

Beverly and set up the office, which enabled me to manage while I was overseas and worldwide tour commitments for many artists. It must have taken some doing to manage the diary of a workaholic, determined to do something new before I had even finished the last project. However, Bev was no different; she was trustworthy, reliable, and always took her work and role seriously. While operating as my P.A., Bev was one of the Peoples Community Radio Line (PCRL) DJs in her spare time, where her delivery standards never diminished. The privilege of working with Bev and the systems we established set me up for what is to come next. Beverly moved on to bigger and better things with my blessings. Hence, we have remained good friends over the years.

Having said this, in 2018, I was directing the musical 'Mirrors and Makeup'. I asked Beverly if she could include her daughter and niece in the dance scenes, which she approved. I later worked with both her daughter and niece, providing vocal coaching as well as providing them with insight into what a music career would look like.

I had moved the operation to Birchwood Crescent, Mosely, Birmingham. The business had become too much for me to manage, so I asked Joycelyn St Juste to attend an interview, and the rest was history. Joycelyn was perfect. Not only an excellent friend but also similar to Beverly in terms of loyalty and trustworthiness. In a previous role, Joycelyn had worked with word processors and newly on-the-market fax machines, which our business was internationally heading and taking place. Again, Joycelyn was able to manage the workaholic that was me.

Nevertheless, I always felt Joyce was talented and would go on to different things. I always encouraged her to be the best I thought she could be. Now, one of my best friends, alongside Keith, I began teaching Joycelyn the business of music and how contracts worked. This enabled Joycelyn to negotiate shows, contracts, and riders for performances locally and abroad and provide artists with monthly statement taxation receipts and VAT returns.

Joycelyn eventually worked as a lecturer in one of Birmingham's colleges. We are still very close friends.

The administration's role in the music and industry business was imperative for the artists I managed. The business aspects and ensuring smooth operations are embedded within the management contract.

Having said this, a clear set of aims and objectives and dos and don'ts can assist with the process of resolution but sometimes avoid it altogether; in this case, a clause in your contract can provide you with a starting point for a three-way meeting where all parties come together as well as incorporate the areas listed below. These responsibilities include:

Licensing and Royalties: Administrators manage music licensing for various uses, such as films, commercials, and streaming services. They ensure that royalties are correctly calculated and distributed to artists, songwriters, and producers.

Contract Management: They handle contracts between artists, record labels, producers, and other stakeholders, ensuring all parties fulfil their obligations and their rights are protected.

Financial Management: This involves budgeting, accounting, and financial planning to ensure profitability and sustainability. Administrators track income and expenses, manage payments, and oversee monetary reporting.

Rights Management: Administrators ensure that intellectual property rights, including copyrights, trademarks, and performance rights, are protected and managed. This also involves registering works with relevant rights organisations.

Tour and Event Management: They organise and coordinate tours, concerts, and promotional events, handling logistics such as booking venues, scheduling, travel arrangements, and staffing.

Marketing and Promotion: While primarily a role of marketing departments, administrators often coordinate promotional activities, ensuring alignment with overall business strategies.

Compliance and Legal: Ensuring that all activities comply with relevant laws and regulations, including labour laws, copyright laws, and industry standards.

Data Management: Administrators manage data related to sales, streaming, airplay, and other metrics to inform strategic decisions and marketing efforts.

Artist Relations: They maintain relationships with artists, supporting and ensuring their needs are met to foster a positive working environment and effective collaboration.

Having said this, administration in the music industry is essential for maintaining order, ensuring legal and financial responsibilities are met, and supporting the creative processes that drive the industry and constitute its successful management. However, I have set out below the areas that underpin the effective delivery of outputs and outcomes:

Planning I set out a process of brainstorming the goals I thought the artist and I could achieve within a given period based on the artist's or band's talent, considering the available resources needed to achieve those goals.

Organisation This area could include the employment of a trainer or coach or placing the artist in venues where they could test their abilities according to the type of artist they believe themselves to be or the type of artist they are at the time. In addition, this could include feedback and developing a system where they measure themselves against a set of factors achieved by established successful artists.

I found this area complex mainly because I had to communicate my vision—one that would provide energy, get up and go, and believe.

That might sound simple, but it could be more complex. The ability to inspire and motivate people using vision calls for the effective use of experience, passion, and efficient communication skills.

Staffing As mentioned earlier, selecting the right artist or band is a recruitment skill. In this case, although it's the creative music industry, a would-be manager still needs to generate an application process together with some person's specifications for the position or position within the organisation.

Evaluation This area must be recognised. Within most competitive industries, things change quickly, so constant assessment of your goals is crucial for changing direction if needed, improving performance, and taking appropriate action. I have always used the three E's: effectiveness, efficiency, and sound economics.

Emotional Intelligence (EQ)

Effective managers understand the context and culture of leadership. What enables these managers to succeed? It is simple: understanding EQ (emotional intelligence) (the competencies in each dimension of emotional intelligence).

Those four dimensions are high self-awareness, social awareness, self-management, and good social skills. These essential competencies lead to great connections with people and more robust and effective managerial performance. EQ is a critical component in excelling as a supervisor.

The manager's job is to find a way to turn a team member's skill and talent into a higher level of performance. This idea doesn't suggest manipulation at all. Instead, it is about maximising an individual's potential, one team member at a time. It is as much art as it is science.

Chapter 10

Pato Banton

While in Los Angeles, I was asked if I could secure a spot for Pato Banton as a supporting act for Ziggy Marley's tour. I had meetings scheduled, including one at the William Morris Agency to explore this possibility. A friend connected me with the right person, and after presenting the business case, we were chosen to support Ziggy on the entire California leg of the tour. However, this created a scheduling conflict, as Pato was also committed to play at the Reggae on The River festival in northern California, booked nearly five months earlier.

Pato and I lived not far from each other in Balsall Heath, Birmingham, UK. At that time, Pato was a well-known young man passionate about dancing. I remember a popular dance at the time called 'Skanking'. Pato was quite a dab hand at 'Skanking' and would display his ability in the dance halls and clubs around the city. After some time had passed, Pato could be found chatting lyrics on almost every sound system in Birmingham. However, he could be seen more often or not on the microphone of Kris Kennedy Jr's (KKJs) Club Roadshow and 'Radics', a sound system led by the legendary Dolphus Welsh of Jah Massigan sound system, which was the resident sound system at the Earl Grey, a public house in the heart of Balsall Heath, Birmingham.

Not long after this, Pato took part in a band based in Balsall Heath, Birmingham, called Crucial Music, whose membership included:

Bass - Jaffa
Drums - Chinna
Congo's & Percussion - Charge
Guitar - Soloman
Vocalist - Pato

I was asked to assist Crucial Music when they learned I had a van and was reliable enough to pick up their equipment and transport it to musical venues where they were gigging. One particular journey has always stayed in my mind and provided me with the experience that has served me well since then. The band was invited to play in Holland, which meant we had to drive from Birmingham to Dover and board the ferry to Zeebrugge in Belgium and drive to the hotel near the venue. I remember there was a lot of driving, but the experience was worth it; the gig was great, and we all had a good time and then headed back to Birmingham.

On another level, Pato became famous as an MC; he engaged in **'Battles'** like many other MCs. The evening this came to a head, Pato was engaged in a battle with some of Birmingham's best, General CP, Bosey Peter and Judah (RIP), who all came from Handsworth. Pato, being from Balsall Heath or (Bitter Creek), was the odd one out! By nature, this battle became one of not only who was the best but also one of territory. Following this 'battle', it was announced that a decider called **'The Salt Fish Dance'** would be held at the famous Oaklands Sports and Community Centre in the heart of Handsworth, Birmingham.

Around this time, Pato and I had become friends, mainly because he used to MC on my roadshow **GT 600** now and again. We had a neat arrangement because, at that time, Pato's brother Winston, better known as Major' (RIP), was a member. Winston would ask Pato to attend some of our gigs when we played close by where Pato used to live, so he would grace us with his presence and add that spark for our audience. It was a treat. To cut a long story short, I was at the Red Cow public house in Smethwick, Sandwell, West Midlands; as I was leaving, Pato asked if I was going home; as

I was, I gave him a lift and whilst on our way, I stated I would give him a lift to Oaklands, for the intimidating night of the final. The winner would receive money and a cup, and the loser would receive a large salt fish, which they had to take home and cook.

As mentioned in chapter 8. It came the night of the clash, and Pato sent me word, letting me know where to pick him up. On our way, I asked Pato how he felt, and he replied that he was worried that losing would be the end of his career as an MC. I responded by stating that I didn't believe he would lose. I told him that he and Judah were great MCs and continued by asking how many new lyrics he had. I was surprised by Pato's reply, one he announced, and I answered, wow! I followed quickly by asking him to recite it to me. When he had finished, I said, that's the best lyric you have, to which Pato agreed. I have an idea, I said when Pato replied, what do you think? I answered, saying. 'You need to chat (sing, spit) the new one first, to which Pato replied, first! Are you mad? I responded by telling Pato that my strategy was based on Judah and the audience; hearing that lyric, you would get massive applause, which in turn would lead them to think there was a lot more to come; all Pato had to do then was to rearrange the rest of his lyrics differently to suite the rhythms that were being played. So said and done, Pato won the **'Battle'** Cup and became Birmingham's best MC.

Pato and where he lived was within walking distance of my house. We would meet once or twice a week, and he would give me a copy of a demo tape he had just recorded or tell me about the next thing. Then, one day, a very determined Pato said to me that he had sent a demo to Fashion Records in London and that they were interested in recording two songs, 'The Boss' and 'It Ain't What You Do, It's The Way That You Do It'. I wasn't with him at this recording, but Pato told me it went well and that Chris Lane and John MacGulvary hoped to release them soon. It wasn't too long before they were released. The 12' single boasted a good front picture sleeve cover and did pretty well for an introduction to the Reggae market and in the Reggae charts. It also got some reasonable reviews and a place at one of the premier all-dayers staged at the Lyceum Theatre in London's West End.

I arrived there with Smiley Culture, and Pato had already performed. I asked Pato if he had performed yet, and he replied yes. He continued by saying that it wasn't his crowd, but the crowd responded OK and that he was about to leave London and head to where we would sleep that night.

On the way home to Birmingham, Pato and I talked about the show and the responses from the audience. Pato mentioned that he would need a manager, and I replied don't worry, I'll manage you, which Pato and I found amusing. We both felt it would be a big step for someone who hadn't previously managed someone in the music industry. I was even more surprised when Pato paused and said yes, okay then. With that, I got to work and immediately put some shows together and got a few interviews arranged with Tony Williams and David Rodigan. It didn't take long for the news of what Pato had achieved to reach Birmingham. Almost a day later, Pato signalled to radio DJs and promoters, contacting him to call me to organise appointments. Fortunately, I was aided with a Panasonic answerphone, which prevented me from missing a call. It was pretty funny thinking back now; answer phones were new to people from my neck of the woods. People found it difficult to speak to machines that didn't respond. It took time, but people got used to it in the end.

Several record companies wanted to sign Pato, my phone kept ringing. I remember spending days in London trying to cut the right deal while embarking on a crash course reading books on management and the music business. I remember teaching myself the cut and thrust of recording contracts, publishing, and percentages. I remember sitting in a meeting at Island Records with Suzette Newman and Pato, looking at me in amazement. When asked why we didn't sign with Island, the key thing for me was Papa Levi. At that time, Levi had signed with Island for three singles with an option for an album. I feared that although it was a good thing for Island to sign 'Allo Tosh' and make it a hit, Pato would not have been priority, mainly because they had just signed Papa Levi and Suzette Newman could not give me any assurances that this would not have been the case. Another niggling point in my mind was that Pato had begun to write lyrics that were different from the tongue and cheek style of 'Allo Tosh'. I could not forget those words said by Pato, "I can't chat that lyric G, it was just written as a joke". After discussing this with Pato, we agreed not to go with the Island deal. I was sure that with a little working out that I would solicit a couple of non-exclusive deals whilst Pato continued to write new songs the within his authentic range and worked on becoming the artist he wanted to be.

The next time Pato and I met, he told me that Don Christie was willing to lend him the money to produce and record 'Allo Tosh' and that I would need to work out terms with him. We secured Ranking Roger to make the song and went to work. That done, I agreed on producer points with Roger and his manager Tarquin, then met up with Don and decided that the copyrights would remain with us.

1, Don Christie

2, Allo Tosh Original Label

3, Don Christie Record Shop

Ranking Roger

Ranking Roger opened many doors for Pato (as two MCs). They struck up a friendship that led Pato to feature on two songs of The Beat (the English Beat, so-called in America). 'Special Beat Service' album. However, this did not stop there. Roger and his American manager, Bob Berger, continued as friends to us way beyond the business, supporting every move we made; so thankful to them for that.

Although the Record label stated Don Christie Records, it was a way of advertising his shop, which we saw as a small price to pay for his help.

Don liked us both and wanted to help. The monetary return would only go as far as to rescue the funds we borrowed to get the single recorded and pressed, which amounted to 1,000 pounds.

As the story goes, 'Allo Tosh' hit sales of over seventeen thousand copies and hit number two in the reggae charts, held off the number one spot by Wayne Smith's 'Sleng Teng'. Everyone was happy; Don Christie had been reimbursed and thanked for his loan. With the song doing so well, the focus reemerged, and the Record Companies wanted to sign Pato and license 'Allo Tosh'. After many hours of meetings, I secured three non-exclusive licences with Virgin Records, IRS/MCA records in the US, and a French independent label. A good bit of business to which Pato is still collecting royalties today.

Pato Banton, (Dancers) Smurf and Audrey

1, Ranking Roger and I

2, Roger his son, Bob Berger and I

3, Bob Berger Manager and Roger

I will always remember taking Pato to Birmingham Car Auctions and helping him choose a car he wanted to buy. As he became more popular, Pato needed to be more mobile. Pato chose a Ford Cortina, but I didn't know he couldn't drive. So, we need to sort out the motor insurance and road tax, and I set about teaching him to drive for the next seven days or so. Pato passed his driving test in no time, which enabled him to become more mobile while saving a lot of money on taxi fares.

Sometime between the UB40 Baggariddim Album and 1985, Mikey Virtue (UB40) suggested that I provide him with an artist package that he could pass on to a radio DJ in California who loved reggae. The DJ had heard the 'Little Baggariddim EP' that featured Pato and loved it. Having listened to this, I knew my package was ready when Mikey arrived at my flat before their North American and Canadian tour in 1985.

About six months later, I received an answerphone message from Roberto Angotti, a reggae DJ from California of a similar calibre to Tony Williams and David Rodigan, who hosted a weekly reggae show on **KROQ** called Reggae Revolution, the DJ Mikey Virtue had spoken about from California, USA. He had just finished his radio show. Consequently, I missed his call, so we discussed his desire to promote a few shows with Pato in California. Roberto was a talented, well-travelled individual, and he reminded me that he was aware of Saxon and the British MCs; he had visited the UK and attended sound systems playing in the dance halls in London, UK. I was impressed when he said he heard of Tippa Irie, who I also managed, and about the MC clash at Maximilian's, Broad Street, Birmingham.

I explained to Roberto that the best market for Pato was the US because, as a reggae artist, I felt he would become an excellent performer. I stated that he had made an impression on the British audience and had now decided to develop as a performer in culture on the live music circuit in the US. Roberto loved playing music on the Radio but felt he could use his skills and abilities better in publicity and promotion. He told me he was putting together a festival on Catalina Island, off the coast of California, called the 'Splish Splash' and was talking with UB40 about headlining it.

Roberto introduced us to another DJ he worked with on KROQ, the 'Swedish Eagle', who told us about this band doing quite well on the West Coast; they had a good song that was getting airplay. After meeting Pato, he said it felt like a remix that featured Pato would add something special. A few days later, I received a call from Mike Jacobs, the 'Private Domaine' manager, to discuss collaborating on the Absolute Perfection song. To cut a long story short, with the contractual details completed, the song was recorded and released within a month. The song gained daytime, medium rotation airplay on KROQ, and the response was almost immediate; by this time, we had added more dates to Pato's tour, and fans stated that they had bought tickets because they heard 'Absolute Perfection' on KROQ.

Roberto and I recognised the growing interest in Pato's live shows, so we decided to book venues further north. Using the reach of KROQ and the song, we gathered more shows between Los Angeles and San Francisco. Before returning to the UK, we completed shows south of Los Angeles, San, in Jaun Capistrano and San Diago, with the talented set of musicians Roberto had selected and rehearsed for his debut performance at California State University, Long Beach.

When people say the USA is the most challenging market to break into, it's true; it took us two and a half years of travelling to the USA, building an audience to generate the fans and funds to tour with our UK band, the Reggae Revolution (some serious work). Pato's performances and interviews have built a good following on this platform, passing around imported copies of 'Mad Professor Captures Pato Banton', 'Allo Tosh', and some of his British releases.

We covered a lot of ground, travelled thousands

of miles, and were happy with our achievements. However, there was more work; I felt we needed three things to improve: a record deal, Pato's British band of musicians, and a booking agent in the USA who could take responsibility for booking shows in North America and Canada.

Using what we had achieved so far, we developed a good relationship with a record shop owner, Sam Gennaway (now an accomplished author). Sam was encouraged by the sales numbers he had achieved on the consignment of 'Never Give In' we had brought from the UK. This followed the plan I had to get Pato signed with an American record company, which turned out to begin with Primitive Man Records, a subsidiary of IRS records and distributed by MCA records.

Around this time, I didn't sleep too much, mainly because I was hell-bent on concluding the record and publishing contract and establishing an agent who would give the record company more encouragement that the elements were all in place to hit the ground running. I arranged to meet an agent named Rick Bloom, and following that meeting, I engaged him to increase Pato's reach into the college and university market. Roberto was the road manager, and I covered management and the house sound engineer. This arrangement worked well. We managed through networks with the Killer Bees, a good reggae band from Texas.

I had worked out a six-date tour of Texas and the Florida Keys. Pato, the band, Roberto, and I were all set to leave the following day.

We were waiting by the bus when Roberto was delayed and running late. In those days, there were no mobile phones. Roberto arrived but could no longer make the trip due to personal issues. However, after making many phone calls, I decided to leave. It was probably the greatest disappointment of my music career; I was gutted for days. Words couldn't explain how I felt. Most of all, it was the fear of driving two thousand miles to Florida and back. Thankfully, God was with us; as a unit, we all worked together, made it to Texas and Florida in one piece, played some fantastic shows, and had the best time.

As can be imagined, I had to make some difficult decisions. In conversation with Pato, we had to move on. The greatest thing was that I managed to sign Pato to Primitive Man, and after a short internship weekend in the Bay Area, I recruited a graduate from California State University Northridge to a two-year contract as our road manager; the following week, Don and I popped into Ford in Glendale, and I purchased a bus. The aims and objectives behind this decision were based on consistency. It was imperative that if we rented a vehicle for six weeks or more, it would be expensive, the insurance would be excessive, and the possibilities for breakdown could not be relied upon. Renting buses came on a first-come, first-served basis; we needed a vehicle that would always be available and would prioritise the needs of our band. Reliable transportation was vital; a brand-new car would enable us to travel across North America.

Marketing and Promotion

I took the plunge and purchased a new Ford Custom Deluxe. It was fantastic. It had two fuel tanks, which meant we could drive without stopping for six hours. The band was comfortable, which reduced Pato, Don, and my stress levels. I could now establish Pato's strategic plan and artist development, beginning with the Reggae Revolution, on our next trip to America.

The Reggae Revolution Band

From left top: Donavan, Alan, Deco, Raymond, Skins, John, Cotton: James, Tippa Pato Byron and Raymond

The original band that was selected for the American tour was made up of the following members:

Drums - David (Skins)
Bass - Desdale (Amlak) Willmott
Bass - Ray Grant
Bass – Deco Hare
Keys - Glasspole Glasses Sutherland
Keys - Michael Nanton
Trumpet - Duncan Mackay
Trumpet – Alan Francis
Guitar - Richard Reynolds
Guitar – Donavan Newall
Trombone - Steven Morrison
Tenor Saxophone - Byron Bailey
Alto Saxophone - Martyn Phillips

Soprano and Alto Saxophone - James Renford
Percussion – Raymond (Charge) Walker

Not Just Glitz and Glamor

Although the music business seems to some may seem like a dream come true, sadly, it's not all glitz and glamorous. As a young person, travelling to America meant exploration, excitement, great gigs and meeting new people. However, for some, it means loss, loneliness, estrangement and even depression. Most breakups result from artists who leave the country for long periods. Witnessing these issues occur before my eyes following the 98-day tour, which ran over three months.

To contextualise this management aspect, one must consider it similar to an organisation offering 9 to 5 working hours. In 1986/7, the cost of a transatlantic phone call would be one pound per minute; calling home to catch up with a partner and children to check how they were doing could prove very expensive. Problem-solving would meander until the end of the week or would be left until you could see each other face to face. Hence, the personal toll of being away from family and dealing with loneliness is a poignant reminder of the sacrifices in pursuing an artist, musician or manager in the music business; it wasn't easy to make.

This area of my experience managing Pato Banton and navigating the music industry, particularly in the British Reggae scene. It captures the dynamics when touring, the band's camaraderie, and the strategic efforts I encountered to expand Pato's reach. Here are some of the highlights and critical aspects:

The band and I developed a cohesion that produced a family-like bond that expanded, with Don in America and Keith, Bev or Joycelyn back in the UK, which over time became evident.

Each member played a significant role, from Steve Morrison's organisational skills to Skins' reliable presence and Glasses' humour. This camaraderie was crucial for maintaining morale during a long tour. Roberto's last-minute change of plans disappointed me and underscored the unpredictability of touring and managing people's problems. Yet, my decision to proceed with the tour despite the risks demonstrated my resilience and commitment to getting the job done.

I'm not sure whether lookers could see the challenges we faced with booking agents and logistics we faced whilst we were expanding into the broader states of America together with how vast the territory was; however, as well as some harsh, relentless encounters required to develop strategic partnerships (e.g., with Aki and Don in the early stages), Moss from Avalon and Billy Graham in the Bay Area, convinced me that the calculated efforts to increase Pato's visibility and reach would be worth it in the long run.

In the US, the influence of mentors like Miles Copland, Jay Boberge, Sig Sigworth, Moss Jacobs, Barbara Barabino, and others provided guidance and support highlighted for me the importance and value of having a solid support network in the industry.

Working towards the gig at the Whiskey a Go-Go and what came from receiving positive reviews was vital to strengthening the aim of having Pato perform with his British band of musicians (the Reggae Revolution) in America. Prominent publications like the L.A. Times and L.A. Weekly proved to be significant milestones that reflect the hard work that Pato and I undertook together with the strategic efforts taken on that road between Birmingham, England, and California, USA.

The greatest thing for Don Kilbury and I was that we prioritised heading back to our hotel room rather than heading off to another gig or party. In our rooms, we could savour the moments, plan the next steps without interruptions, and savour the joys of visiting New York or Key West in Florida. I had the time and space to reflect on my journey. I realised it was marked by persistence, strategic thinking, and the ability to build and maintain strong relationships within the band and with external partners. Looking back on it now, I recognise that it has painted a comprehensive picture of the highs and lows of managing an artist's career and the multifaceted nature of the British Reggae Industry and the general music industry.

Reggae Sunsplash

Part of the plan in 1987/8 was to establish Pato and Tippa into the reggae territories of the world. This included America, Canada, Europe, and Japan. All was going well. I had set up Tippa on tour supporting Gregory Isaacs and was working on a few ideas for Pato that would further develop our work in the US, keeping up the momentum.

One morning, I received a call from Tony Johnson, one of the directors of Reggae Sunsplash, who was sounding me out about the possibility of including Tippa or Pato as part of the artist package for Reggae Sunsplash. Due to the success of 'Hello Darling' and Tippa's association with Saxon, he was invited as one of the British artists chosen for Sunsplash 87; Tippa had represented the UK at Sting 86 and the Reggae Roll Call festival promoted by Don Hall. Reggae Sunsplash was perfect for them, and it was joined by a British contingent of artists and bands, Aswad, Steel Pulse, and Maxi Priest.

Performing to a tremendous crowd, Tippa jumped on Pato's shoulders and, with microphones in hand, delivered the British fast style at the Bob Marley Centre, Montego Bay, Jamaica. It was the highlight of their performance and one for the record books.

I met Tony again while doing business in Los Angeles through a friend I knew then, Roger Steffens, where we spoke about how he started Reggae Sunsplash; I told him that I was blown away by the lineup of artists that performed year after year and how incredible, he was gracious and humbled with his response telling me that Sunsplash started with five of them some of whom I had the opportunity to meet in 1986 and 7. Tony stated that all Jamaican directors, including Tony Johnson, Don Green, John Wakeling, Ed Barclay, and Ronnie Burke, had formed the company Synergy.

Roger Steffens

Roger was a Vietnam veteran and photographer who impressed me with his vast knowledge of Bob Marley. Roger was like an oracle or an encyclopedia. Roger wore many hats, some at the same time; in addition to his photography, Roger was a host and an MC, toured with Bob and was invited to travel with him and the Wailers band on their tour bus.

Roger hosted a show called the 'Reggae Beat' on **KCRW**. Many times, Pato and I had the opportunity to visit Roger at his home in Los Angeles, where it must be said his collection of Reggae music lined the four corners of the walls of one room, 30ft x 20ft. I could imagine he possessed many rare and unreleased demo recordings of Bob Marley. His t-shirt collection just went on and on. Nevertheless, Roger implored Tony to watch out for Pato, Tippa, and me as we were on the rise.

In August 1987, Pato and Tippa were invited to perform at Reggae Sunsplash: The Bob Marley Centre, Montego Bay, Jamaica; it was a significant milestone for all of us to be present alongside the cream of the crop in reggae music at that time. Pato and Tippa stood alongside Admiral Bailey, Hugo Barrington, Big Youth, Paul Blake & Blood Fire Posse, Dennis Brown, Burning Spears & Burning Band, Chalice, Cocoa Tea, Culture, 809 Band, General Trees, Gwen Guthrie, Half Pint, Derrick Harriot, I-Threes, Gregory Issacs, Killer Bees, Barrington Levy, Lovindeer, Maker, Ziggy Marley & The Melody Makers, Freddie McGregor, Shirley Mclean, Peter Metro, The Mighty Diamonds, Echo Minot, Monty Montgomery, Mutabaruka, Llyod Parks, Maxi Priest, The Sagitarius Band, Sandii & The Sunsetz, Shakaman & Shakeena, Sister Carol,

Sister Charmaine, Sly & Robbie, Tiger, Tonto Metro, U-Roy, Et Webster, and Yellowman. The entire event is an event I will forever treasure in my mind.

1, Grantley GT and Toot's Hibbert's daughters

2, Playing dominos on the tour bus Tony Johnson and Pato Banton

3, Tommy Cowan, GT and Sharon

Before I left for Los Angeles and the UK, Tony and I discussed the inclusion of Tippa and Pato in detail for Sunsplash USA, where it was established that Tippa could not be included on the tour because I had already signed contracts for him to tour Europe with Gregory Isaacs. This meant Pato would be the only artist I managed playing a part in Sunsplash USA. Once nailed down, I asked Keith if he would handle the responsibilities of Tippa in Europe whilst I flew to Jamaica with Pato, covering rehearsals with Derek Barnett and the Sagittarius Band and fine-tuning the logistics and H1 visas. It made sense to fly Pato and me into Jamaica to meet the touring unit rather than to fly into the US from the UK.

Reggae Sunsplash Tour USA: Various Artists, May, 1988

The lineup for Sunsplash USA 1988 consisted of the Band Sagittarius, Pato Banton, Paul Blake & Blood Fire Posse, Carlene Davis, Eddie Fitzroy, Sophia George, Toots Hibbert, Yellowman and MC Tommy Cowans.

Ziggy Marley

I heard Ziggy Marley and The Melody Maker's album One Bright Day in Los Angeles again during a meeting with Miles and Jay, who asked if I could pull a rabbit out of the bag and get one of the Ziggy dates for support. I didn't say much then, but I had several meetings set up; one in particular was at the William Morris agency to explore the possibilities of becoming the support act for Ziggy's tour. This was the next stage in increasing Pato's penetration and reach in southern California. However, as luck would have it, I spoke to a friend from the Ziggy team, who put me in touch with the right person and assisted me in presenting the business case, that Pato would be the perfect choice. The meeting felt like an interview; I had to wait a few weeks for an answer, but eventually, word came back, letting me know that we had been chosen to support Ziggy on not one but the entire Californian leg of their American tour.

1, Ziggy Marley, Grantley GT and a Friend

2, Steven Marley and I

With the tour confirmed, I noticed a clash; Pato was due to play two gigs on the same date. I had committed nearly five months earlier to play Reggae on The River, a significant festival in northern California. Pato and the band were due to come off stage at Reggae on the river on the afternoon of that day and were due for sound check at Irvine Meadows three hours later the same day. The problem was the drive time from Humbolt County to Irvine was nine hours, meaning that we couldn't do both shows and would have to cancel one. It was not an option to forgo the Ziggy dates because as said before, the contract included multiple shows. (There was the added pressure of returning to Miles and Jay, who had agreed to hire a bus with the entire IRS staff to attend the concert, to let them know it wouldn't happen).

1, A group of staff from IRS Records Jay Boberge

2nd from the right. 2, Jay and Miles Copland (dancing)

Reneging on Reggae on the River would not look good either; that decision would almost certainly have led to a lack of trust in my management and, indirectly, team Pato. There was a decision to make, so having slept on it and discussing it with Don (my American personal assistant and road manager), we decided to look at flights. Coming up with nothing, the decision was made to explore private hire, and we rented a seven-seater jet and pilot from a small airport a few miles from the show in northern California to transport us to John Wayne Airport in Orange County. The road crew consisted of eleven, which meant four members could not travel to Humbolt and head back to Irvine after the show the night before. Don and I met with Pato and the band to explain the situation. Thankfully, they were all happy. I was still worried even though the insurance was covered. Despite my internal concerns, all went smoothly; I didn't have the pleasure of feeling okay until the tour bus picked us up at Orange County, and we were all backstage at Irvine.

Touring with Ziggy Marley

As part of the Ziggy Marley aspect of the tour, we covered six dates, which was the entire California leg of the tour with Ziggy Marley and the Melody Makers.

Working with Ziggy Marley and his team was highly professional. They had everything organised in what I call a professional way. What inspired me was that, even more critically, their unit delivered what it said on the tin. Ziggy and Melody Makers presented similarly to us; they were like friends. I got to speak to Rita at least three or four times, and she and I got on well. Rita was impressed with us even though we were the support band. She opened her arms to whatever we needed, and there were no restrictions. Ziggy's engineers, his house engineers, just afforded me everything. There were no restrictions; the rigging engineers were excellent. I knew the backstage manager, Zola Burst (he could do the job in his sleep). I learned so much from Zola and have missed him since his passing. (RIP) Zola. I got on well with the stage engineer, whom I must thank repeatedly for the monitor work he assisted us with. Apart from having our back line and not using Ziggy's, we had no issues with anything.

Pato and I had an opportunity to meet Ziggy personally. We were invited onto Ziggy's tour bus, and it was organised; we made our way to the back, where my question to Ziggy was, "What's your mission?" Ziggy answered, "The truth," and I said, "Anything you'd like to add to that," and he said, "The truth". I think I understood that to mean, in terms of that Grammy-winning album 'One Bright Day', that's all I needed to hear; the message was in the music. Apart from Ziggy and his sisters, who were backing vocalists, Stephen shone like a star. He played congas and bongos and partnered with Ziggy when he became an MC.

I can say that Pato, the rest of the band, and I felt at home around Bob Marley's children and his wife. We learned a lot about Bob because, as well as talking to Rita about the usual production stuff, I also got a chance to speak about Bob, and she was pretty candid with me. I won't go into what we talked about because I don't think it is for this time, but she was sincere, and I noticed she walked with a swagger.

Pato Banton Albums Recorded and Produced:

1, Never Give In - Produced by Pato Banton and Grantley GT Haynes

2, Visions of The Worlds - Produced by Pato Banton and Grantley GT Haynes

3, Wise Up, No Compromise - Produced by Angus (Drummie Zeb) Gaye, Grantley GT Haynes and Pato Banton

4, Pato Banton and The Reggae Revolution, LIVE In The USA and Canada

1, The Album Pato Banton a Reggae Revolution Live

2, Grantley GT and Pato

The band and the team in the UK were all mind-blown by what we had achieved in getting through the stress and absolute joy of completing such a great tour. Not that I didn't, but one of the things I used to do whilst mixing Pato and the band on stage was to record the shows. The shows supporting Ziggy were no different; I paid more attention in sound check to use the outboard gear to the most significant effect, adding compressors and gates on the vocals, turning the EQ on the drums and bass, etc. I remember Don suggesting I purchase a portable Digital Audio Tape (DAT) a few weeks earlier, which could record digital sound. My feelings were focused on the fact that the whole unit had reached the halfway point of a 96-date tour and was operating like a well-oiled machine. The band was pumped up for the gigs supporting Ziggy, so I set up the levels on the DAT recorder ready for each show, praying I would deliver the best live mixes using the house board.

We would always listen to the recording of shows on the bus whilst travelling to the next. We were all surprised when we heard the recording of the Irvine show, mainly because it sounded good and reflected how the band had played. Pato was pleased; I remember him saying we should release this as a LIVE album. I recall pitching it to the record company, but a professional recording using a mobile recording unit would be better. The tapes remained in a well-guarded box in my loft for many years until a few years ago when Pato and I decided to release them. When on form, Pato Banton, as an artist, delivers a vibrant and energetic voice that exudes positivity and charisma. His vocal style is dynamic, with a distinctive blend of reggae, dancehall, and toasting elements. His voice has unique agility, allowing him to transition effortlessly between rapid-fire lyrics and melodic hooks. His delivery is often characterised by infectious enthusiasm and a knack for storytelling, which resonates deeply with audiences.

This album features mixes from the 98-date tour of

the USA & Canada; it brings its audience 10 of the most dynamic live performances ever witnessed by Grammy-nominated British Reggae Artist and the band known as The Reggae Revolution.

Over 12 weeks in 1989, sleeping in over 58 hotel rooms, we travelled over 30,000 miles by road, 9,000 miles by air and seven miles by foot in the company of Ziggy Marley and The Melody Makers, Toots Hibbert, The Sagittarius Band, Steel Pulse, UB40, No Doubt, Big Country, to mention a few! These master tapes were safe but misplaced. Thankfully, they were found and remastered at the legendary Abbey Road Studios in London, England, by Simon Gibson. Now compiled by My Boyz Beatz, for GT's Records to be heard by collectors and fans, the rest is up to you!

We invite you to take a trip with Pato and The Band, delivering their magic on stage; the stage is set. The links are as follows:

Spotify

https://open.spotify.com/album /5VytR2r63hfV5rQhuX6JAo?si=k8T EmPHaSheUMngknQd k8TEmPHaSheUMngknQdHkQ&dl_branch=1

Apple Music

https://music.apple.com/gb/album/my-boyz-beatz-pato-banton-the-reggae-revolution-live/1584502991

Amazon

https://www.amazon.co.uk/dp/B09FH88SDY/ref=cm_sw_r_cp_api_glt_3C07ZJC7D070390DKK9Z

YouTube

https://youtu.be/GfSNljMbGy4

Chapter 11

Tippa Irie

Tippa and I discussed what I could do for him as a manager, with Tippa noting the progress made with Pato. I assured him that his financial situation would improve significantly if I managed him. I promised that he would be driving his desired car within six months. Five months later, I renegotiated his deal with Greensleeves, and Tippa was driving a white GTi Golf Cabriolet, enhancing his mobility and freedom. I kept my promise.

I first met Tippa Irie while he was on Saxon Studio International Sound System as an MC. As a promoter, Pato and I would promote shows in the Birmingham area of Sparkbrook at a public house called The Mermaid. We would rent a room in the pub and hire a sound system. Most of the time, a sound system called King Iwah would provide the sound. Here, Pato and I would have the sound play and offer an open microphone for local artists to come along and promote themselves. Those nights were epic; people would come from all over Birmingham to see what we were doing.

It came to the stage where our promotions had become so successful that we had to move venues. More importantly, we held an MC competition to promote these local artists further into Birmingham. To do this, we moved the venue to a popular venue at that time known as the Rising Star, Mount Pleasant, Bilston, in the West Midlands. We were surprised because we sold the place solidly, with people outside who needed help to gain entry. Following the success of that night, we decided to hold the competition final. On the bill would be the finest up-and-coming MCs from all over Birmingham and the West Midlands at that time: Lieutenant Mellow, Fancy Fitzy, Zod Man, Colonel Valentine, KKJ, and judges Tippa Irie and Papa Levi. It was an incredible night and one I'll never forget.

I had not long signed a management contract with Pato Banton and, a few months later, Tippa Irie. We were going to Woolwich, London, for a meeting with Papa Levi. Continuing the journey, Tippa and I began discussing what I thought I could do for him as a manager. I remember saying to him, "Is there something that you would like me to do for you, and he replied yeah". Tippa had seen the progress made with Pato and continued, what would it mean? I talked about terms and what I thought I could do, and I remember asking how much money you have in the bank right now, stating that whatever the figure, if I managed you, it would change.

I assured him I would deliver over and above what the contract stated, equivalent to his performance and songwriting ability. I also assured him he would drive his desired car within six months. Talking about setting myself a target, I set myself to work; five months later, I had renegotiated his deal with Greensleeves, and Tippa was driving a white GTi Golf Cabriolet.

In my previous life, I must have been a driving instructor. About a year prior, I had taken Pato to Birmingham Car Auctions and helped him choose a car he liked. I did the same thing with Tippa. Saxon was up and down the country, and he was now booked to headline shows across the UK and needed more than ever to be more mobile. Together, we purchased Tippa's first car, a Volkswagen Polo. In Tippa's case, I knew he couldn't drive. Sorting out motor insurance and road tax over six weeks, I set about teaching him to drive for the next two weeks. Tippa passed his driving test for the first time, increasing his mobility and personal freedom.

Greensleeves Records UK's UK Bubblers

I met with Chris Cracknell and Chris Sedgwick at Greensleeves Records to establish the direction and focus for Tippa's artistic development. I was impressed with the direction mainly because the company was behind him; Greensleeves were ready to drop the second solo, 'Complain Neighbour'. He stated they would be looking at releasing a couple more singles before dropping the album **'Is It Happening To Me'**. With this in hand, I met with Chris Sedwick, head of operations and joint director of Greensleeves Records, regarding the songwriting element and publishing territories. Somewhat happy with the arrangement, based on Tippa's position in the market back then, we decided to remain with Greensleeves. I needed to prioritise the area of publishing in my first year with Tippa, particularly because I planned to progress his career outside of the UK. At that time, many artists and musicians didn't understand the concept of the music business.

Nevertheless, I saw the recording aspect, studio time and associated costs differently. Songwriting, PRS, publishing, where there would be a contract for this area and finally, Performances and Tours, where there would be separate contracts. The role of the music manager must ensure the above elements are met in the artist's best interests, either with a lawyer or someone with the skills and expertise.

Marketing, Press, and Publicity

At Greensleeves, Margot was head of the press and publicity department. She was effective, efficient, and helpful, with a diary filled with a wide-ranging list of contacts. Press and publicity were her thing, as was understanding the benefits of networks and networking with DJs who could generate bridges that generate national chart airplay.

Tippa recorded something almost every week, either for the album or tracks we felt could be one-away singles. Around the same time, we were looking for a title for the album. Of a few, 'Is it Really Happening To Me' became the most favoured choice. At the time, Tippa had a song typifying an aspect of a part of his life that needed a few adjustments before recording it in the studio. In our favour, several songs were recorded that would make the final cut for the album at the time: 'The Best', 'Complain Neighbour', 'Football Hooligan' and 'Hello Darling', which are still at the demo stage.

Hello Darling

No matter where I go, those who remember the 1980s love **'Hello Darling'**. I remember it well; even at the demo stage, it sounded like a hit. The title, the melody, and the musical composition lifted all those concerned, making them feel good.

Before my tenure, I believed that Greensleeves Records had signed Tippa with a plan to develop him into a crossover artist and the pop field. However, I am still determining whether or not Tippa was evident in this direction when he signed his original contract before my tenure. I say this because there was a clear distinction between the Tippa Irie one might find spitting fire on his sound system, Saxon and the production sound in songs like 'The Best' and 'Complain Neighbour'.

Greensleeves had established a reputation in the UK and the rest of the world as a company known for releasing authentic reggae music, launching and progressing the careers of artists like Dennis Brown, Gregory Isaacs, The Mighty Diamonds, and Shabba Ranks. The production sound behind Tippa's compositions could be described as distinctively British. I came to know Patrick Donagon of (The Reggae Regulars), from vast amount of studio sessions I was at where he took part as the associate producer.

Nevertheless, I had reservations. Tippa loves many musical genres, but his favourite by far is reggae, which gets him out of bed. Having said this, Chris and I had many conversations in which we concluded that Tippa would always have the creative talent to write a pop song. Authenticity as an artist, whatever the genre, comes down to who the artist is and what drives them.

In preparation for Tippa's next single, Chris Cracknell and I agreed on a budget and booked Easy Street Recording Studios for a jam session; he stated that he could not be there and Patrick would take charge in his absence. One of the songs the musicians worked on was 'Hello Darling'. On Saxon, Tippa would generally sing on the version of Marcia Griffiths 'Feel Like Jumping'; however, when it came to delivering it in the studio, it didn't seem to work as it did in the dancehall. The musicians worked well, but something didn't fit. After some time, I asked if I could say something. I asked Drumtan Ward if he could play a swing pattern on the hi-hat whilst maintaining a one-drop foundation beat; I then asked the bass player to play a two-step jazz pattern, four beats to the bar, and finally asked Tippa to sing the lyrics to that pattern, Patrick from here on directed the band to develop finer details of the demo.

Later that week, Chris telephoned, letting us know that he would progress the recording of 'Hello Darling' but would be using Mark Angelo and an engineer named Lindell Lewis. Lindell was a skilled music studio engineer who would become very useful later.

Chris and Patrick were excited about the song, and, as a result, Chris increased the recording budget, making it possible to add overdubs: keyboards by Lindell, Saxophone by Ray Carlos and Guitar by Melvin (Ciyo) Brown. With the composition complete, Tippa returned to the studio to voice the final vocal recording and harmonies coached by Lindell. Following the final mix, Chris invited me to Virgin Records Town House Studios, where Tony Cousins mastered 'Hello Darling' for pressing. I can't thank Chris and the team for allowing me to be part of something that, to this very day, I use aspects of what I learnt back then in my productions today.

In those days, following the production, mix and mastering stages, the next step focused on getting the song heard. Radio 1, Capital and Kiss would be prioritised for a song like' Hello Darling'. To achieve this adequate record, companies would hire pluggers. The job would be to take the record to club DJs, radio stations, and other partners to get them to listen to the song. Understanding this, Margot set up a method of generating feedback focussing on the mailouts she had carried out. We had enough support with the plugger to get onto playlists at Radio One. Janice Long and John Peel loved playing it.

Tony Williams, David Rodigon and David (Kidd) Jenson supported it, achieving the Capital Radio playlist and enabling us to gain a mid-week chart position, followed by a UK chart entry of number 22 on that Sunday in the summer of 1986. and following that midweek position, it would progress to an opportunity to get on top of the pops. Everything fell into place regarding coopting selective DJs who could take the song's future through airplay. When John Sachs and Chris Tarrant started to play, it was clear we had a hit on our hands, and the next call we would receive would be from 'Top of The Pops'.

Although very happy, I was concerned. Although strong album tracks were recorded, no team member felt there was a strong enough song that could become a follow-up to the success of 'Hello Darling'.

'Hello Darling' was a tongue-in-cheek song featuring one of those cockney phrases that everyone can relate to, underpinned by a swing beat. Greensleeves felt we needed something in the middle to launch the album with another single, but we didn't have one ready. Hence, we spent quite a long time, probably too much time, trying to find it.

Ultimately, this called for a cover song or a new song. Opting to record a new song called for Tippa to finish a song he had started called 'Heartbeat' and for anyone who has achieved a hit song of any description can become a double-edged sword, in that it can propel you towards the next hit or can send you into meltdown. The problem, as I saw it for us, was that by the time Heartbeat was released, we had lost the momentum generated by Hello Darling; there were six months between both songs, which, in my opinion, was too long.

Top of The Pops

Having spent most of my teenage years watching Top of the Pops, with the family walking through those doors at BBC Television Centre, Shepards Bush, London, to be there was surreal and aright of passage. My excitement faded once Tippa and I were shown to his dressing room. Walking down the corridor to his room was another experience. Passing the dressing rooms of Legends Queen, Cliff Richard, Stevie Wonder, Atlantic Starr, and newcomers Samantha Fox and Tippa was a moment I will never forget. I remember one of the things Top of the Pops insisted on: all performers had to mime their performance, which Tippa did not like; however, it was mime or a showing of the video. One of the benefits of performing live was the opportunity to network with managers, assistants and some of the staff at the BBC.

A song usually lasts between 2 and 3 minutes; however, we spent the whole day there. We met with one of the staff who introduced us to Mike

Reid (Radio 1 DJ). Who explained how the running order would go, and the rest of the time was spent talking to the other artists. I remember having a long conversation with Samantha Fox and her manager about how busy she was and how she was finding the music business. What was helpful was that other managers told me the sales of 'Hello Darling' would increase following Tippa's performance. They were right; from a chart position of 33, Pippa moved up to 27 the following week.

Sting 1986, Jamaica

That moment came when, in 1986, I met up with Mandingo, a staunch reggae promoter and African-Caribbean activist who was charged with the responsibility of negotiating the delivery of Tippa Irie on behalf of Isaiah Laing and Tommy Cowan for his performance at **Sting 86,** cinema 2, New Kingston, Jamaica.

I met and talked with Tony Johnson, one of the Directors of the iconic Reggae Sunsplash. He stated he was considering bringing Tippa Irie to Jamaica for Sunsplash 1987, a significant anniversary that would include British Reggae artist Maxi Priest and bands Aswad and Steel Pulse. I remembered that the planning would take some time to make the above happen, but that was for another day.

Arriving in Kingston, Jamaica and meeting with Laing and his team was a welcoming experience. Laing was humorous; Tippa and I were impressed with how he carried out business alongside the addition of the personal touch he earned from those who worked with him. Laing had laid on meet and greets with VIPs and other performers, visits to Jammy's recording studio, rehearsals with the Sagittarius band, and interviews.

I remember before Tippa and I flew out to Jamaica, people told me I needed to be careful going to Jamaica due to the level of crime and shootings taking place at the time. I'm not sure if I was fearless or what, but the things I had seen in my life up until that point led me to understand I needed to conduct myself in a particular way when faced with danger. Having said this, I was hanging out with Isaiah Laing one afternoon in a district called Jungle when he received a call telling him that his police friend and colleague Cornell 'Bigga' Ford had been shot. Right there and then, Laing said to me, "GT, come"! He quickly grabbed a few items, jumped into his car and drove around Jungle and Tivoli Gardens. We didn't stop, but Laing later asked me if I was worried. My response to him was yes, of course I was. I told him that throughout my life, I have learned that fear can be your greatest weapon when your back is against the wall; you do all you can to stay alive; don't talk or think. Later that day, Tippa asked where I had been; Laing explained that we had been and to check out a few things, letting Tippa know he approved of the man he was taking care of his business. Can't forget Laing, a great supporter of British MCs and their music.

That night, Laing took Tippa and me to a Metro Media dance nearby; it was there that I first experienced what is known as shots being fired,' into the air. This would happen when someone heard something they liked in the dance hall. That was an experience of a lifetime. The only other time I experienced gunshots was in the territorial army.

Tippa, Barrington Levy & his brother, Sting 86

Sting is a fantastic event, world-renowned for its annual event highlighting the world's best reggae singers and dancehall MCs. Tippa performed incomparably, delivering his British chart hit 'Hello Darling'. Before leaving the stage, he represented the UK by delivering rapid rounds of fast-style fire fashioned by his sound system Saxon Studio International in London, to which he received a tumultuous round of applause.

Reggae Sunsplash 1987

My eagerness to push the boundaries came when I met Tony Johnson, one of the directors of Reggae Sunsplash, who was sounding me out about the possibility of Tippa and Pato joining the British contingent package for Reggae Sunsplash 1987. Due to the success of 'Hello Darling' and Tippa's association with Saxon, he was invited as one of the British artists chosen for Sunsplash 87; Tippa had represented the UK at Sting 86 and the Reggae Roll Call festival promoted by Don Hall. Reggae Sunsplash was perfect for them, and it was joined by a British contingent of artists and bands, Aswad, Steel Pulse, and Maxi Priest. Performing to a fantastic crowd, Tippa jumped on Pato's shoulders and, with microphones in hand, delivered the British fast style at the Bob Marley Centre, Montego Bay, Jamaica. It was the highlight of their performance and one for the record books.

I met Tony again while on business in Los Angeles through a friend I knew then, Roger Steffens, where we spoke about how he started Reggae Sunsplash; I told him that I was blown away by the lineup of artists that performed year after year and how incredible, he was gracious and humbled with his response telling me that Sunsplash started with five of them some of whom I had the opportunity to meet in 1986 and 7. Tony stated that five directors, all Jamaican, including Tony Johnson, Don Green, John Wakeling, Ed Barclay, and Ronnie Burke, had formed a company named Synergy.

Reggae Sunsplash Festival: Bob Marley Centre, Montego Bay, Jamaica, August 1987

Following the success of 'Hello Darling', Tippa was invited to appear at Reggae Sunsplash along with other British Reggae contingents: Pato Banton, Aswad, Steel Pulse, and Maxi Priest.

As referred to in chapter 10, Synergy had decided that due to British artist's rise in popularity and worldwide appeal, 1987 would be the year they sought to include the UK and America in the reggae capital of the world, Jamaica, mainly because it was their strategy to tour the world with the Reggae Sunsplash Brand. Artists such as Admiral Bailey Hugo Barrington, Big Youth, Paul Blake & Blood Fire Posse, Dennis Brown, Burning Spears & Burning Band, Chalice, Cocoa Tea, Culture, 809 Band, General Trees, Gwen Guthrie, Half Pint, Derrick Harriot, I-Threes, Gregory Isaacs, Killer Bees, Barrington Levy,

Lovindeer, Maker, Ziggy Marley & The Melody Makers, Freddie McGregor, Shirley Mclean, Peter Metro, The Mighty Diamonds, Echo Minot, Monty Montgomery, Mutabaruka, Llyod Parks, The Sagitarius Band, Sandii & The Sunsetz, Shakaman & Shakeena, Sister Carol, Sister Charmaine, Sly & Robbie, Tiger, Tonto Metro, U-Roy, Et Webster, and Yellowman also graced the stage throughout the festival.

Before I left Los Angeles for the UK, Tony and I discussed the inclusion of Tippa and Pato in detail. It was established that Tippa could not be included on the tour because I had already signed contracts for him to tour Europe with Gregory Issacs. This meant Pato would be the only artist under my management to cover Sunsplash USA. In the UK, Keith handled the responsibilities of Tippa in Europe, and I flew to Jamaica with Pato.

Paris, France

Due to the success of 'Hello Darling, ' utilising opportunities became part of my DNA. I woke up every morning with a mission: to break into a new territory on the world map. My strategy for Tippa in 1987/8 included some huge world record-selling markets: America, Canada, Europe, and Japan. All was going well. Tippa was set up to support Gregory Isaacs on his European tour covering Austria, France, Spain and Germany.

It may not have been clear to Tippa then, but in the back of my mind, the plan for Tippa was bigger. I aimed to support a licensing agreement between Greensleeves Records and Blue Moon Records based in Paris, France. The relationship was established two years prior when Blue Moons director John Cotton was about to release 'Hello Darling'. At the time, reggae was a well-established movement in France. The tour with Gregory would improve Tippa's profile as an MC on Saxon and a serious artist who toured the world.

'Hello, Darling' became successful in France, utilising Blue Moon's skilful marketing and promotion of radio stations like Europe 1 and collaborations with high-end brands at the time. One such performance included artists such as Grace Jones, George Michael, the Pet Shop Boys and Paul Young, to name a few. This occurred after a promotional event at a Sky Resort in the French Alps.

There was little time for getting star-struck; John introduced me to the manager of a famous French band, Bill Baxter, who expressed his intention for Tippa and his band to collaborate on a recording. The deal included Virgin Records France (the band's record company), Greensleeves Records and Blue Moon Records. In addition to promoting 'Hello Darling, ' the recording of the song 'Bienvenue A Paris' (welcome to Paris), a pop genre track released in 1987, Tippa and I must have travelled to France every other week for about four or five months. Tippa's was becoming a household name in France, doing his penetration into Europe no harm. To this end, his profile gathered momentum, not to mention the high-profile invitations resulting from the chart position 'Bienvenue A Paris' achieved in France.

America

Tippa toured America briefly with the Saxon sound system in his youth, including a performance at Tilden Ballroom in Brooklyn, New York.

To establish longevity and following his recent chart success in the UK and his media profile, we decided to work towards establishing a presence in the US and I had built up a network as a solo artist. Tippa would be introduced with a debut performance at a profile venue. Like Pato, Tippa had a grassroots presence in America, forming a significant aspect of his biography.

Most introductory venues, particularly Los Angeles, New York, and Chicago, were encouraged to book British acts that had a presence in their hometown, especially if you were from the UK. Because of this, we chose Los Angeles. Pato had established a following there and there, and I had built up a network that would be a valuable asset for Tippa's introduction. The artist pack included information and cuttings from the New Musical Express (NME), Record Mirror and Black Echos; we also added cuttings from British Music Press and Newspapers at the time. British magazines helped raise Tippa and Pato's profiles and enabled us to secure the debut show at the Whiskey A Go-Go on Sunset Boulevard, California.

Both Tippa and Pato had agreed to support each other in territories. The other would provide support where one was strong, and vice versa. This way, I could utilise the benefits of collaboration on shows and tours worldwide. This worked well for Pato when it came to Jamaica and Tippa when it came to the US. With the boys concentrating on what they did best, Roberto and I focused on assisting the venue in promoting the show and selling tickets. Doing all we could muster, we set about inviting local opinion formers, artists, musicians, agents, lawyers and record company A&R representatives executives to get them both signed to major labels in the US.

As history would have it, this took some time. America is unlike the UK. The distance between the North and South of the UK covers about 700 miles. However, America is vast. By contrast, the distance between New York and Los Angeles covers about 3,500 miles. In terms of size, you can't compare America to the UK. It's just too vast to compare. If you drove from Birmingham to London, talking about 130 miles in time could take two and a half to 3 hours. Travelling between Los Angeles and New York would take about three and a half days.

To build a presence, an artist and their team must approach this beast state-by-state. I decided to play some of the most essential venues or those less well-known, get our foot in the door, leave an impression, and return a year later, either selling more tickets or playing a more profile date. I remember the Midwest because although you can't leave out, there was a method of performing there that one had to bear in mind: the challenges experienced by ethnic minorities. We would always encounter racism, but we didn't let it affect our overall aim, which was to sleep in the next bed and play the next show.

Working intensively with record companies, agents and lawyers at the time, I remember getting a call from one of our lawyers at the time, Ron Dinacola, who advised me that George Jackson, a film producer, was shooting a Michael Schultz movie with the rap group the 'The Fat Boys' called 'Disorderlies'. The set location was in a mansion in the Beverly Hills area of California, which was surreal. The cast included Tony Plana, Ralph Bellamy and Don Ameche.

Ron suggested it would be good for us all to meet George, one of the clients he represented at the time. We were looking at several films where he might need your help.' 'I'm having a BBQ over the weekend. I'd like you to come.'

It was a great afternoon and a quiet party. We met 'The Fat Boys,' 'Heavy D', and a whole host of individuals from the movie industry. This led to an unexpected meeting with Quincy Jones and a glimpse of Michael Jackson's rehearsing.

1, Michael Sch

3, The Fat Boys all on the set of the 'Disorderlies.'

Over the years, I got used to meeting people on the spur of the moment, mainly when IRS Records was situated on the Universal Studio site, Lankershim Boulevard, in California. I was privileged to meet stars like Peter Falk, Danny Murphy, and John Ritter. The parties and drugs didn't interest me; I was never one for being up until the early morning hours when there was work to do the following day. I always wanted to be pretty sharp for meetings in my diary and moments that came along unexpectedly.

We were doing something right: opportunities continued to present themselves at every juncture, Tippa was up for the challenge, and we continued to play the right shows at the suitable venues, edging closer and closer to significant festivals such as Bob Marley Day in Los Angeles. Where we didn't do that, we chose venues up and down the coast of southern California. Many shows of this type were poorly paid; however, we could utilise these as loss leaders. As said previously, we needed to go out on tour and start to penetrate the US. We barely made enough money to cover hotel expenses and per diems; the critical factors for us were to maintain the task of moving across the US, get good rest, and eat a good breakfast.

One of the most challenging features of touring the US is how they perform. Most venues require entertainers to perform two sets in a night. This would mean you hit the stage for the first set of 45 minutes and return for the second set after a 30-minute break. Tippa wasn't a fan of these engagements, and they didn't sit comfortably with him. He was missing family, girlfriends and his mother, as his father had returned to Jamaica.

As a break from the tour took place, Tippa returned to the UK. A new tour began; however, Pato and I continued. I think consistency became a beneficial factor where, as the tour went on, things got better; opportunities came in the form of momentum, which generated shows where I could factor in escalation clauses in the contract, which was supported by the music press, reviews were getting better which was reflected by the uplift of tickets sales and continued with us hitting percentages.

Percentages are a vital factor when booking shows. It allows a promoter who takes the risk of booking an artist to recoup the gross potential of the minimum guarantee and promotion expenses. At that stage, there would be a breakpoint where all takings after that the artist would receive a 50-50 split with the promotor door takings or equivalent.

Japan - Tokyo, Osaka, and Nagoya

In June 1991, we embarked on a tour of Japan, the 'Original Raggamuffin' Japanese tour, produced by Parco Tachyon Co. Ltd, with the **Rough House Crew**; what a tour!

Across eight days, we toured as a unit and enjoyed every minute. We played at three venues in Tokyo, Osaka, and Nagoya. On arrival in Japan, we all experienced culture shock; what I mean is that I was walking down some steps, looking out, and I saw a mass of people with the same black hair. Similarly, one afternoon, it was raining heavily, and again, I saw a mass of black umbrellas different from anything I had experienced before; it was almost as if I could walk on those umbrellas and get where I was going, and if that wasn't enough, the Bullet Trains in Japan took me out of this world! The only thing disappointing was the price of a Coke a Cola, which you could buy in the UK at the time for twenty-five pence, was on sale for one pound.

All Pictures of Original Raggamuffin Japan Tour (images courtesy of Parco Tachyon Co. Ltd)

The sound engineers' abilities blew me away. Before our arrival, I had faxed the stage plan, plot, and channel list to the head engineer. Usually, as the house engineer, I would have to make minor adjustments; they not only had the stage set as requested but also rooted the channels I requested to the board and patched in the outboard effects.

I was in heaven. Aware of the set list for everyone, the sound check went well.

We were communicating by fax and phone to Sweetie and Legend, his father. Hence, Sweetie felt comfortable dropping on tour and collaborating with Peter on songs 'On and On' and 'Smile'. The band rehearsed the remainder of Sweeties set in Birmingham, which saved time with travel and logistics. Steven Clark, our drummer, played an excellent role as the musical director, assisting me in delivering on that aspect of the production. Myki Tuff opened all the shows, performing songs such as 'Work', 'Mr Tuff ah Come', 'Bible', and other favourites. The **Rough House Crew** did not have an acoustic bass player; we used two brilliant keyboard players, which gave us a tight sound; it was lovely. I provided the band members with the list of songs from which they learned the songs as the musical director. To cut costs, we doubled up by combining soundchecks and rehearsals.

With Myki's performance ending, Myki introduced Peter, who performed for twenty minutes, delivering his best-known tracks to an incredible welcome, 'Love Affair', 'I'll Be There' Jah Promise and 'Don't Leave Me Lonely'.

Returning to the stage, collaborating with the headliners Sweetie Irie and Tippa Irie, the energy of both MCs was on top' the audience knew all the songs; Tippa gave them 'Girl of My Best Friend', 'Raggamuffin Girl', and 'Stand By Me' and the fast style, the noise at times was too much, in a good way. The shows were incredible and will forever be one of my most memorable times in reggae music. I learnt that Sweetie was excellent with a band and brought something unique each night. What a performer, and all credit to Tippa, Peter, Myki Tuff as opener, and the band.

Tippa Irie - UK Dancehall Pioneer

In 2023, GT's Records released a compilation of My Boys Beatz recordings for the Grammy-nominated Reggae artist Tippa Irie. I have always considered Tippa one of the most lyrically talented, influential, and melodically gifted artists of the Windrush generation.

I remember the first time I spoke with him about his time so far in music. We both recounted how unimaginable it was that a 19-year-old could drive thousands of young people around the UK to create sounds reminiscent of an earthquake and create queues that circled buildings that could come from such humble beginnings.

Saxon Studio International provided Tippa with the perfect platform to make his mark in the music industry; from then on, nothing would stop him from coughing up fire.

"I'm an African" tells you where his heart is, "Saxon Studio International" talks of loyalty, and his Grammy Award nomination tells you about his songwriting abilities and collaboration that's "Hey Mama" with the Black-Eyed Peas.

"Hello, Darling," assisted Tippa to recognise his popularity and the household name he had become in the United Kingdom. I noted how rewarding the business could become worldwide if we had the wherewithal to seize the opportunities.

The album marks a milestone in Tippa's career and the body of work he has amassed over his 35-year career; from the shy, talented young person out of South London came the "opposite" and much more. My Boyz Beatz brings you the "UK Dancehall."

Links:

Spotify

*https://open.spotify.com/album/
2B1zhSPyq7BhtmK6Vj9Zx3?si=jtPJbwv2TECLTFYiilOhRQ*

Apple Music

https://music.apple.com/gb/album/uk-dancehall-pioneer/1683480229

Amazon

https://amazon.co.uk/music/player/albums/

Chapter 12

Peter Spence

After promoting a night of British talent, I met Peter Spence after a big night DJing at Mary Street Church Hall, Balsall Heath, Birmingham. I bumped into Peter outside Earl Grey in Balsall Heath, Birmingham, where he played some demos for me in my car, including "Don't Leave Me Lonely" and "Frivolous Woman," which stood out. I booked a studio, brought in musicians, and worked on beats, basslines, and drum patterns. My love for chord progressions and strings shaped the production style, laying the foundations for many of my songs. Peter and I ended up collaborating for 13 years.

My first memory of Peter Spence as a musician/vocalist was Night at Mary Street Church Hall, situated on the corner of Edward Road and Mary Street, Balsall Heath Birmingham. GT 600 was playing a community event against the Sound system called Take Two. For some reason, we weren't expected to do that well because Take-Two was a larger outfit in the sound system fraternity, and they had a lot more power and sound system boxes. However, never to be one to shy away from her challenge, I told the lads to listen. We have this going for us: Sound quality, a double-deck system, and Music, and we know how to play Records. We had to select suitable records for the audience, which was in our favour. We didn't know much about Take Two; we light young people then. I guess we were just fearless. We just wanted a good time and knew we'd have reasonable support.

We were even, and both of us played some great tunes. However, closer to the end of the night, it was about 10.30 pm when I asked Winston, Pato's brother, to check if he was at home (he lived within walking distance from the venue). Not too long after Winston and Pato returned, with his hand held out, Pato said give me the riddim. I quickly turned over Marcia Griffiths 'Feel Like Jumping', and Pato obliterated the dance; just as soon as he came, he left us with the memory.

A crowd gathered around the GT 600s record decks following Pato's performance. However, two or three individuals shouted, "Let Peter sing, not to keep them waiting." I handed the microphone to Peter. The place erupted when he took the microphone and uttered the first few lines. Peter graced the audience with a few bars and left. The crowd interactions continued to buzz. It was just astonishing. The place was on fire. The anticipation had risen, and we played admirably.

It must've been adrenaline or something because I don't know where the record selection came from, but I remember playing 'Roots Natty' by Johnny Clark. The audience from them or from then on was we had them in our hands, and we ended that night victorious.

I always remember that night, and somehow, I knew I would work with Peter Spence sometime in the future. That voice, that's all I could remember. Not too long after that, I moved to London for work. Here, I got to experience different aspects of music, reggae, etc. It came to a time after I had begun managing Pato, and as a team, Pato and I had started to focus on promoting British talent from our hometown, Birmingham.

I was outside of the Earl Grey in Balsall Heath Birmingham when I saw Peter and casually got talking to him about what he was up to. Peter stated that he had some demons he could play for me, so we got into my car and listened to them. He said I've been working on these with a friend called

Gary Chisholm, and we've come up with this. One of the songs was 'Don't Leave Me Lonely', and another was 'Frivolous Woman'. Those two songs caught my attention; the others I heard were good but needed more work.

Sometime after 'Allo Tosh' became successful, I began producing much more. I hired a studio and got some musicians in and work on beats that had come to my mind, you know, baseline here, drum patterns there called progressions in many different places; however, what I loved was chord progressions and strings, and I think has never left my production style.

Having said that, because of the relationship between Peter's parents and me, even though I was about three years older than Peter, I remember him attending the same church as my family. I think it helped that my father was also a Christian because our parents had a relationship. Peter's dad used to go to church; hence, I felt I needed to ask Peter's parents if it were ok for Peter and me to work together in the music business with a contract. Having said that. One evening, I went to Peter's house, Balsall Heath Birmingham, and asked his dad. Is it okay if I manage your son? His dad replied that's up to Peter. Pete said yes, and we started from there. I put together a contract, and I gave it to his dad to have a look at. I explained it, and Pete and I got to work.

The first song we worked on was 'Frivolous Woman', which I released on my label, Moving Records. It did well because it got into the local charts and ended up relatively high. It also entered the Black Echo reggae chart but didn't enter the top 10. It wasn't a song that resonated with its audience, so it did pretty well in terms of a local hit.

I needed more experience as a producer and record label before releasing my next song. I produced two songs using the musicians Derek Frivia and Patrick Donegon, so instead of releasing the second, I licensed 'Don't Leave Me Lonely' to Greensleeves Records, a UK bubblers label. Chris Cracknell liked 'Don't Leave Me Lonely' and thought it would add to the growth and consistency of the lover's rock end of the UK Bubblers Label and its parent company, Greensleeves Records. It was also cost-effective for Chris; he didn't have to go through the costly experience of recording 'Don't Leave Me Lonely' from scratch in the studio.

The song became a hit for Peter, placing him in front of the right people in the reggae music business fraternity and its affluent audience. Consequently, Peter earned the Best Newcomer award at Tony Williams's British Reggae Music Awards in London. Unselfishly, I gave the producer credits to Patrick Donegan, a reggae producer and British Reggae Regulars band member. The strategy worked.

'Don't Leave Me Lonely' put Peter on the right path; his profile gathered momentum with another strategic release, a new song called 'Love Affair', utilising the lyrics of Sugar Minott's Lovers Rock', which took to the market and became a popular song loved by the Lovers Rock genre. The next step was to determine what would move next. We needed another hit. Peter needed another hit; this came when I had the idea that a family would be watching the TV, and films, including Elvis Presley, were shown on the TV. One of my mom's favourite songs by Elvis was 'Girl of My Best Friend'. I had an idea, so I spoke with Pato, who had assembled a demo studio in his apartment. I called together a few musicians and put down the basics of what would become the rhythm for 'Girl of My Best Friend'. Once, I played this to Peter and explained that I wanted him to cover this Elvis Presley song; Peter learned it within a couple of days.

I recorded Peter's vocals very quickly, shortly after I booked 'Rich Bitch Studios' on Bristol Road, Birmingham and mixed the track. However, at the time, I felt he needed something else. I played the song to a few people to get some feedback and realised that most people liked it. Everybody I played it to fell in love with the idea, but I still felt it needed something else before I released it.

Days later, Tippa Irie was in town, which gave me the idea for a remix. I played the song to Tippa, who loved it, stating it was a good song; I turned to it and said it needs you to feature on it, to which he replied, yeah, no problem. I said no, no, no, and I would like you to respond to Peter's desire to have your girl. Tippa replied oh, I get you. The rest is history. Tippa came up with the lines. 'What's the matter with him…? When done, I released it, and it just sold and sold; that song would become the Anker for Peter's album. This enabled Peter to tour the west midlands and the country, becoming a reggae household name.

What followed was the release of Peter's album, 'I'll Be There,' which was ready to release. We had so many tracks. 'I'll Be There', 'Jah Promise', 'Girl, My Best Friend', 'Love Affair', etc. The album went on to do very well. It became a top 10 Hit album, generating a feature 'Black Echoes' review. Peter's career had solidified as a British male Reggae lovers rock Vocalist. We put together impressive run-off shows and a national personal appearance tour that solidified Peter's statement on the market and promoted the album.

1, I'll Be There (The Album)

2, Peter performing at the Hummingbird

2, I'll Be There (The CD)

Unlike Pato Banton and Tippa Irie, Peter's music fell into the category of lover's rock. However, he wasn't alone; I also managed a talented singer, Annette B' at the time. I commissioned Derek Frivier to work with her and produce some songs. He came up with two good singles, which I signed to Greensleeves, UK Bubblers. Between Keith and I, we garnished so much work for Peter that he became a full-time artist for at least four years; we would place Annette as a full-time hair stylist, by day would support Peter on the same shows in a part-time capacity, which enabled us to introduce her to the market.

To further Pete's career outside of the UK, I felt the way forward was to record two songs, 'Give A Little Love' and 'Situation Crazy' featuring Peter collaborating with Pato on his 'Visions of the World' album. This enabled Peter to tour the US with Pato. With the appropriate H1 visa. I released 'I'll Be There' in America as a US release.

As you can imagine, a lot was going on for Peter at the time because I had just negotiated the deal to sign with Island Records, and 'The Girl of My Best Friend' was one of the first singles, followed by 'Stand by Me', which became the second Single. Things were definitely on the offer for Peter, and we were utilising the whole team to establish a unified approach to several different areas within the British Reggae music industry, both at home and abroad.

Japan

As mentioned in the previous chapter, In June 1991, Peter joined Tippa and Sweetie Irie on a tour of Japan, the 'Original Raggamuffin' Japanese tour, the Rough House Crew, produced by Parco Tachyon Co. Ltd. What a tour across eight days as a unit. We played at three venues in Tokyo, Osaka, and Nagoya. As the front-of-house mix engineer, I was aware of Tippa and Peter's set list; I had only communicated via phone with Sweetie and General, his father, at the time and, as a result, worked Sweeite's hits and album tracks. I provided the band members with the list of songs from which they learned the songs as the musical director. It was also agreed that we would double up and use extended soundchecks as rehearsals. Myki Tuff opened the show, closely followed by Peter performing a twenty-minute set of his songs, 'Love Affair', 'I'll Be There' Jah Promise and 'Don't Leave Me Lonely'. He then collaborated with Sweetie on the songs 'On and On' and 'Smile' and, at the same time, collaborated with Tippa on 'Girl of My Best Friend', 'Raggamuffin Girl', and 'Stand By Me'. The shows were fantastic and will forever be one of my most memorable times in reggae music.

3, GT, Peter, Sweetie and Tippa

Throughout his career, Spence has worked with various prominent producers and artists within the reggae industry and has continued to release music that resonates with fans of lovers of rock and reggae music. His smooth vocal style and passionate delivery have made him a beloved figure in the genre.

My Boyz Beatz ft Peter Spence long awaited 27 track Album - Song Book.

Following my hiatus from the music industry from 1992 to 2014, Peter and I reestablished our relationship with the release of 'The Grace of God' and 'Lift Your Hands'. These two songs came about because Peter listened to the radio and heard 'Let's Just Be Friends' sung by fourteen-year-old Lucy Tennyson. Around that time, Peter had entered a quiet period and had some ideas he wanted to record. Lucy, who someone who I was a fourteen-year-old young person who I had met while delivering outreach sessions in shared End, Birmingham, and had begun a course of coaching sessions with. (who I will discuss later).

We achieved popularity with a remake of Maxi Preist's 'Best of Me', featuring Tippa Irie on the remix, which generated a lot of air-play, especially in London and Birmingham. I had just formed My Boyz Beatz, a production company primarily designed to release songs recorded with young people I coached.

Peter telephoned me and requested the instrumentals so that he could begin writing lyrics to the beats. He planned to return to my studio, where I would record and produce his vocals. While recording 'The Grace of God' and 'Lift Your Hands', Peter needed something lyrical for the final 60 seconds. As a writer, I suggested Peter add 'Better Days Will Come' to complete the communication narrative of the song, completing both songs, which was to become Peter's comeback EP. James and I finished the mix and mastered all of the songs recorded on what I called 'My Boyz One Riddim'.

'Story Book'

Story Book covers the majority of recordings released by GT's Records under the auspices of My Boyz Beatz and produced mainly through me. It features 27 tracks, creating a diverse and extensive music collection over 20 years, a testament to dedication and hard work.

The album offers a unique blend of old and new songs, providing listeners with various musical experiences. With such many tracks, there's bound to be something for everyone's taste. It's great to hear that some tracks have been released as singles and others are yet to be released, allowing individual songs to stand out and gain wider recognition.

Sharing creative work with the world is always a thrilling experience, both for the artists who poured their passion into the project and for the audience who eagerly awaits the opportunity to enjoy and connect with the music. The hope is that the album **'Story Book'** resonates with the audience and provides a memorable listening experience for all who engage.

Links:

https://open.spotify.com/album /5fRboD6QjsU4RNKsM1yKkl?si=HUTzT97xQi-eHDj6JngB0g
iTunes - Apple Music
https://music.apple.com/gb/album/story-book/1684813375
Amazon
https://amazon.co.uk/music/player/albums/ B0C3JNP31M?marketplaceId=A1F83G8C2ARO7P&musicTerritory=GB&ref=dm_ sh_98EGR7LZtZHhbMgxeyVdUNuq5

YouTube

https://youtu.be/uGaE8Gur1bE

https://youtu.be/4rBCh10x-pI

https://youtu.be/Y60lVMBdV5Q

https://youtu.be/AgZYo9YeVBU

Chapter 13

Music Promotion

The MC Clash at Maximilian's Night Club on Broad Street, Birmingham, featuring Pato, Tippa, Levi, and Macka B, highlighted my career as a British Reggae promoter. It had everything: buildup, atmosphere, and a thrilling showdown. It's often hailed as the most celebrated and well-known MC clash in the UK, drawing fans from Manchester, Liverpool, London, Wolverhampton, and Birmingham. A roadblock caused the police to threaten closure of the event unless I controlled the situation outside. Thinking quickly, I asked Zukie of Master Blaster to announce that parking tickets and vehicle removal were in progress. It was a risk, but it got the desired effect. Cars were moved, and the situation was brought under control.

It is a vocation that taught me an enormous amount about the reggae music business. It began with Pato and I getting together to showcase talents for the West Midlands to form GT and PB promotions. Both he and I had experience working with young talent. Later, as Pato became busy as an artist, I continued on my own as GT promotions.

Following the development of GT 600 and its success as a roadshow, I naturally developed a taste for putting on events. Knowing Pato, we naturally got talking about putting on events that would support and encourage people from our area to become musicians or artists. At this point, I was learning and reflecting; I was glad I listened to my dad and studied my lessons at school hard; reading, writing, and arithmetic were crucial in working out the gross potential and, therefore, understanding what the break-even would amount to as well as the likelihood of profit might look like.

The Mermaid

Pato and I decided to promote a local talent show at the Mermaid Public House on Stratford Road, Birmingham. We booked the venue, printed flyers, and created a marketing plan. Having spoken to some local acts, we ascertained they wanted to perform. Local acts such as Bonito Star, Michael Ellis, Sargent Nobel, Lieutenant Mellow and Fancy

Fitzy came along on a night and joined the open mic session.

These sessions would take place on a Monday or Tuesday night, acting similar to a youth centre program but with a specific agenda that included a sound system. The venue provided us with one of the function rooms with minimal lighting. We would sell tickets and collect money at the door. We also hired the door security, known by his nickname (Animal). I knew him from school, so I could trust him to carry out his role with the right mindset. He could also be described as a gentle giant. We made a good team, and promoters liked him, as did our regular customers.

I used my supervisory management qualification, the National Examination Board for Supervisory Management Certificate Programme (NEBSM) course content, which assisted me with managing people and the side hustle. My head chef encouraged me to enrol if I wanted to become a head chef at some point in the future. At that time, I didn't realise that skills could be transferable.

Pato and I completed four to five performances at the Mermaid. They would always sell out and be rammed. Sometimes, there wasn't any room to walk, and at other times, the rafters would be sweating due to crowds of 250 to 300 people. We needed to move our operation somewhere else.

Master Blaster

I sought to extend the team with a sound system; having said that, I was seeking a sound system I could develop that could become popular in Birmingham, provide an annexe that could be used as a public address system and one that I could tour the world with.

In my opinion, Master Blaster could have achieved this with some work and investment. We started well with a show at Oaklands, then one at Bilston, Winson Green, and the following was the big one at Maximillion's Birmingham. Zukie, Billy, Tin Tin, Beaver Millitant, and Stylee were young, motivated MasterBlaster sound-system members who were disciplined and willing to listen.

We sold out of most venues in Birmingham and the surrounding areas. Needing to step things up, we decided to take our promotions to Henry's Night Spot, Bilston, West Midlands. **(now known as Robin 2)**, well known for live gigs. **Da Dah**, the manager, was impressed with us because what we said would happen happened, and more importantly, we paid the fees and sold a lot of drinks.

> **THE LONG AWAITED M.C. CLASH!!!!**
> TO TAKE PLACE AT
> **HENRY'S NIGHT CLUB** (Bilston)
> (formally known as RISING STAR)
> **MON. 1ST APRIL 1985** 8 pm – 3 am
>
> From LONDON — **TIPPA IRIE** The Best & From LONDON — **PAPA LEVI** Massive & Hail
> v's
> From BIRMINGHAM — **PATO BANTON** Afro Tash / From WOLVERHAMPTON — **MAKABEE** Bible Reader
>
> Laying down the riddim will be
> **KRIS KENNEDY JUNIOR** AND CLUB ROADSHOW
> Guest P.A.'s From London, **KERNAL FLUX**, (Pirate loves to criticise!)
> **SISTER CANDY + MISS IRIE** (Keep Bubbling)
>
> Guest P.A.'s From B'ham, **ADMIRAL JERRY, LUITENANT MELLOW, + ZOD MAN**
>
> RATE AT GATE £3.00
> THIS SESSION WILL BE VIDEO'D
> COACHES LEAVE ALL STAKE PUB / GOOCH ST. 10.00 pm

The original flyer intended to hold the event at Henry's Night Club. However, tickets were selling so fast that we had oversold the event three weeks prior. Therefore, I moved the event to Maximillions Night Club, Broad Street, Birmingham City Centre.

We hired Henry's and put together a promotion consisting of MCs and singers; it was rammed solid; we invited Kris Kennedy Jr (KKJ), who was the Reggae on BRMB Radio at the time, and we also put Des Mitchell, the Reggae DJ on BBC Pebble Mill Studios alongside a host of artists performing, it made perfect sense. People loved it, so instead of attracting 250 - 300 people to our promotions, we stepped things up, and now we're pulling seven (700) eight (800) hundred people.

The Midlands MC Competition

GT and PB promotions were doing well; our name was growing outside of Birmingham, and people would come from miles to venues like Henry's Night Club in Bilston to witness some of the exciting MC battles we were putting together. We delivered on the audience's expectations, and the up-and-coming young MC rappers became more widespread until the moment came when we decided to promote a Midlands competition. Papa Levi and Tippa Irie are Britain's most well-known Saxon MCs to judge the event.

It was a big deal. We raised the gate's price to cover the gross potential of costs. There was a worry that the cost might affect the sales, but there was no need for the cover charge to be appropriate to the event. Nevertheless, it still was rammed solid to the rafters and sold out.

The local MCs contending was Fancy Fitzy, Colonel Valentine, Lieutenant Mellow, and Zodman. Valentine, popular with the public and the ladies, was the favourite to win. However, Zodman was so well prepared that, as the underdog, he won with some excellent lyrics and MC flow. His lyrical bars and how he performed them did it for the judges and me. For the other MCs, it was a body blow; members of the public who were present still talk about it today, and it will never be forgotten.

It was similar to the 'Salt Fish Clash' between Pato and Judah; the MC who was expected to run away with it didn't win, career ended. I suppose this was the night I became one of Birmingham's well-known reggae promotors, having achieved that event. I recall Tippa telling me some time later that it was the fact that I had successfully promoted that event, which assisted his decision when it came to choosing me as his manager. He recounted that he saw somebody who could get the job done, be organised, manage, and understand how to use money.

Marketing and promotion are good starting points and valuable assets to people in the music business at the time, especially artists.

Pato became a very busy artist, so it became impossible for him to continue with the promotion business, so I continued on my own. I promoted numerous events in Birmingham and collaborated with clubs and independent promoters. I remember promoting Aswad, Saxon Studio International, Smiley Culture, and Maxi Priest until, even for me, I no longer had the time due to commitments outside of the UK.

Lloyd G Blake - The Hummingbird Birmingham UK

Birmingham: As I said, Lloyd Blake is one of Birmingham's premier league Reggae Promoters. You would find Lloyd and colleague Eric almost every weekend by the fountain in Birmingham City Centre handing out flyers for up-and-coming events and many venues across the city.

Birmingham has produced some exceptional community-based promoters who have led the development of British reggae music in the UK.

Lloyd Blake is an individual that we grew up as boys and young boys promoting grassroots. He would hand out flyers for shows and events he was producing. Everybody seemed to know who Lloyd Blake was. He spoke well and clearly, and by the same measure, he knew what he was doing because he understood the business from a British concept and Jamaica, where Reggae music was born. I first met Lloyd Blake when I was part of Duke Wally Soundsystem. Lloyd came around and met up with Vincent Gordon (crooks) and booked (Duke Wally) the Sound for what would usually be known as a sound clash competition, where two or three youth sounds played against each other in one particular venue.

This didn't stop as I moved through the music business from being a DJ with GT 600, especially when I started managing artists in reggae music. Lloyd Blake would call me up and book one of my artists.

Lloyd became someone I could ask for advice; he was never shy when inviting me into his office and allowing me to sit down and hear what he had to say. He was good like that, so as time passed, Lloyd became more than just a business person or partner. He became somewhat of a mentor and a friend, and that's how we've continued up to today.

From left: 1, Tony Garfield (Beshara), Trevor (Gatecrash),Grantley GT, Lloyd Blake and Sensi

2, Quaker City, Grantley GT

It came when Lloyd took over the management of the Hummingbird Venue, Dale End, Birmingham. This was an exciting time for Birmingham because the Hummingbird became the go-to venue for reggae music and other musical genres. Reggae music was at the heart of Lloyd Blake, so you would find some inspiring dances or promotions happening at the Hummingbird. You know they were legendary. We're talking about Shabba Ranks and Dennis Brown: Gregory Isaacs, The Wailers, Musical Youth, Aswad, and Steel Pulse. I remember taking my mom to The Mighty Sparrow; he was the Calypso King of Trinidad and the Caribbean. Hence, at the heart of the Windrush generation, like Lord Kitchener, people from that era adored these artists from the West Indies.

The Hummingbird First Annual Awards 1987/88. I was presented with a special achievement award for outstanding services to Black Music; two years later, I received the Best Producer award. Peter Spence won best male vocalist album, 'I'LL Be There,' and Annette B won best female Vocal and single at the Hummingbird's third annual awards in 1989/90. Again, I thank the judging panel and members of the public who voted.

1, Peter Spence, Annette B and Grantley GT at The Hummingbird Awards`

2, Grantley GT and Annette B

To give an example of the spirit and passion that Lloyd Blake had and the philanthropy he had for British reggae music, Lloyd sought to award artists, musicians, and producers with Hummingbird awards. This credited several individuals for their hard work and contributions to British Reggae Music and sent a message to others who desired to achieve similar standards. Lloyd Blake, Tony Owens, and Bernie Dixon can never be forgotten. The Hummingbird became a place we called our own, which was pivotal to our development and crucial to our growth. The presentation of awards gave us a legacy.

Cecil Morrison - Peoples Community Radio Line(PCRL), Birmingham UK

Many of you reading this book may have heard about Cecil Morrison; however, for those who have not, Cecil Morrison or (Music Master) became a pioneer of pirate radio in the 1980s. If you love reggae music and had spent time in Birmingham between 1984 and 1992, you could not have missed the impact that PCRL achieved.

	Midnite-3AM	3-6AM	6-9 AM	9-Noon	12-3 PM	3-6 PM	6-8 PM	8-10 PM	10-12
MON	Tony Roots	Tape	Mickey Nold	Angel A	Mr Romantic	Little Richie	Tony Dendy	Stevie G	Zuk
TUE	Festas	E Double D	Chicken George	Chicken George	Mr Romantic	Little Richie	Cherry Festas	Rankin Bev	Stevie
WED	Tony Roots	Fablo	Mickey Nold	Chicken George	Miss P	Little Richie	Angel A	Miki Studio	Che
THU	Miki Studio	Tape	Chicken George	Tony Roots	Mr Romantic	Little Richie	John Saunders	Gilly Iris	Ran Be
FRI	Tape	Tape	Mickey Nold	E Double D	Chicken George	Chicken George	Tape	Trevor Ranks	Zuk
SAT	Steve Williams	Miki Studio	Chicken George	Joy & Bobbles (10-12)	David Vincent (12-2) Sunday (2-4)	Gilly Iris (4-6)	Big John	TC Shore	Paul Be
SUN	DJ Fuse	Fablo	CJ (8-10)	Gilly Iris (10-12)	Steve Williams (12- ?)/Cherry+4	Miss P (4-6)	David Vincent	CJ Gospel	To Ro 11
	Reggae	Soul	Jazz	Talk	Gospel	Soca	Childrens

An example of a typical PCRL radio weekly program of events

PCRL became the heart of the African Caribbean community, the go-to radio station for news, current affairs, events, community fun days, and parties. It brought people together in a very positive way. Cecil Morrison and his deputy Pilot were the men and trailblazers behind the radio station. They managed the selection of DJs, some still active today. It was a twenty-four-hour machine.

Cecil started his dream from humble beginnings. Earlier in his career, recognising the role of communication with African Caribbeans, he explored community television. However, he was plagued by legalities and red tape, so he concentrated on the radio before pausing briefly. Still, he took only some of what he had mustered to formulate PCRL and the inception of the pirate radio revolution, which ran right across the UK.

Cecil became a pioneer of the pirate radio revolution in Birmingham. To his credit, PCRL is necessary for whatever I achieved as a promoter, manager, or producer to hit the mark as it did. The audience PCRL created led to local community movements that I last saw a long time ago; the council had to take notice and listen to the issues presented by the African Caribbean community.

This led to radio stations such as the BBC and local independent stations reprogramming their broadcasts to accommodate shows that responded to the needs of the whole community.

Annette B

Annette B, a reggae singer, is known for her soulful voice and contributions to the music scene, particularly during the early 1980s. Since then, she has gained recognition as one of the prominent female voices in reggae, often celebrated for her emotional and powerful vocal delivery. Annette B. worked with various artists and producers, contributing to the genre's rich tapestry.

I began working with Annette in 1984, just after she completed work with Phillip Gad, who released the single 'Love Affair', and shortly after this, I began managing Annette. Apart from Annette's melodic voice, I have always respected the businesswoman in Annette, particularly because she always maintained a full-time job while at the same time carrying out her musical career after her 9 – 5 (a hairdresser stylist) at Scissor Trick in Birmingham over the weekends. My first role as her manager was to look for the most appropriate music producer. I wanted to work with someone who would collaborate with Annette, write songs, and develop her next single. This opportunity came about quicker than I thought. I had met Derek Frivier earlier that year while producing two songs with Peter Spence. Derek and Annette developed 'I Found Love', released on Greensleeves Records, UK Bubblers label, in 1986. However, Chris Cracknell clarified that the single would require me to assist with promoting Annette up and down the country with shows. This wasn't a difficult task for me to achieve as one of Birmingham's promotors at the time, as well as a manager of three prominent artists at the time; I was able to place Annette on shows, which would have been a struggle for others to achieve.

Keith Brown took responsibility for the logistical aspects and shows I could not attend. This sentiment goes to the management team we created utilising the personal assistant qualities of Ranking Bev and Joycelyn St Juste, who assisted us with the artist booking system. Songs like 'I Need You Now' followed this program of work and established Annette as a credible female vocalist in the sub-genre we call Lovers Rock.

Annette and I had to move on; I was constantly abroad, so my time was limited. However, the production team continued, including Derek Frivier, who, between him and Annette, continued recording songs years after. Annette B's melodic voice encouraged Neil Frazer (Ariwa) to release 'Fairy God Mother', around this time, she was noticed by reggae music Clement Dodd, aka Coxsone Dodd, who invited Annette to America to record an album for his Studio One Label. Annette took the opportunity to record the album.

In 1987, Annette and I worked together again to record a cover of Louisa Marks 'Six Street,' which received a lot of air-play on radio. This was followed up with a collaboration with Masterblaster sound systems MC Corporal Billy Spice, with the cover of 15, 16, 17s classic hit 'Black Skin Boy' and 'Wah Dis Pon Mi', again generating significant airplay. Annette also recorded the John Holt classic 'Sweetie'.

All tracks are available on GT's Records – My Boyz Beatz on Corporal Billy Spice EP 'QueensPoundSystem' and 'My Boyz Beatz, The Beginning The Vaults' featured below, before giving her heart to the Lord.

1, Corporal Billy Spice

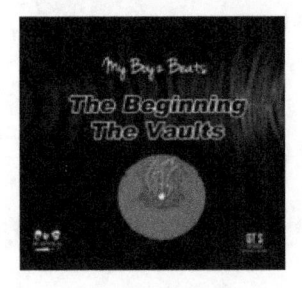

2, The Album GTs Record

3, Annette B

In 2001, Annette became a Christian. Her new purpose led her to embark on an independent project, which resulted in the release of the album When I Wake Up **in 2013.** The single **'Pop God's Style' followed,** propelling her career to this day.

The MC Clash - Maximilian's Night Club, Broad Street, Birmingham - Pato, Tippa, Levi and Macka B

It was one of the proudest moments in my career as a British Reggae promoter. The clash had everything: the build-up, the atmosphere and the showdown. People always congratulate me on putting on that show no matter where I go. By far, the most celebrated and well-known MC clash in the UK. One of England's best MCs was facing off against the next in each corner.

People came from Manchester, Liverpool, London, Wolverhampton, and, of course, Birmingham. I wanted something central so I hired a central venue at the time called Maximillian on Broad Street, in the heart of Birmingham. By ten o'clock, it was a roadblock on Broad Street; nothing could move one way or the other; we had problems, and the police warned that unless I got things under control, it was looking like they would have to shut down the event, which was the last thing I needed. Responding to this, I asked Zukie to announce over the microphone that people needed to move their cars or the police would go to move them. A few good friends of mine helped the police to navigate cars to more appropriate spaces and let others know the event was **'sold out'**.

Master Blaster set the scene with some good music, then Birmingham MC 'Admiral Jerry' came with a topical, Tongue 'n' Cheek lyrical number called, 'Who Ah Go Feel It'. The crowd never stopped bawling for a restart. They were licking wood and all sorts. Then it was time for me as the promoter to introduce the lineup of MCs Pato Banton, Tippa Irie, Papa Levi and Macka B.

It was awesome. All the lyrics deserved that night were brand new and up to date. Every MC was on par and represented their tuff; it was two and a half hours of sure-shot delivery at the highest level. There were no winners or losers for the first time in dancehall history, just back-to-back-lyrical tennis.

I had a few problems at the door, but overall, what a fantastic show! Unfortunately, it will never be repeated. However, those who wish to view it can find it on YouTube. The management of music promotion and the door required careful handling. The door and its management couldn't simply be automated and left to run smoothly. It had to be closely monitored and managed according to certain principles, almost on a 10-minute basis.

This promotion was no exception; we took steps to secure the funds collected by depositing them into the bank safety deposit box to prevent any issues with theft. Additionally, we controlled the number of people entering and exiting by personally managing and tracking familiar individuals throughout the night.

Waiting for Levi to turn up, time was getting short. Pato picked up the microphone and began; Tippa came back heavy, just as the audience expected, and started the fire with some classics. With his unique style, Macka B followed up with tact and diplomacy. The sound system rewound and came repeatedly, pulling up the rhythm for crowd satisfaction; it was awesome. It was like that all night; as anybody would have, Levi turned up right at the end when the dance ended. He couldn't even chat. The fun factor was so high that no one noticed until well into the night, and Papa Levi hadn't turned up yet. However, Tippa continued alone until near the end, when Papa Levi walked through the door.

I just remembered being worn out. I think it was pure adrenaline and joy that got me through, which is why when I entered the field of substance misuse, I understood the impact of adrenaline, fight or flight, and the mental addiction some drugs can provide for individuals., hence music is my drug of choice until this very day.

Chapter 14

GT's Records – The Early Years and The Releases

Part of GTs Records' early years involved collaboration with many musicians, including Steven Clark. Keith Brown and I paid off a loan in exchange for Steve's future work as an engineer, purchasing drums and other musical equipment from America. Keith received a 10% share in GTs Records, and our production team was named The Rough House Crew. After a successful American and Japanese tour, the loan issue was resolved when I took a break from the business.

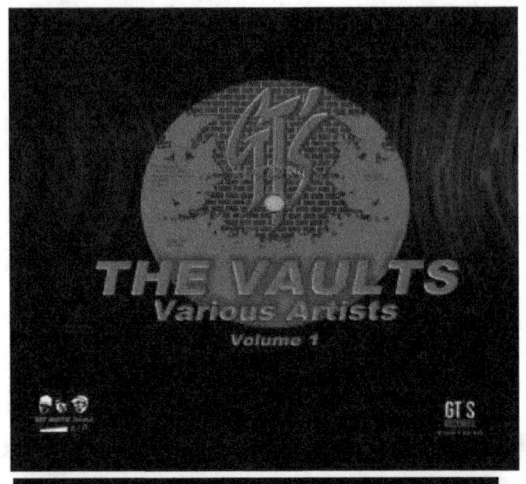

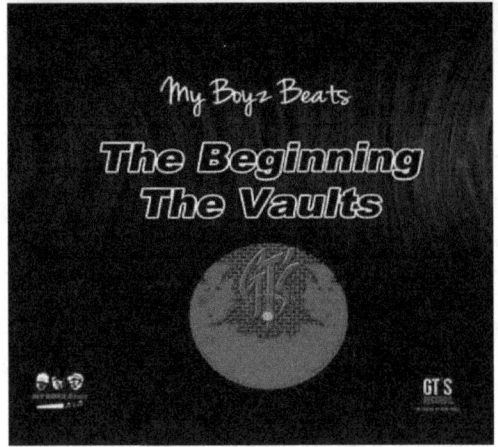

GTs Records embarked on a project that included work with Stephen and Paul, who became members of the Rough House Crew. This came about because Steve had taken up a loan from a friend, and because of several factors, he needed help to repay the loan within the term. The purpose of the loan was to enable Steve to purchase a studio. Faced with returning the items, I suggested to

Steve that Keith Brown and I would pay off the loan and allow him to pay Keith by working as a musician and engineer in the studio. Part of the bargain was that I would cut Keith a percentage share in GT's Records.

I don't play a musical instrument. However, before 'Hello Darling' by Tippa Irie, I took saxophone lessons from Birmingham legendary Andy Hamilton. It taught me that I could work out notes, chords and progressions, things I had learnt from listening to my dad's records and having him explain a good singer from a great singer. The overarching learning outcome came with the understanding that I could hum notes and melodies with my voice, enabling me to write songs by communicating notes I wanted musicians to play, attributes that assisted me in later years when I would become a music producer and later still for My Boyz Beatz.

However, Keith has continued as an owner of GT's Records until this day.

GT's Records – The Early Years and The Releases Discography

1992

Fiona Harriot & Peter Hunnigale – Mind-Blowing Decisions

Major Popular – Don't Worry

Juki Ranks – Pop-Up

1993

Ruff House Crew – Lovin's Got Me "Crazy"

Peter Spence – Love Affair

Annette 'B' - Six Street

1988

Tippa Irie – Two Sides of Tippa Irie (Album)

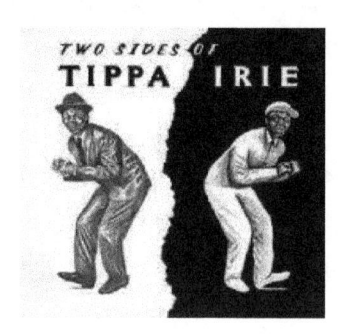

Various Artists – Great British DJ's Roll Call '89 (LP, Sampler)

1989

Peter Spence – Love Affair

French Kiss - Missing You

Peter Spence – I'll Be There (Album)

Mikey Tuff – Dougoo - Dougoo / True We Black

(Single)

Peter Spence – Heart and Soul / One In Ten

1991

Annette B & Corporal Billy - Stop Your Lying

Various Artists – Great British Reggae DJs & Singers Roll Call '89 (Album)

Various – Great British Reggae Rappers & Singers Roll Call Volume 2 (Album)

Peter Spence & Tippa Irie – Saphire and Steel (Album)

Tippa Irie – Ah-Me-Dis (Album)

1990

Charisma – Yo-Yo

Nerious Joseph – It's Over

French Kiss – Missing You

Chapter 15

My Boyz Beatz – GTs Records

I founded My Boyz Beatz in 2013/4. This production pathway intends to provide an end-to-end development program for young people, the Wheeler Street Midnight Bus project (who worked in the community around safety and anti-social behaviour). This development program became so successful that it stretched beyond its original remit into the wider entertainment industry for vocalists and musicians. My Boyz Beatz now works alongside world-class musicians, offering artist development, songwriting, production, and composition services. As a notable figure in the British reggae scene, I worked with prominent artists and bands in Birmingham, England.

The first two years of Wheeler Street were a special team that achieved funding for many programs. The success of our work led to a meeting with His Royal Highness, The Prince of Wales, who recognised us as a team and congratulated some of the young people we worked with.

His Royal Highness, The Prince of Wales', Lucy Tennyson & Grantley GT

Deciding to re-establish or rebrand GT's Records after such a long hiatus, I began with discussions with key people. These included Tippa Irie, Jbeatz0121, Keith Brown, James Crosdale, Trevor Ranks, Little Ritchie, Kennedy Wilkinson, Stevie J and Major Popular. I got together with each of them and expressed what I wanted to achieve, and they all gave me a similar response, which was if you're going to come back after such a long break, you need to remember that things have changed and the market wasn't the same as how I left it in 1992. After explaining that I recognised that things had changed and that I wasn't divorced from understanding that the Internet had started, the birth of the MP3 had taken place. People could now send music over the Internet and by email; having said this, I think they got the message. What was valuable was that after undergoing these months of preparation conversations, the scale of what I wanted to achieve became more apparent. However, the process taught me a lot. It was good to discuss details with people I greatly respected and who were willing to provide me with feedback on how to improve the things I intended to approach. I explained that I wanted to work with young people to develop a new style and form of Reggae, a fresh-sounding progressive set of beats I hoped the market would listen to.

I commented that I was working with James Crosdale and would be including Jbeatz0121, indicating that there was no chance that songs would sound similar to those I had released in the 80s or 90s; the productions would be different. I explained that my vision included digital marketing, and I would be working with Matt Flint, the CEO of Yoghurt Top Marketing Limited. I saved money utilising my skills in digital photography form gained from some courses and experience I had with my digital camera. I found this helpful when working with Robin

Giorno, designing the artwork for music cover art, and uploading songs to CD Baby, my digital distribution company.

In this respect, I spoke with a few DJs in the business and played regularly on the radio in London and Birmingham.

These were Commander B, Daddy Ernie, Colin (Cee Bee) Brown, Ranking Bev, Levi Washington, Bionic Steel, Big John, Little Richie, Wayne Irie, and Trevor Ranks. I spoke with Lady Destiny and asked her to review the song **'I Love You,'** featuring Keziasoul, before its final mix. Her feedback gave me what I needed to decide which song to release first and re-enter the British reggae music industry as a producer.

Before the final mailouts, I sat down with Trevor Ranks, a DJ I greatly respected who hosted a show on Birmingham's Sting radio. Trevor interviewed me, stating my return and endorsing the new music the audience was due to hear in 2014. He commented that he felt the productions were on par with what was currently being played on radio stations across the United Kingdom and the world. Trevor never stopped there. He outlined that some of the vocalists were young and still at school.

Artists, musicians, producers, and those in the retail world of musical compositions will tell you that becoming successful in the music business requires successful marketing and promotional campaigns.

Keith Brown, Major Popular, and I sat down with honesty at heart many times. Major is well known for his exploits as an MC with Birmingham's Observer sound system.

I recorded him using Fashions A Class studio in London, producing songs like 'Tempa' and 'Fire', found on the British MC's Album on GT's Records, alongside **'Crazy Love'** with Fiona Harriott. The production relationship between us was cut short due to the demands that took me outside the UK following the international success of Pato Banton and Tippa Irie.

1, Lucy Tennyson & Grantley GT

2, Lucy Tennyson, Grantley GT and Miss Aliya

However, returning to the business in 2014, I re-recorded Major, collaborating on songs we produced that featured Keziasoul, Miss Aaliyah, Jbeatz0121 and himself. Major was a great help in assisting me with productions I felt were ready for release; what I liked was his straightforward honesty. He didn't mince his words. If he didn't feel it, he would say he didn't feel it. Major assisted me with alerting DJs with up-and-coming releases and sharing emails with DJs he felt would benefit from playing the songs on their shows.

To this end, I can't thank him enough. I was able to offer my assistance to Major regarding becoming social media savvy. I provided him with a breakdown of the benefits of Facebook and Instagram, explaining how essential it was for any artist seeking to become successful in the music industry. I recounted everything I had learnt in six months about the Internet, Facebook, and Instagram to assist him with promoting himself around the areas in which he wanted to become proficient. I thought sharing our knowledge and experience served us well, and to a certain extent, it strengthened our relationship. Consequently, conversations like these enabled me to move forward in a business I had spent 12 years away from.

Development Program for Young Artists and Jazz Café Show 2015

Similarly, when James and I thought we had completed the composition for 'I Love You' and Best of Me'. I played it to Tippa, who said he didn't know if it hit the mark. I also played it to Keith Brown, who felt it sounded old. However, I took both feedback elements on board, returning to the studio the following week and completing a much-improved rhythm that impressed me. Even though I was involved, listening to it, I must agree James wasn't convinced; however, by the time we had changed two or three of the instruments, James was over the moon, and it didn't take long to get to the point where I could represent the rhythm to Tippa and Keith once again. On this occasion, I was happy with the feedback from both individuals, which allowed me to immediately set a date for recording Lucy's vocals for the song 'Best of Me'.

Lucy was shy but had a good tone. Recording Kezia's vocals was an event in which I found I could draw out the best in Kezia, whose voice I would describe as a mix of silk and chocolate. Both songs provided a pathway to My Boyz Beatz and the return of GT's Records to the British Reggae music arena.

Major Popular is an artist capable of unique expressions and quick-witted bars. I have often said that Major's ability could be described as an MC, a host, and a promotor. I am pleased to say that Major has done all three as an accomplished MC. He has hosted many events, notably his own, Four DJs and a Box of Records, which has become highly successful.

He continues to MC mostly with James Crosdale, who, to date, has delivered one of my favourite songs by him called 'Prettiest Girl'. I am so proud of his unique commentary on particular affairs in the current domain.

As mentioned earlier in this book, I had worked as a manager (Engineer) and record producer in the music business and founded GTs Records for over 40 years. However, I was now helping young people explore their musical and professional art ideas. It didn't matter whether or not they were musically gifted or talented. What matters is that they had an interest in the performing arts, acting, singing, and writing areas; however, what was found is that some young people were interested in Dance, and some young people were very interested in singing and rap.

Within the production sessions on the Midnight Bus, I could utilise a laptop computer and interface unit and a Digital Audio workstation to record the young people's ideas and produce a quick MP3 file for them to take away. With the range of talent that came through, it was clear that there was a grey need for work with some of these young people to take place; hence, the opportunity I was now providing separate sessions where these young people could be introduced to the professional world of the music studio and recording.

This was done separately with the agreement of the parents of young people to allow their children to work in capacity with me to coach and produce professionally recorded records. Some young people who came out of this separate development program have recorded some tracks, which are displayed below. Those Artists are Lucy Tennyson, Miss Leah Darshae McKenzie, Mike, Mikey, and John.

These tests have been recognised on significant platforms such as Spotify, Apple Music, Instagram, and TikTok and have received National recognition awards.

Through My Boyz Beatz starting and developing this program with young people, My Boyz Beatz has gone on since 2014 to work with hundreds of national and international solo acts. As a digital marketing consultant, Matt Flint played a crucial role in helping me develop brand awareness. He encouraged me to leverage my background in the music industry to create meaningful value for others who could benefit from my experiences. I vividly recall an engaging conversation with him about the far-reaching influence of reggae. Despite not knowing exactly who the typical reggae fan might be, we concluded that the audience was broad; the key was figuring out how best to present it.

I remember having a long conversation with George Graham, Frank McLintock, Keith Lemon and Stephen Graham about reggae; when they asked what I did, I talked about substance misuse and crime. They showed much interest; however, when I mentioned reggae, their eyes lit up, and they asked me many questions. George and especially Stephen told me they were Tippa Irie and Pato Banton fans. Please see below:

1, Miss Aliya, Lucy Tennyson, Grantley GT & Jbeatz0121

2, Matt Flint, Lucy Tennyson, Grantley GT & Keziasoul

3, Keziasoul, Ashley Walters & Grantley GT

The British Reggae Music Industry. A Windrush Legacy. My Story

1, Grantley GT, Stephen Graham

2, Matt Flint, His Team, Keith Lemon, Will Mellor & Grantley

3, Frank McLintock, Grantley GT and GT George Graham

Traditional Record Companies No Longer Exist

Record companies like the Big Four (Universal Music Group, EMI, Warner Music Group, and Sony BMG) no longer exist as they did years ago. This is related to how people listen to the music they love.

Before the birth of the mp3, there were vinyl and CDs, followed by mp3s and downloads. As said before, Napster, LimeWire, and Kazaa produced a method by which people could download music for free, closely followed by streaming sites such as YouTube, Spotify, iTunes and Apple Music. This wiped out the profit margins that record labels and companies would generally make; however, the big four bought shares in the leading streaming sites, as mentioned previously. Like anything, if you own a proportion of a product or service, you naturally have a vested interest, meaning that, in many ways, you get to shape the trajectory of its development and delivery.

This has also affected the music, film, and high street industries. So, back to the earning potential of record companies, one thousand streams generated on Spotify or YouTube, for instance, will earn a songwriting team between sixty and 90 pence. A new artist may struggle to generate twenty thousand streams and still only achieve the best part of twenty pounds.

These figures skew the vision that most artists have to make a living out of the music industry and, more importantly, record labels with ambitions of becoming large companies.

Independent Artists

Some artists have broken through the glass ceiling and become independent. However, they still need teams to assist with production, mastering, photography, imaging, promotion, marketing, and publicity. These professionals need payments. This means that independent artists must become small record companies wanting to achieve streams above two hundred thousand or more.

The founding of My Boyz Beatz was explicitly geared towards assisting young, talented artists in becoming independent. Their development included music business education, vocal coaching, studio recording, and performing live at clubs and festivals. The first was Lucy Tennyson, with other professional artists who did not need development coaching but were produced by My Boyz Beatz, such as some of those mentioned below.

Lucy Tennyson
Keziasoul
Miss Alyah
Jbeatz0121
Sophia Lee Soul
Dennis Lloyd

Major Popular
Peter Spence
Sandra Cross
Terence Wallen

Chapter 16

Social Media and the Music Industry

Social media and the music industry underwent a significant shift between 1998 and 2001, with platforms like Napster enabling the free exchange of music files. Since the British Reggae Industry began in the 1970s, reggae has often been discussed as a passion rather than a business. Unlike genres such as Pop, Rock, R&B, Grime, and Afrobeat, which emphasise profit and loss, reggae conversations rarely focus on financial aspects outside concert promotion and major record companies. This disconnect between passion and business in reggae is a subject of intrigue.

The Internet started in 1983, Linked-in began in 2003, Myspace in 2003, Facebook in 2004, Instagram in 2010, Snapchat in 2011 and TicTok in 2016. All of the above have, in one shape or another, led to a 'C' in the way people communicate and the way music is currently consumed.

In the past, traditional media was distributed and accessed through television, radio, or print channels. On the other hand, new media is distributed and accessed through digital channels, such as social media, search engines like Google, and email. How we absorb and communicate information and news online has changed drastically since social media was born. For one, traditional media is no longer a one-way avenue of communication: now, consumers can participate in the conversation and influence the news. Social media has also allowed news to be accessed in real-time, for instance, just seconds after a big event happens. Social media can also be used to identify trends and make predictions based on conversations in ways that would need to be done before forking out thousands of dollars on surveys. Lastly, the shelf life of an article or story and its reach has skyrocketed with the help of social sharing techniques.

How Do Young People Get News

The public can now consume news and information on multiple platforms as soon as it happens. Our demand to know what's happening in the news now makes it crucial for news outlets to post on social media, but it's not always the official source that gets to the news first. As we've seen with live events (sports and entertainment), natural disasters and political announcements, social media platforms such as Twitter and Facebook allow the public to contribute to and control the news, reaching a tuned-in audience in real-time, often faster than any traditional news outlet has time to publish a story. Since listeners can curate their news feeds by following specific Twitter handles and Facebook/Instagram accounts, this specified access to immediate news and headlines makes it more difficult for news outlets to reach a large audience and more accessible for consumers to digest the news they want. For instance, as I get into the office each morning, I skim my Twitter feed and click on which headlines grasp my attention. The headline or the tweet is more important than ever to get us to click through to a story. Given this immediate access to headlines and breaking news, our attention span has gotten smaller and smaller, so small, bite-sized content is crucial for brands and outlets to capture their audiences. And now that Facebook and Instagram deliver content based on algorithms that match consumers' interests, it's becoming more difficult for brands and news outlets to guarantee they'll reach their audiences.

Everyone Matters

The most significant effect of social media on traditional media and content is that now everyone feels like they have a voice. Whether through Facebook, Periscope, Snapchat or Medium, social media has provided a public forum for anyone with an opinion. While this has created an overwhelmingly saturated social atmosphere, it has also led to a genuine wave of voices and influencers on social media.

Social media has also proved a valuable tool for marketers to search, track and analyse conversations and trends. PR professionals can use social media monitoring tools up front, utilising social media data to influence PR strategies and report on competitors and public sentiment and engagement following and during a campaign.

Being Seen and Heard

Last, social media is an easy tool for boosting an article's reach. Simply tweeting or posting a link to a story can reach hundreds to thousands of new eyeballs depending on the number of followers, and you will likely encourage others to share the articles, reaching their followers as well. Nowadays, online outlets publish a story and post it on their Twitter feed so that their social followers will click on it (refer back to my earlier statement about finding our news on social media). Quick note: When you're working with a journalist, find out if that's typical practice for their outlet, and be sure to retweet/repost once it's live so that your brand's followers will see the articles as well. There are many ways that social media has enhanced traditional media, and in fact, the two go hand-in-hand now. While you're coming up with your conventional media strategies for your brand, consider how social media can be incorporated for a more creative and ultimately successful campaign, and keep a finger on the pulse of the changing media industry and how social plays into it.

Has The Reggae Music Industry Changed Since the Internet?

The initial stage (from approximately 1998 to 2001) of the digital music revolution was the emergence of individuals listening to music with others via a network that allowed the free exchange of music files (such as Napster).

Since the inception of the British Reggae Industry in the 1970s and where we are today in 2024, most people talk about reggae as a passion, a labour of love or something they love to do. By contrast, when I speak to people in the industry, I very seldom hear people talk about finance, business or management outside of the area of concert and festival promotion and the boardrooms of the big four record companies. I am somewhat mystified that both concepts must be inextricably linked within those conversations. Here is why: if we look at pop, rock, R&B, grime and even the arrival of afrobeat. There is a clear focus on the area of profit and loss.

One clear difference is the package that artists and bands highlighted in the genres above present and the presentation of their reggae counterparts. We can all understand that the birth of the internet presented the entire music industry with challenges, such as the departure of analogue recording studios, tape cassettes, vinyl records, and CDs, as well as the introduction of MP3, downloads, and streaming. Technology has increased, embracing hard disk recorders onto highly developed digital audio workstations such as Logic and Pro Tools (DAWs). What is true is that British Reggae has moved with this change and is not part of my debate.

However, my thoughts focus more on the difference I see in how artists and bands present themselves and their products on social media platforms like Instagram, TikTok, Facebook, and Twitter, as well as those whose genre of choice is reggae. My concerns and fears run deep here because what it suggests is that something is missing.

When I think of social media, I see opportunities first and foremost: free advertising, low-cost baseline promotion, and direct marketing to a chosen audience. A straightforward factor could be seen in photos and videos. Thirty years ago, record companies would have to spend an arm and a leg in photo session costs to develop new artists. Today, with the right apps, it can be done with a smartphone. To put this into context, as of the time of writing this book, Sabrina Carpenter, 'Espresso', Tate McRae, 'Greedy' Kehlani, 'After Hours 'Billie Eilish' 'Birds of a Feather parts of the video were shot with a smartphone. The same applies to Afrobeat with artists like Burna Boy, 'Last Last' Wizkids, 'Essence', and we could go on and on.

The key factor associated with marketing is content. The fact remains for budding artists, especially how creative they can be when generating content. New artists still need great songs; those songs need to correlate with a fanbase to promote or secure bookings, which is where social media and presence occur; why? This is where your loving fans hope to find you; this is where promoters and advertising agents will look for you before they call you directly. It is also worth remembering that these people might be looking for you but come across someone more appropriate for your business. Getting back to the fans, their needs are slightly different but correlate with the business of profit, loss and branding. Whichever side the coins land, followers want to know who you are, what you look like, and what you do.

Most people would describe the key factors for developing a fanbase, which is fundamental for selling products and concerts.

Is Music Production Simpler Now?

The internet has also made it much easier for musicians to produce their music. Thanks to Wi-Fi broadband and faster internet speeds, it is now more accessible to download music production software and work on projects remotely.

For example, a musician can now collaborate with other musicians and producers worldwide without leaving their home studio. Similarly, software such as Pro Tools, Logic Pro X, and Ableton Live has simplified the process of recording and editing music, allowing musicians to do more with less. In addition, shared file storage services such as Dropbox, Google Drive, and iCloud have made sharing files with other musicians and getting feedback on their work easier. This has been a great way to simplify and streamline the process of creating music.

Nowadays, musicians can combine different genres, so it is impossible to identify them apart.

Old songs heavily depended on melody; the composers took their time to create their specific music. Making a new song could take several years. Composers often only take a few hours to compose their latest songs.

Piracy

The internet has made it much easier to combat piracy. Services such as Apple Music, Spotify, and Tidal have drastically reduced the need to download music illegally. These services allow consumers to access an extensive music library at a fraction of the price they would pay to buy an album. This has benefited both consumers and the music industry, as it reduces the amount of piracy and provides a more reliable source of income for musicians.

While the internet has largely been a force for good in the music industry, it has drawbacks. It is essential to understand both the positives and negatives to get a clear picture of the true impact of the internet on the music industry.

Competition

One of the internet's most significant drawbacks is that it has increased competition among musicians. It is now easier than ever for new artists to gain exposure, and as a result, there is an influx of new music. This has made it much harder for musicians to stand out from the crowd and get recognition. Music piracy is still an issue despite the efforts of streaming services. This can harm independent artists, who often need more funds to fight piracy.

People still use Torrents or illegal streaming sites to access music without paying for it, which can significantly reduce an artist's income. This is a significant issue in countries where laws are not enforced, and citizens can access music without paying.

For example, in countries such as India, music piracy is still prevalent and is a major issue for many musicians. This highlights the need to continue fighting against piracy and ensure that musicians are being fairly compensated for their work.

Declining Music Figures

The internet has also caused a decline in album sales as digital music downloads have become the dominant form of music consumption. Many now opt to download individual songs from an album instead of purchasing the entire album. This has caused a decline in revenue for the music industry, as they make significantly less money from digital downloads than physical albums.

Retail Record Shop Closures

The internet has caused many retail music stores to close down. In the early 2000s, music fans flocked to stores like HMV, Our Price, Virgin, chains like Boots, supermarkets in the UK, and Tower Records to buy CDs or vinyl records. However, with the rise of digital music, these stores are no longer necessary and have been closing down worldwide. What was once a huge market has now gone.

This results in unemployment for the employees and financial losses for the stores. It can also hurt the music industry by decreasing physical album sales and revenue.

Loss of Revenue

Finally, the internet has made it much harder for musicians to make a living from their music. Streaming services such as Spotify and Apple Music pay out meagre royalties, making it difficult for musicians to make a living from their music. This has caused many independent and emerging musicians to struggle financially, as they need help to make enough money from streaming services. This has been a major issue for the music industry and still needs to be addressed.

Chapter 17

Music Past, Present and Future

Music has evolved significantly over time. Early 20th-century radio revolutionised the industry by broadening music's reach, giving rise to genres like jazz, blues, and rock and roll. The Internet has made music sharing and downloading easy, leading to widespread piracy. This shift caused a dramatic decline in music industry revenue.

For people like me. Not one day goes by that you haven't heard at least one song on the radio or another device. But what are the differences between the 60s, 80s, 90s, and now music? Music can be like therapy; music has different styles, genres and feelings. But music can also entertain, educate, and inform. Of course, the music in the 60s isn't the same as it is now; there have been a lot of differences over the years.

The "old" music was produced using simple instruments like cello, viola, tuba and trumpet. Of course, there were many other instruments, but these are the most important ones because music and music sales began with sheet music and concerts. Composers like Motzart, Strusse and Beethoven were the pioneers. These days, you can open a computer program and play live tracks or MIDI sounds, and the program will enable you to mix them with or without vocals into something worthy of someone's listening ear. This has led to a new area in music: you don't need a musical education; you only need a feeling for music and the ability to record it. We still use musical instruments, but electronic music is becoming increasingly popular.

Genre

Back then, the genre was apparent to hear and to tell which genre it was. There was either Western or Indian, but not a combination. Nowadays, musicians can fit different genres together, so it is impossible to identify them apart. Old songs heavily depended on melody; the composers took their time to create their specific music. Making a new song could take several years. Now, composers often only compose their new songs for a few hours. This is possible thanks to our current knowledge of technology. While the old songs are a lot better in quality than the new ones, there are a lot of songs of lousy quality, be they old or new. It's up to us what we choose to hear and enjoy.

Music in the 60's

In the 60s, there was a massive rise in popular music styles. In the 50s, rock music began. However, several years later, in the 60s, there were new popular styles, such as jazz, pop, and folk music. Folk music was reborn in the 60's thanks to several performers who wanted to rescue the musical form from what they saw it was. Bob Dylan, Jimmy Hendricks, Mark Knopfler, and Don McLean adopted folk styles. They played simple musical arrangements on acoustic instruments, but the songs were filled with political commentary on contemporary issues. Their songs addressed the problems of the civil rights movement and the Vietnam War. As the decade continued, folk music merged into folk rock as performers used electrified instruments and more sophisticated songwriting. The starters of this genre were Bob Dylan and the group Simon and Garfunkel. However, rock and roll music was dominated by one group: The Beatles.

Music in the 80's

The biggest news about music in the 80's was probably the coming of a television network about music called MTV.

The cable channel soon made the music video very popular and essential. Almost single-handedly, MTV made stars of names we know these days, such as Michael Jackson, Madonna UB40 and U2. It also helped bring rap music to the mainstream. The single best-known performer was Michael Jackson. His 1983 album Thriller, with its singles 'Billy Jean' and 'Beat It', made the former child star a millionaire. Other famous names in the 80s are Whitney Houston, Prince and Bruce Springsteen. Springsteen's song 'Born in the USA' became an alternative national anthem after its release in 1984.

Music in the 20th Century

There was a massive rise in other genres, such as Classical Reggae, Lovers Rock, British Dancehall, Bhangra, Jungle, and Drum and Bass. New bands were formed around this time. We saw the peak of CD sales worldwide. For young kids, a CD (Compact Disc) is a digital optical disc storage device for storing and playing digital audio recordings.

These days, the most popular genres are still classical, country, electronic, jazz, Latin, heavy metal, hip hop, and rock. The most famous artists still make music and are played daily on one of the many radio stations in the world: Taylor Swift, Justin Bieber, The Weekend, Tate McCray, Bruno

Mars, Rhianna, Eminem, Biggie Ed Sheeran, Burna Boy, and Tayla, to name a few.

Enter The 21st Century.

Radio allows music to be broadcast to a broader audience, making it more accessible. This led to the emergence of popular music genres, such as jazz, blues, and rock and roll. The internet has become advanced enough that users can share and download music online. Pirating music no longer demanded dubbing tapes and burning CDs. People could download virtually any song they wanted through file-sharing platforms for free. This caused revenue in the music industry to plummet.

As said previously, the pirates got there first. In 1999, Napster provided a straightforward peer-to-peer file-sharing system that gave users free access to millions of tracks. Technology has transformed the music industry in many ways, including production, making producing music from home more accessible and affordable. Distribution: Making it more accessible to distribute music online. Consumption: Making it possible to listen to music anywhere, at any time, and to create personalised playlists. Social media in the music industry is assisting in the growth and evolution of the industry in many aspects. From allowing access to international audiences at the touch of a button to giving direct engagement between artists and fans, the accessibility social media allows is revolutionising marketing strategies.

For one, traditional media is no longer a one-way avenue of communication: now, consumers can participate in the conversation and influence the news. Social media has also allowed news to be accessed in real-time, for instance, just seconds after a big event happens.

The TikTok algorithm often picks similar-sounding hooks and audio that inevitably go viral, causing a homogenisation of musical tastes. This algorithm may restrict the diversity of music that becomes mainstream on the app and, consequently, into the broader music industry.

The Future, A Hobby or A Business

While the overall effect has been positive, many issues, such as piracy and low revenues for musicians, still need to be addressed. As the internet continues to evolve, the music industry must continue adapting and ensuring that musicians are fairly compensated for their work. By doing so, we can ensure that the music industry remains a viable and vibrant segment for many years.

The music industry is undergoing significant changes, and while streaming has democratised access to music, it has also posed challenges for artists seeking to earn a sustainable income. The future of the music industry will likely continue to evolve around several key trends and opportunities. Here's a look at how artists and musicians can adapt and thrive in the 21st century:

Generating Income and Revenue Streams

Artists and musicians today should focus on diversifying their income streams through digital sales, merchandising, crowdfunding, and educational content. Leveraging platforms like Patreon, streaming services, and online marketplaces is crucial, while NFTs offer new opportunities for selling unique digital assets. Additionally, licensing work for use in media, engaging directly with fans via social media or live streaming, and seeking grants or residencies can provide financial support. Collaborations with brands or other creators and offering exclusive fan experiences also help create a sustainable and resilient income base.

Live Performances and Touring: Even though the COVID-19 pandemic temporarily disrupted many live events, concerts and **tours** remain one of the artists' most lucrative income sources. Unique, immersive live experiences or, more minor, intimate performances can attract dedicated fans.

Merchandise Sales: Selling merchandise online or at live events allows artists to capitalise on their brand. Limited edition items like vinyl limited edition sales, collaborations with visual artists, and exclusive fan club offerings can enhance revenue.

External Funding and Direct Fan Support: Platforms like Patreon, Kickstarter, and Bandcamp allow fans to support their favourite artists directly. Exclusive content, early releases, or personalised experiences can incentivise fan contributions.

Sync Licensing: Licensing music in films, television, commercials, video games, and online content can be a substantial revenue source and help reach new audiences.

Teaching and Workshops: Many musicians have turned to teaching, whether through online platforms, private lessons, or workshops. This not only provides income but also helps in building a community around their work.

Building a Strong Personal Brand

Building a solid personal brand as an artist is essential in today's competitive and interconnected world. A well-defined brand distinguishes you from countless other creatives, making your work instantly recognisable and memorable. It helps convey your unique artistic vision, values, and personality, fostering a deeper connection with your audience. A strong brand can also open doors to more opportunities, such as collaborations, exhibitions, and sponsorships, as it signals professionalism and consistency. In an era where social media and digital platforms are potent tools for self-promotion, having a cohesive personal brand is crucial for gaining visibility, attracting patrons, and ultimately achieving long-term success in art.

Social Media Engagement: Artists who actively engage with their audience on platforms like Instagram, TikTok, YouTube, and X (Twitter) can build a loyal fan base. Regular content that showcases both their music and personality can strengthen fan relationships.

Content Creation: Beyond music, creating content like vlogs, podcasts, tutorials, or behind-the-scenes footage can attract a broader audience and provide additional revenue through ad placements or sponsorships.

Innovative Use of Technology

NFTs and Blockchain: Non-fungible tokens (NFTs) have opened new avenues for artists to sell their work as digital collectables. Blockchain technology can also ensure more transparent and direct royalty payments to artists.

Virtual Concerts and Metaverse: With the rise of virtual worlds and the metaverse, artists can perform in digital spaces, reaching global audiences without geographical limitations. Virtual concert tickets, digital merchandise, and exclusive virtual experiences can become new revenue streams.

Collaborations and Partnerships

Brand Endorsements: Partnering with brands and procuring endorsements, sponsorships, or collaborations can be very lucrative. Authentic partnerships that align with the artist's image resonate more with audiences.

Cross-Industry Collaborations: Collaborating with visual artists, fashion designers, or tech companies can create unique projects that attract attention and revenue from different sectors.

Ownership and Control

Retaining Rights: Artists increasingly understand the importance of purchasing masters and owning publishing rights. This control ensures they receive a larger share of the profits from work they have participated in.

Independent Distribution: Using platforms like Distro Kid, TuneCore, or Bandcamp allows artists to distribute their music independently, keeping a more significant portion of the revenue.

Focus on Niche Markets

Cultivating a Dedicated Fan Base: Artists who focus on niche markets and build a robust and dedicated fan base can sustain their careers even without mainstream success. Niche audiences often provide more consistent support through purchases, event attendance, and direct contributions.

The Future of British Reggae

British reggae music production is declining due to the emergence of streaming platforms and declining sales of vinyl recordings. It can also be forgotten that in direct contrast to the birth of British reggae in the 1970s and terrestrial radio airplay, digital audio broadcasting has completely transformed the world, and the small number of radio stations that played reggae years ago might have something to do with its decline.

Nevertheless, young people have been critical consumers of British reggae since its inception, with trailblazers like Dennis Bovell, Janet Kay, Aswad, Steel Pulse and Maxi Priest. The question has to be asked: Where is British reggae in 2024, and where does its future lie?

British reggae, once a vibrant and influential

genre with global appeal, has undoubtedly seen a decline in mainstream visibility, particularly when compared to its peak during the 1970s and 1980s with iconic bands like Steel Pulse, Aswad, and UB40. Several factors have contributed to this, including changes in how music is consumed, the advent of digital streaming platforms, shifts in audience preferences, and the proliferation of radio stations, many of which offer niche programming that can sometimes fragment audiences.

Reggae, especially British reggae, may need help to compete with the mass appeal of mainstream genres that dominate these platforms. Additionally, the algorithms used by streaming services tend to favour chart-topping, mainstream music over niche genres like reggae, which affects its discoverability.

Radio and Digital Audio Broadcasting (DAB)

As I pointed out, radio has also shifted significantly. In the 1970s, terrestrial radio was a key platform for promoting British reggae, with DJs and sound systems playing a significant role in shaping the sound and visibility of the genre. Digital audio broadcasting (DAB) has increased the number of stations and segments available, but in doing so, it has also dispersed the audience across a broader range of channels. While there are still reggae-specific shows and stations, these are often overshadowed by more commercial music formats, making it harder for British reggae to maintain a prominent place on the airwaves.

The Youth Market

Despite these challenges, British reggae has historically resonated with younger generations. Bands like Steel Pulse and Aswad broke new ground by fusing reggae with local cultural influences and addressing social issues, which attracted a dedicated youth following. While youth still engage with reggae, their tastes have shifted, with newer genres like grime, drill, and Afrobeats gaining more traction in the UK. These genres speak more directly to the contemporary social and political landscape, which British reggae once did in its prime.

Where is British Reggae in 2024?

In 2024, British reggae exists primarily in more underground or niche scenes, though some artists still push boundaries and maintain the genre's legacy. Emerging artists like Amaria BB, Kiko Bun, Lucy Tennyson, Miss Ayliah, Keziasoul, Aleighcia Scott, Jbeatz0121, Claire Angel, Hollie Cook, Haile, WSTRN, SeSe Foster and, of course, Stefflon Don continue to keep the British reggae flame alive, blending traditional sounds with modern influences. Festivals such as 'Rototom Sunsplash', 'One Love', 'City Splash', 'Reggae Land and 'Simmerdown' still offer spaces for reggae to thrive, albeit more as a celebration of nostalgia than a space for genre evolution.

Grantley GT, Holly Cook, Horseman & Tippa Irie

The Future of British Reggae

The future of British reggae likely depends on its ability to evolve and engage with modern musical trends. Fusion with other genres, such as incorporating elements of grime, Afrobeats, or electronic music, could breathe new life into the scene. Reggae's roots in social justice and activism resonate with contemporary struggles, and there's also potential for it to continue thriving in grassroots and independent movements.

However, for British reggae to regain its footing in the mainstream, it will likely require significant media support, including radio and streaming playlists, and a fresh wave of talent willing to innovate while honouring the genre's deep cultural heritage.

Conclusion

The future of the music industry overall will likely continue to see artists needing to be more entrepreneurial, build teams, and leverage a combination of traditional revenue streams and new opportunities enabled by technology. While streaming may not provide a living wage for most, diversifying income, building a solid personal brand, and utilising new technologies will be critical strategies for artists and musicians to sustain and grow their careers in the 21st century.

Chapter 18

Mirrors and Makeup – The Musical

The concept of Mirrors and Makeup aimed to guide young artists into a broader field of performing arts using a professional style of coaching and mentoring. It was hoped that the young people we cast may have chosen the field of acting or musical theatre sometime in the future, using Mirrors and Makeup as a springboard. Rem Conway and I used music from My Boyz Beatz to develop a story and created a program to train young people in this artistic process alongside the challenge to balance dance, acting, singing, and performing roles. This difference in skill requires.

Mirrors and Makeup (The Musical) is one of the most challenging things I have done since entering the performing arts and music area. It's not for the faint-hearted, and directing a musical is not for the faint-hearted, but it can be advantageous.

The concept of Mirrors and Makeup came from wanting to develop young artists into a field where they could, where they probably hadn't done any drama at school, singing, or dancing. Still, I wanted to help them gain experience in a group setting and with guidance from people I knew and those who had done it previously, although there weren't many.

I engaged with a guy called Rem Conway, who, between him and I, worked it out using the music from My Boyz Beatz that we had produced. We could develop a story around those songs. We took it extremely seriously because we created a program to train young people on how to approach casting and the process of being an Artist. They both acted and sang at the same time. This was very challenging for them because, you know, learning lyrics for a song is one thing, but learning lyrics and words for an acting role was difficult for them. You know, you might think that it's an easy thing to do. Still, one of the things we got going is helping them to see their character within themselves. Acting a role that is as the person as closely to who they are as individuals or if that couldn't be developed to put themselves in the position of somebody similar to that was difficult for some of them. We didn't move on from there; we trained them to learn their lines.

1, South & City College 2016 Promo

2, Crescent Theatre 2019 Promo

3, CRE 8 Dancers

This was hard; it wasn't easy for me because the director needed to learn everybody's lines and understand where people came in and out. Rem Conway was excellent because he has done it before. We put exercises in place that stretched all actors, assisting them with concentration and focusing on moving their bodies into positions that would engage the audience more effectively. Facial actions that enhanced the direction of the script. I used a flipchart to demonstrate the blocking I was looking for, highlighting at the same time methods of learning their lines quickly. Because the actors had never acted, I set up a WhatsApp group where I referenced YouTube videos to highlight what I was looking for.

One excellent thing was getting people to work in pairs and groups of three. It assisted them with their lines and, gradually, the entire script.

This was crucial because we had to prepare for the unexpected, knowing we would only sometimes have the whole cast present at rehearsals. Having cast members who could step into someone else's role was essential to managing this.

Cast members were encouraged to learn the whole script, making understanding their cues and those of their co-members more accessible. We were working with two groups of young people, Northfield Youth Service, a group brought together by Wheeler Street. Both groups worked well together, assisting with the movement of props, positioning young people in the right place at the right time and blocking. However, it was tricky because most people had never acted in the field of performing arts and preparing for a performance in front of 400 hundred people.

1, Cre 8 Dancers with Saffron Rosie (Top far right)

2, Cre 8 Dancers at 9th Black Tie Ball

The storyline of Mirrors and Makeup starts with a young girl who could be more confident at school. She achieves this because she is an outstanding singer. However, she doesn't look like an artist or an individual who could develop into a chart-topping vocalist.

The scene is set with famous "top" students in a school or college. A girl engages with one of the top boys, who encourages her to enter a singing competition. She befriends another girl, who seems supportive but is deceitful. This false friend manipulates her, secretly enters the competition, and wins. The girl is devastated by the betrayal, but the boy who helped her initially warns her of the other girl's true nature. Despite facing threats from a school gang, he supports her. Eventually, the girl confronts her fake friend during the competition, revealing the betrayal in front of the judges, who then suggest they sing together.

The script relates to real-life scenarios frequently occurring in the global and British Reggae music industries. The task for any artist or band confronted with such deceit is to reach out to mentors and professionals who are part of the production team and who can handle these issues sensitively in the first instance.

Following the dress rehearsal, the production ran at the matinee in front of a live audience. This proved a beneficial opportunity, as a successful, sold-out turnout and a fantastic performance met the following performance later in the evening.

Elements of Mirrors and Makeup The performance can be found on YouTube, as well as individual recorded singles and albums by My Boyz Beatz featuring cast members Jbeatz0121, Keziasoul, Darshae and Miss Aliya.

Appendix 1

My Boyz Beatz, GTs Records - Digital Release Discography

Lately - 1EYE ft Tippa Irie (My Boyz Beatz Remix)

I've Landed, Empress P -: Digital **Album**

'live' At the Glee Club Birmingham, ft Keziasoul -: Digital **Album**

I Want You, ft Lytie -

Stranger ft Mason Noise -: Digital Single

Perfect, ft Micki & Iked - (Remix): Digital Single

We Need to Talk, Modern Minds -: Digital **Album**

Are You Real ft Jbeatz0121 & Lucy Tennyson) Digital Single

Best of Me, ft Lucy Tennyson Digital Single

I Love You, ft Keziasoul: Digital Single

It Is What It Is, ft Jbeatz0121 & Lucy Tennyson) Digital **Album**

Let's Be Friends, ft Lucy Tennyson, Digital Single

Lift Your Hands, ft Peter Spence): Digital **Album**

"The Reggae Sessions" My Boyz Presents ft Keziasoul Digital **Album**

Triple Riddim Album My Boyz Beatz ft Various Artists Digital **Album**

Baby Boy ft Miss Aliya -: Digital Single

Be Strong ft Lucy Tennyson -: Digital Single

Best Life!! ft Juki Ranks & Jbeatz0121 -: Digital

Blessings in Disguise ft Keziasoul -: Digital Single

Chain Smoker ft Tippa Irie -: Digital Single

Don't Sniff Coke (Live at the Greek Theatre, C.A. USA) Pato Banton and The Reggae Revolution -: Digital Single

Dread at the Mic ft Myki Tuff: Digital **Album**

Emotions ft Lucy Tennyson -: Digital **Album**

Feeling Is Real ft Marcia Mellis -: Digital Single

Four Leaf Clover ft Judy Blu & Sue Brown -: Digital Single

Girl of My Best Friend ft Peter Spence & Tippa Irie -: Digital Single

Good Boy Bad Boy ft Jasonia Johnson -: Digital Single

Gwarn (Live at Irvine Medows, CA, USA) ft Pato Banton and The Reggae Revolution -: Digital Single

Heart & Soul ft Peter Spence -: Digital Single

Huss La ft Juki Ranks & Lucy Tennyson: Digital Single

I Got You: Digital Single

I Love You ft Keziasoul & Tippa Irie (Remix) -: Digital Single

I See ft LXG -: Digital Single

I Will Always Be Your Girl ft Leah Logan, Jbeatz0121 & Juki Ranks: Digital Single

If I Give My Heart to You ft Lucy Tennyson 3 Mixes: Digital Singles

Original Reggae Mix

Acoustic Mix

Dance Mix

If I Give My Heart to You ft Peter Spence -: Digital Single

In Love with My God ft Peter Spence -: Digital

Jah Promise ft Peter Spence -: Digital Single

Jbeatz0121 ft Jbeatz0121: Digital Album

Jennie's Dream ft Jude: Digital Single

Just Like a King ft Jude: Digital Single

Laidback But Serious ft My Boyz Beatz: Digital Single

Lift Your Hands ft Peter Spence -: Digital Single

Love Affair ft Peter Spence -: Digital Single

Love Is the Answer ft Sophia Lee Soul -: Digital Single

Love Is the Answer ft Sophia Lee Soul (Reggae Remix): Digital Single

Love Struck ft Lucy Tennyson & Mason Noise: Digital Single

Memories ft Sandra Cross: Digital Single

Mi Name Sensi ft Myki Tuff: Digital Single

Mind Blowing Decisions ft Peter Hunnigale & Fiona Harriott: Digital Single

Mind How You Step ft Juki Ranks: Digital Single

Mr Tuff ft Mad Professor & Myki Tuff: Digital Single

Mr Postman ft Vy -: Digital Single

Live in the USA & Canada -: Pato Banton & the Reggae Revolution Digital **Album**

My Boyz One Riddim, ft My Boyz Beatz -: Digital **Album**

My Boyz Two & You Riddim, ft My Boyz Beatz -: Digital **Album**

My Only Lover ft Papa Crook & Major Popular -: Digital Single

My Opinion (Live Reggae on the River, C.A. USA Pato Banton & the Reggae Revolution -: Digital

No Coming Back ft Darshae -: Digital Single

Not the Way ft Terence Wallen -: Digital Single

One in Ten ft Peter Spence - : Digital Single

One Love ft Jude -: Digital Single

Operator Yuh FI Rope Een Set Speed Intermede ft Tippa Irie: Digital Single

Operator Yuh Fi Rope Een Set Speed Intermede (Jungle Remix) ft Tippa Irie: Digital Single

Optimistic ft Keziasoul, Peter Spence & Jbeatz0121 -: Digital Single

People Live ft Tippa Irie -: Digital Single

Put the Guns Down ft Jbeatz0121 -: Digital Single

Put the Guns Down ft Jbeatz0121 & General Levy (Drum and Bass Mix) -: Digital Single

Put the Knifes Down ft Jbeatz0121 (Reggae Mix) -: Digital Single

Put the Knives Down ft Jbeatz0121 & General Levy (Drum and Bass Mix) -: Digital Single

Queen's Poundsystem ft Corporal Billy Spice -: Digital **Album**

Reggae Got Soul ft Keziasoul -: Digital **Album**

Running Back to Me ft Sandra Cross -: Digital Single

Say Goodbye ft Jasonia Jonson (Reggae Remix) -: Digital Single

Serious Times ft Johnny2Bad -: Digital Single

Should I ft Peter Spence -: Digital Single

Smokey Blues ft Sandra Cross -: Digital Single

So Whiney Whiney ft Jbeatz0121 -: Digital Single

So Whiney Whiney ft Darshae & Jbeatz0121 (Remix) -: Digital Single

Spotlight Love ft Johnny2Bad -: Digital Single

Story Book ft Peter Spence: Digital Album

Sweetest Kiss ft Lucy Tennyson -: Digital Single

The Beginning - The Vaults ft Peter Hunnigale, Peter Spence, Tippa Irie, Myki Tuff, Vivian Jones, Corporal Billy Spice, Major Popular, Rose Capri, Lytie, Pocket Size, Nerious Joseph Annette B, The Rough House Crew & Fiona Harriot -: Digital **Album**

The Bible, Mad Professor & Myki Tuff -: Digital

The Discussion Riddim My Boyz Beatz Tippa Irie, General Levy, Macka B, Keziasoul, Sophia Lee Soul (Various) -: Digital **Album**

The Grace of God ft Peter Spence -: Digital Single

The Johnny2bad Experience ft Johnny2Bad -: Digital Album

The Mission ft Jbeatz0121 -: Digital Single

The My Way Riddim ft Jbeatz0121, Peter Spence, Keziasoul, Darshae, Sandra Cross, Miss Aliya, Judah, Lucy Tennyson & My Boyz Beatz -: Digital Album

The Singles Sampler, Vol. 1 Peter Spence, Sandra Cross & Lucy Tennyson -: Digital **Album**

The Sound of Soul ft Judy Blu -: Digital Single

The Sunshine Riddim ft Darshae, Keziasoul, Miss Aliya, Jbeatz0121, Major Popular & Lucy Tennyson -: Digital **Album**

The Youths Are Being Hypnotised ft Macka B -: Digital Single

The Youths Are Being Hypnotised ft Macka B (Jungle Remix): Digital Single

Time Fi Di Come Up ft General Levy -: Digital Single

Time Fi Di Come Up ft General Levy & Tippa Irie (Remix) -: Digital Single

Trapped Inside Your Love ft Keziasoul (Acoustic Remix): Digital Single

Twenty First Century Jungle My Boyz Beatz & Exile ft General Levy, Tippa Irie, Macka B, Keziasoul & Jbeatz0121 -: Digital **Album**

UK Dancehall Pioneer ft Tippa Irie -: Digital **Album**

I'll Be There ft Corporal Billy Spice & Peter Spence -: Digital Single

When Will It Stop ft Tippa Irie -: (Original Mix) Digital Single

When Will It Stop ft Tippa Irie -: (Jungle Mix) Digital Single

When You Say You Love Me ft Sophia Lee Soul -: Digital Single

Whisper My Name ft Vy -: Digital Single

Shot Up ft Papa Levi -: Digital Single

I've Got a Praise (My Boyz Beatz Presents) The Projects Digital Album

The Vaults, Vol. 1: Various Artists ft ft Peter Hunnigale, Peter Spence, Samantha, Tippa Irie, Myki Tuff, Vivian Jones, Corporal Billy Spice, Major Popular, Rose Capri, Pocket Size, Nerious Joseph Annette B, The Rough House Crew & Fiona Harriot Digital **Album**

Young Girl ft Johnny2Bad -: Digital Single

Young Entertainers (My Boyz Beatz Presents) ft Modern Minds, Keziasoul, Lucy Tennyson, Miss aliya Jbeatz0121, T'Zion, Lucy Shaw, Darshae, Blaise Duncan, & Maisie Robertson Digital **Album**

Appendix 2

The UK Reggae Charts - British Reggae Music Discography 1974 - 1987

The cottage industry of reggae songs entering the UK national charts began to create a buzz, which led to a demand for the manufacture of reggae records licensed from Jamaica and later the development of the emerging 'Lovers Rock' genre, which began with a British-born singer from London named **Louisa Mark**, with a cover of Robert Parkers, **'Caught You In A Lie'**, reached number one in the reggae charts. Louisa followed it up with, **'All My Loving' in 1975**, **'Even Though You're Gone' and 'Six Street' in 1978** on Safari Records.

In April 1974, the first UK reggae record was sung by a white working-class male singer, Judge Dread, with a song called 'Dr Kitch' on Trojan Records. He was the first British home-grown artist to hit the charts, and he manufactured and sold in record shops throughout the UK.

British Reggae Top 10 Hit Singles and Albums

1974

Judge Dread - Dr. Kitch/Molly - Trojan

Matumbi - Reggae Stuff - Horse

The Cimarons - Over The Rainbow - Trojan

Judge Dread - Big Nine - Big Shot

1975

Louisa Mark - Caught You In A Lie - Safari

T. T. Ross - Single Girl - DIP

T.T. Ross - Take Me Make Me - DIP Aswad - Back To Africa - Island

1976.

Aswad - Back To Africa - Island

Matumbi - After Tonight - Safari

T.T. Ross - Misty Blue - Lucky

Albums

Aswad - Aswad - Island

Singles

The Cimarons - On The Rock - Vulcan

1978

Aswad - Stranger - Grove

Heptics - Natural Woman - D Roy

Tradition - Breezing - RCA

Matumbi - Empire Road - Harvest 12"

Cool Notes - My Tune - Jama

Albums

Matumbi - Seven Seals - Harvest

Singles

Capital Letters - Smoking My Ganja - Greensleeves

Louisa Mark - Six Street - Bush Ranger

15 16 17 - Good Times - DEB Music

Louisa Mark - Six Street - Bushays

Capital Letters - Smoking My Ganja - Greensleeves

1979

Guardian Angel - China Gate - Matumbi

Heptics - Little Girl - D-Roy

True Harmony - Don't Let It Go

To Your Head - Freedom Sounds

16. 15 16 17 - I'm Hurt - DEB

Sonia - Ooh Baby Baby - D-Roy 12"

The Jewells - Love And Livity - Cash And Carry

Brown Sugar - Our Reggae Music - Studio 16

Sister Love - Goodbye Little Man - Cool Rockers

Sonia - Ooh Baby Baby - D-Roy

Cassandra - Sitting In The Park - D-Roy

Barry Brown - Conscious Girl - D-Roy

Sheila Hylton - Breakfast In Bed - Ballistic

Albums

Aswad - Hulet - Grove

Singles

Simplicity - Been In Love - Ital Music Force

Storm - It's My House - Soundoff

One Blood - Sparkle In Your Eyes - Neville King

Matumbi - Point Of View - MR

Sonia - Ooh Baby Baby - D-Roy

Albums

Matumbi - Point Of View - Matumbi

Singles

Janet Kay - Rock To The Rhythm - Arawak

1980

Blood Sisters - What About Me - Sound City

Eargasm - This Is Lovers Rock - Venture

One Blood - Sparkle In My Eyes - Neville King

Papa Levi And Augustus Pablo - Run Come In A De Dance - International Rockers

Treddy Lincoln - If It's Love That You're Looking For - CAM

Paul Dawkins - To Love Someone - Arawak

Papa Levi - Run Come In A De Dance - Rockers

Love And Unity - I Adore You - Studio 16

Investigators - Baby I'm Yours - Inner City

Carmen Barnet - Make It With You - Hawkeye

Investigators - Baby I'm Yours - Inner City

Vivian Jones - Good Morning - Third World

Private I's - Folk Song - Cruise

Storm - Today Is My Birthday - Soundoff

Private I's - Folk Song - Cruise

Rod Taylor - Moving Out Ever - Unity

Rod Taylor - Night In September - Nigger Kojak

Investigators - Baby I'm Yours - Inner City

Charmaine Burnett - Gonna Make It With You - Hawkeye

Albums

Linton Johnson - Bass Culture - Island

Singles

Sonja - Magic Lady - D-Roy

Jackie - Boyfriend - Cha Cha

Albums

Tradition - Runaway Love - RCA

Heptics - Little Girl - D-Roy

Singles

Desi Roots - Weed Fields - Hawkeye

Singles

Alpha - Can't Get Over You - Cool Rockers

Pre-Release 45

Glen Brown - Crisp As A Ball (Assack Lawn) - South East Music

Bionic Steve - Bermuda Triangle - Crystal

Ruddy Thomas - When I Think Of You - Hawkeye

Tyrone - I Need A Woman Tonight - Ambassador

Albums

Black Slate - Amigo - Tcd

Discomix 45

Marie Taylor - I Love You Always - K And K

15 16 17 - I Need A Man - Cha Cha

Pre-Release 45

Archie And Lyn - Rat In The Centre - High Note

Discomix 45

Sadonians - Disappointment - Freedom Sounds

Albums

Misty In Roots - AZ

Discomix 45

One Blood - House Is Not A Home - Neville King

Claire Maclean - Back Together Again - Mobassa

Marie Taylor - I Love You Always - K And K

Ruddy Thomas - When I Think Of You - Hawkeye

Albums

Misty Live - AZ

Pre-Release 45

Rod Taylor - Night In September - Nigger Kojak

Discomix

Blood Sisters - My Guy - Sound City

Discomix 45

Corner Shot - Promise To Love You - CB

Love Structure - Doorway Of Love - De Luxe

Movement - No Man Is An Island - Ballistic

Maria Taylor - I Love You Always - KK

Albums

Misty In Roots - AZ

Black Slate - Amigo - Slate

Pre-Release

Archie And Lyn - Rat In The Centre - High Note

Sister Jan - A Man Like You - Rockers International

Delroy Melody - Mister Brown - Marcus

Captain Sinbad And Little John - A1 Sound - Youth In Progress

Discomix 45

Dee Sharpe - Let's Dub It Up - Fashion

Maria Taylor - I Love You Always - KK

One Blood - A House Is Not A Home - Neville

King

Ruddy Thomas - When I Think Of You - Hawkeye

Pre-Release 45

Earl 16 - Changing World - Rockers

Disco 45

Aswad - Warrior Charge - Island

Carol Thompson - I'm So Sorry - Santic

Investigators - Close To You - Inner City

Albums

Misty In Roots - AZ

Disco 45

Carol Thompson - I'm So Sorry - Santic

Dee Sharpe - Let's Dub It Up - Fashion

Pre-Release

Paulette - My True Love - Solomonic

Disco 45

Aswad - Warrior Charge - Island

Carol Thompson - I'm So Sorry – Santic

Discomix

Investigators - Close To You - Inner City

Janet Kay - Feel No Way - Arawak

Pre-Release

Paulette - My True Love - Solomonic

Angela Prince - My Man Is Gone - Studio One

Lajeune Williams - Hello Stranger - Mandingo

Vincent Marsh - Things Are Come To Bump - Arabic International

Disco 45

Love And Unity - Just Don't Care - Studio 16

Mellow Rose - Imitation Love - Studio 16

Disco 45

Badoo - Rocking Of The 5000 - K & G

In-Crowd - Freak Man - Solid Gold

Albums

One Blood - In Love - NK

Disco 45

In-Crowd - Sweet Man - Solid Gold

Disco 45

Mellow Rose - Imitation Love - Studio 16

Nathan Skyers - Leave Bad Company- - Mandingo

Disco 45

Techniques - Go Away Girl - Techniques

Albums

One Blood - In Love - Neville King

Singles

Desi Roots - Go Deh Right - Hawkeye

Albums

Desi Roots - Doing It Right - Hawkeye

Disco 45

Desi Roots - Go Deh Right – Hawkeye

1981

PRE-RELEASE 45:

Nathan Skyers - Leave Bad Company- - Mandingo

Disco 45

Carroll Thompson - Simply In Love - Santic

Victor Romero - At The Club - Special Request

Simplicity - Loving Kind - Neville King

Jean Adebambo - Paradise - Santic

Albums

One Blood - One Blood In Love - Neville King

Disco 45

Victor Romero - At The Club - Special Request

Albums

One Blood - In Love - Neville King

Disco 45

Love and Unity and Ranking Unity - Put It On - Studio 16

Love and Unity - Just Don't Care - Studio 16

The Albians - Who's Gonna Love Me? - K And K

Carol Thompson - Simply In Love - Santic

Disco 45

Victor Romero - At The Club - Special Request

Albums

One Blood - In Love - Neville King

Disco 45

Victor Romero - At The Club - Special Request

Chosen Few - Love Between A Boy And Girl - Love And Unity

Hugh Porter - Love TKO - Rub A Dub

Simplicity - Loving Kind - Inner City

Albums

Sylvia Tella - Spell - Sarge

Disco 45

Victor Romero - At The Club - Special Request

Chosen Few - Love Between A Boy And A Girl - Love And Unity

Simplicity - Loving Kind - Inner City

Barbara Jones - Just When I Needed You Most - GG (pre)

Chosen Few - Love Between A Boy And A Girl - Love And Unity

Dee Sharp - Follow Your Heart / Swing And Dine - Fashion

Love And Unity - Put It On - Studio 16

Barbara Jones - Just When I Needed You Most - GG

Samantha Rose - Together In Love - Nature

Chosen Few - Love Between A Boy And A Girl - Love And Unity

Family Love - Anniversary - Inner City

Paul Dawkins - One More Step - Arawak

Love And Unity - Just Don't Care - Studio 16

Victor Romero - At The Club - Special Request

Dee Sharp - Swing And Dine - Fashion

Love And Unity - Put It On - Studio 16

Dee Sharp - Follow Your Heart / Swing And Dine - Fashion

Donna Rhoden - Be Kind To My Man - Santic

Aswad - Babylon - Grove

Portia Morgan - Let Me Be Your Angel - Hawkeye

Albums

Aswad - Showcase - Grove

Disco 45

Investigators - Love Is What You Make It - Ice

Donna Rhoden - Be Kind To My Man - Santic

Yvonne Douglas - In The Middle Of The Night - S & G

Erroll Bellot - Babylon - S & G

Carrol Thompson - Hopelessly Without You - S & G

Dee Sharp - Swing And Dine - Fashion

Albums

Aswad - Aswad Showcase - Island

Disco 45

Donna Rhoden - Be Kind To My Man - Santic

Aswad - Babylon - Island

Investigators - Love Is What You Make It - Inner City

Carrol Thompson - Hopelessly Without You - SG

Love And Unity - Can't Let You Go - Studio 16

Sylvia Tella - Spell - Sarge

Investigators - Love Is What You Make It - Inner City

Carrol Thompson - Hopelessly In Love - SG

Carroll Thompson - Hopelessly / You're The One I Love - S&G

Yvonne Douglas - In The Middle Of The Night - S&G

Heather - I'll Always Love You - Mass Media Music

Love And Unity - Can't Let You Go - Studio 16

Samantha Rose - Can't Believe I'm Losing You - Paradise

Donna Rhoden - It's True - Santic

Carroll Thompson - Hopelessly/You're The One I Love - S&G

Yvonne Douglas - In The Middle Of The Night - S&G

Claudia Fontaine - Natural High - JB

The Investigators - Love Is What You Make It - Inner City

Albums

Carroll Thompson - Hopelessly In Love - Carib Gems

Slim Smith - Very Best Of - Stars

Carroll Thompson - Hopelessly In Love - Carib Gems

Disco 45

Lorraine - I've Got To Let Him Know - S&G

Dennis Pinnock - I Want To Be - S&G

DISCO 45

Aswad - Finger Gun Style - CBS

Misty - Peace And Love - People Unite

The Investigators - Summer Time Blues - Inner City

Samantha Rose - Tell Me Why - Live And Love

Black Slate - Sirens In The City - Ensign

One Blood - Show Some Love - Inner City

One Blood - Show Some Love - Neville King

Johnny Osbourne / Aswad - 13 Dead (Nothing Said) - Simba

Simplicity - Waiting - King City

Victor Romero - I Need A Girl Tonight - Epic

Carroll Thompson - Happy Song - S&G

Carroll Thompson - Just A Little Bit - S&G

Jennifer Benjamin - This Feeling's Killing Me - SS

Nia Natty - One Love Style - S&G

Victor Romero - I Need A Girl Tonight - Epic

Instigators - Let's Make Love - Love Bird

1982

Albums

Aswad - New Chapter - CBS

Disco 45

Matic 16 - Jah Hova - Music Hive

Derek Lara - Come On Over - Hawkeye

Carlton And His Shoes - Mood For Love - Fashion

Arema - In Love - City Boy

Janet Kay - You Bring The Sun Out - Black Roots

Papa Face - In A Jamaica Style - Top Notch 10"

Derek Lara - Come On Over - Hawkeye

Charisma - Open Up The Door - King And City

Albums

One Blood - Super Showcase - Neville King

Janet Kay - Capricorn Woman - Solid Groove

Ruddy Thomas - Key To The World - Hawkeye

Victor Romero - Miss Attractive - Epic

Samantha Rose - Go Away Little Boy - Paradise

John McClean And Toyan - Starliner - Musical Lovers

The Techniques - I'll Never Fall In Love Again - Black Joy

Sandra Reid - Ooh Boy - Sir George

Albums

Aswad - Not Satisfied - CBS

Disco 45

Carrol Thompson - Your Love - S&G

Papa Face - Dance Pon De Corner / Girls - Fashion

Musical Youth - Pass The Dutchie - MCA

Albums

The Investigators - First Case - Inner City

Leroy Simmons - At The Dance - NK

Albums

The Investigators - First Case - Inner City

Disco 45

Aswad - Roots Rocking - Simba

Papa Face - Jamming Modeller - Top Notch 10"

1983

Albums

Ruddy Thomas - Very Best Of Ruddy Thomas -

Mobiliser

Jean Adebambo - Feelings - Ade J

Disco 45

Dennis Brown / Aswad - Promised Land - Simba

Aswad - Roots Rocking - Simba

Dee Sharpe - Rising To The Top - Fashion

Investigators - Living In A World Of Magic - Private Eye

Albums

Sandra Reid - If Dreams Were Red - Sir George

Investigators - Living In A World Of Magic - Investigators

Pre-Release

Papa Face / Bionic Rona - Too The Bump - Fashion

Philip Levi - Mi God Mi King - Bad Breath

Interns - Nothing Is Impossible - Reilly

Albums

Aswad - Live and Direct - Island

1984

DISCO 45

Natural Touch - Gimme Good Loving - NK

Philip Levi - Mi God Mi King - Level Vibes

Papa Face/Bionic Rona - To The Bump - Fashion

Albums

Aswad - Live And Direct - Island

Pre-Release

Philip Levi - Mi God Mi King - Bad Breed

Disco 45

Maxi Priest And Philip Levi - Sensi, Mi God Mi King - Bad Breed

Papa Face / Bionic Rona - To The Bump - Fashion

Albums

The Robotics - Massive Rock - A Class

Disco 45

Natural Touch - Gimme Good Loving - Neville King

Papa Face / Bionic Rona - Too The Bump - Fashion

Philip Levi - Sensimilia (Mi God Mi King) - Level

Vibes

Pre-Release

The Robotics - Massive Rock - A Class

Disco 45

Aswad - Chasing The Breeze - Island

Christine Lewin - Juicy Fruit - Kufe

One Blood - Get In Touch With Me - Sound City

Raymond Simpson - Dance In Time - Tads

Disco 45

Aswad - Gave You My Love - Island

Aswad - Chasing For The Breeze / Gave You My Love - Island

Natural Touch - That Funny Feeling - Neville King

Smiley Culture - Cockney Translation / Slam Bam - Arthur Daley Intl.

Sandra Reid - Feel So Good - Sir George

Smiley Culture - Cockney Translation - Arthur Daley Intl

Fenton Smith - Boom It Up - Fashion

Maxi Priest - Throw Me Corn - Level Vibes

Louisa Marks - Hello There - Oak Sound

Cynthia Schloss - As If I Didn't Know - Review

Philip Levi - Bonny And Clyde - Island

Clarence Parks - Gun Man - Atomic Boom

Sir George Posse - Touch A Four Leaf Clover - Sir George

The Investigators - Woman I Need Your Loving - Private Eye

Reprobates - Name That Tune - Fashion

Asher Senator - Abbreviation Qualification / Fast Style Origination - Fashion

Papa Face / Bionic Rhona - Pon The Street / Bubbling Hot - Fashion

Tippa Irie & The Colonel - Just A Speak - UK Bubblers

Peter Culture - Facing The Fight - Ariwa

The Investigators - Woman I Need Your Loving - Private Eye

Papa Face And Bionic Rhona - We're Bubbling Hot / Pon The Street - Fashion

Paulette Tajah - 'Cos You Love Me Baby - Raiders

Barry Boom - Smile - Level Vibes

Aswad - 54, 46 - Island

Paulette Tajah - Cos You Love Me Baby - Raiders Music

Levy Roots - It A Fe Burn - Conqueror

Mikey General - Baby Mother - Conqueror

Smiley Culture - Police Officer / Shan A Shan - Fashion

Philip Levi - Big And Broad - Island

Jean Adebambo - This Will Be - Ade J

Sister Candy - Keep Bubbling - Raider

Fenton Smith / Reprobate - Girl / Take A Tip From We - Fashion

Albums

Aswad - Rebel Souls - Island

Disco 45

The Massive Horns - Merry Melodies - Fashion

Smiley Culture - Police Officer / Shan A Shan - Fashion

Maxi Priest - Should I? - Level Vibes

Aswad - I Need Your Love - Island

The Instigator - Five-O - Shuttle

Albums

Asher Senator And Johnny Ringo - JA To UK MC Clash - Fashion

Aswad - Rebel Soul - Island

Disco 45

One Blood - Running Around - Sound City

Sandra Reid - We Belong Together - Sir George

Paula - Jazzy Lady (Baby) - Rock And Groove

Investigators - Doubts To The Wind - Private Eye

Albums

Aswad - Rebel Souls - Island

Saxon Posse - Coughing Up Fire - UK Bubblers

Disco 45

Tipper Irie - The Best - UK Bubblers

The Instigators – Five 'O' - Shuttle

Danny Dread - Sensi Nice - Marcus

1985

Pato - Allo Tosh - Christie

Albums

In Crowd - Man From New Guinea - Island

Disco 45

Smiley Culture - Entertainer Entertainer / Roots Reality / Cockney Translation - Fashion

Patrick Andy And Aswad - Struggle - Simba

Sandra Cross - Country Living - Ariwa

Natural Touch - Hold Me Tight - Level King

Peter King - Step On The Gaff - Fashion

Janet Kay - Fight Life - Soho

Dennis Gregory - After The Party - Sound City

Horse Man - Horse Move - Raiders

Andrew Paul - Who's Going To Make The Dance Ram? - Fashion

Mikey General - Singer With A Flavour - Jah Life

Macka B - Bible Reader / Huge Mi Huge - Fashion

Natural Ites - Picture On The Wall - CSA

Albums

Maxi Priest And The Caution Band - You're Safe - Ten

Disco 45

Nerious Joseph - Sensi Crisis - Fashion

Pato Banton - The Boss/It Ain't What You Do - Fashion

Tipper Irie - Complain Neighbour - Greensleeves

Outer Limits - Cruising - Sir George

Albums

Maxi Priest - You're Safe - Ten

Disco 45

Nerious Joseph - Sensi Crisis - Fashion

Aswad - Bubbling - Island

Andrew Paul - Who's Going To Make The Dance Ram? - Fashion

Tipper Irie - Complain Neighbour - Greensleeves

Sister Audrey - I Love You - Ariwa

Aswad - Bubbling - Island

Nerious Joseph - Sensi Crisis - Fashion

The Heptics - Spend Some Time Together - Starlight

Albums

Maxi Priest And Caution - You're Safe - 10

Disco 45

Horse Man - Chicken Flap - Magic Shoot

Aswad - Bubbling - Simba

Pato Banton - Mash Up The Telly - UK Bubblers

Albums

Maxi Priest - You're Safe - 10

Pre-Release

Home T-4 And Papa Levi - Dear Pastor - S&R

Disco 45

Lorna G - Gotta Find A Way - Ariwa

Albums

Mad Professor - Captures Pato Banton - Ariwa

Disco 45

Aswad - Bubbling - Simba

Albums

Pato Banton - Mad Professor Captures - Ariwa

Disco 45

Papa Levi - Riot In Birmingham - Island

Lorna Gee - Got To Find A Way - Ariwa

Albums

Jah Shaka And Aswad - Jah Shaka Meets Aswad In Addis Ababa Studios - Shaka Music

Mad Professor - Captures Pato Banton - Ariwa

Disco 45

Sandra Cross - You're Lying - Ariwa

Aswad - Bubbling (remix) - Simba

Asher Senator - Match Of The Day / Asher At The Auction - Fashion

Lorna Gee - Got To Find A Way - Ariwa

Tippa Irie - Telephone - UK Bubblers

Albums

Mad Professor And Pato Banton - Mad Professor Captures Pato Banton - Ariwa

Jah Shaka And Aswad - Jah Shaka Meets Aswad - Jah Shaka Music

Maxi Priest - You're Safe - 10

Disco 45

Tippa Irie - Telephone - UK Bubblers

Smiley Culture - Nuff Personality - Culture

Albums

Mad Professor - Captures Pato Banton - Ariwa

Disco 45

Sandra Cross - You're Lying - Ariwa

Norma Jean - Got To Find A Way - Ariwa

Undivided Roots - Party Night - Entente

Audrey Hall - One Dance Won't Do - Germain

Asher Senator - The Big Match - Fashion

Andrew Paul - Hustle Dem A Hustle - Fashion

Albums

Gussie Prento - Raw Rub A Dub Inna Fashion - Top Notch

Massive Horns - Merry Melodies - Top Notch

Disco 45

Audrey Hall - One Dance Won't Do - Germain

One Blood - I'm A Changed Man - Level Vibes

Just Dale And The Robotics - Until You Come Back To Me - Craze Face

Tippa Irie And Pato Banton - Dance Hall Moves - UK Bubblers

Albums

Steel Pulse - Babylon The Bandit - Elektra

Disco 45

Tippa Irie - Hello Darling - UK Bubblers

Audrey Hall - One Dance Won't Do - Germain

Jean Adebambo - Pain - Now

Albums

Steel Pulse - Babylon The Bandit - Elektra

Pre-Release

Top Cat - Them Haffe Chase Me - Scorpio

Disco 45

Tippa Irie - Hello Darling - UK Bubblers

Maxi Priest - Strolling On - 10

Toyan Adikale - Here I Go Again - Criminal

Bonito Starr - Can't Buy Me Love - Now

Albums

Steel Pulse - Babylon The Bandit - Elektra

Disco 45

Tippa Irie - Hello Darling - UK Bubblers

Maxi Priest - Strolling On - 10

One Blood - I'm A Changed Man / It's A Romance - Level Vibes

Toyan Adekale - Here I Go Again - Criminal Record

Bonito Starr - Can't Buy Me Love - New Generation

Asher Senator - Bubble With I - Fashion

Sandra Cross - It's You - Ariwa

Winsome - Am I The Same Girl? - Fine Style

Albums

The Reprobates - Rubble Dub - Rubble Music

Sylvia Tella - Spell - Sarge

Disco 45

Aswad - Haul And Pull Up - Simba

Pato Banton - Secret Thunderbird Drinker - UK Bubblers

Benjamin Zephaniah - Free South Africa - A&A

Albums

Macka B - Sign Of The Times - Ariwa

The Robotics - My Computer Is Acting Strabge -

Ariwa

Disco 45

Aswad - Haul And Pull Up - Simba

Macka B - Wet Look Crazy - Ariwa

Albums

Macka B - Sign Of The Times - Ariwa

1986

Albums

Macka B - Sign Of The Times - Ariwa

Aswad - To The Top - Simba

The Reprobates - Rubble Dub - Rubble Music

Disco 45

Winsome - Born Free - Fine Style

Michael Gordon - Magic Feeling - Fine Style

Peter Hunnigale - Be My Lady - Street Vibes

Axeman - Africa - Fashion

Albums

Macka B - Sign Of The Times - Ariwa

Disco 45

Sandra Cross - You're Lying - Ariwa

Mikey General - Sound Doctor/Jump & Shout - Fashion

Nerious Joseph - Special Lady/Danger Man - Fashion

Aswad - Kool Nuh - Simba

Aswad - Kool Nuh - Simba

Mikey General - I Say No - Omega

Undivided Roots - Party Night - Entente

Wayne Marshall - Give Me The Mix - Jah Tubby

Nerious Joseph - Special Lady/Danger Man - Fashion

Mikey General - I Said No - MGR

Albums

Steel Pulse - Babylon The Bandits - Elektra

Disco 45

Aswad - Kool Nuh - Simba

Aisha - The Creator - Ariwa

Albums

Mad Professor - Taste of Caribbean Technology - Ariwa

Disco 45

Nerious Joseph - Special Lady - Fashion

Aswad - Kool Nuh - Simba

The Blackstones - Sweet Feelings - World International

Mikey General - Jump And Shout - Fashion

Albums

Steel Pulse - Babylon The Bandits - Elektra

Gussie Prento - Raw Rub A Dub - Top Notch

Natural Touch - Collectors Item - NK Records

Aisha - The Creator - Ariwa

Aswad - Kool Nuh - Simba

Pre-release

Slim Smith - Watch This Sound - Striker Lee

Disco 45

Aisha - Dancing Time - Ariwa

Mother Nature - Short Man - Ariwa

Aswad - Kool Nuh - Simba

One Blood - I'm A Changed Man/It's A Romance - Level Vibes

Aswad - Kool Nuh - Simba

Just Dale And The Robotics - Until You Come Back To Me – Ariwa

One Blood - I'm A Changed Man - Level Vibes

Just Dale And The Robotics - Until You Come Back To Me - Craze Face

Tippa Irie And Pato Banton - Dance Hall Moves - UK Bubblers

Tippa Irie - Hello Darling - UK Bubblers

Jean Adebambo - Pain - Now

One Blood - I'm A Changed Man/It's A Romance - Level Vibes

Jean Adebambo - Pain - Now

Undivided Roots - Party Night - Entente

Michael Gordon - Love Is In The Air - Fine Style

Pre-release

Top Cat - Them Haffe Chase Me - Scorpio

Disco 45

Bonito Starr - Can't Buy Me Love - Now

Toyan Adekale - Here I Go Again - Criminal Record

Bonito Starr - Can't Buy Me Love - New Generation

Asher Senator - Bubble With I - Fashion

Disco 45

Sandra Cross - It's You - Ariwa

Ricky Ranking - Digital Rock - Levy Roots

Maxi Priest - Strolling On - 10

Asher Senator - Bubble With I/I'm The Man - Fashion

Sandra Cross - It's You - Ariwa

Winsome - Am I The Same Girl? - Fine Style

Disco

Maxi Priest - Strolling On - 10

Winsome - Am I The Same Girl - Fine Style

Sandra Cross - It's You - Ariwa

Toyen - Here I Go Again - Criminal Records

Tippa Irie - Hello Darling - UK Bubblers

One Blood - I'm A Changed Man/It's A Romance - Level Vibes

Sandra Cross - It's You - Ariwa

Albums

Macka B - Sign Of The Times - Ariwa

Disco 45

Toyen - Here I Go Again - Criminal Records

Aswad - Haul And Pull Up - Simba

Pato Banton - Secret Thunderbird Drinker - UK Bubblers

Lorna G - Don't Go Crazy - Ariwa

Benjamin Zephaniah - Free South Africa - A&A

Albums

The Robotics - My Computer Is Acting Strabge - Ariwa

Disco 45

Winsome - Am I The Same Girl - Fine Style

Aswad - Haul And Pull Up - Simba

Asher Senator - Bubble Wit I - Fashion

Albums

Macka B - Sign Of The Times - Ariwa

The Reprobates - Rubble Dub - Rubble Music

Disco 45

Aswad - Haul And Pull Up - Simba

Macka B - Wet Look Crazy - Ariwa

Debbie G - You're My Sugar - UK Bubblers

Albums

Macka B - Sign Of The Times - Ariwa

Albums

Macka B - Sign Of The Times - Ariwa

Aswad - To The Top - Simba

The Reprobates - Rubble Dub - Rubble Music

Disco 45

Macka B - Wet Look Crazy – Ariwa

Disco 45

Maxi Priest - Crazy Love - 10

The Administrators - Hand Clapping Foot Stomping Music - Groove And A Quarter

Winsome And Nerious Joseph - Rock With Me Baby - Fine Style

The Natural Ites - Lately - Realistic

Barbara Jones - Please Mr Please - Charm

Debbie Glasgow - Knight In Shining Armour - UK Bubblers

Barry Boom - Come Follow Me - On Top

Peter Hunnigale - Fool For You - Street Vibes

Albums

Maxi Priest - Intentions - 10

Sandra Cross - Country Living - Ariwa

Andrew Paul and Mikey General - Sound Boy Burial - Digikal

Asher Senator - Born To Chat - Fashion

The Investigators - First Case - Inner City/Private Eye

Jacob Miller - Each One Teach One - Rockers

Disco 45

Winsome - Homebreaker - Fine Style

Aswad - Hooked On You/Gimme The Dub - Simba

The Administrators - Hand Clapping Foot

Stomping Music - Groove And A Quarter

Albums

Maxi Priest - Intentions - 10

Mikey General & Andrew Paul - Sound Bwoy Burial - Digikal

Investigators - First Case - Private Eye

Disco 45

Maxi Priest - Let Me Know/I Dream - 10

Winsome - Home Breaker - Fine Style

Nerious Joseph - No One Night Stand - Fine Style

Aswad - Hooked On You/Gimme The Dub - Simba

Joseph Cotton - No Touch The Style - Fashion

Albums

Undivided Roots - Ultimate Experience - Entente

Disco 45

Senior Sandy - Public Enemy Number One - Saxon

Aisha - Prophecy (Vocal) - Ariwa

Joseph Cotton - No Touch The Style - Fashion

Albums

Undivided Roots - Ultimate Experience – Entente

Joseph Cotton - No Touch The Style - Fashion

Ernest Wilson - Promise Me - Techniques

Maxi Priest - Let Me Know - Ten

Judy Boucher - Can't Be With You Tonight - Orbitone

Nerious Joseph - No One Night Stand - Fine Style

Mikey General - Kuff'n Dem - Digikal

Conrad Crystal - True Love - Legal Light

Janet Kenton - Don't Stay Away - High Power

Disco 45

Maxi Priest - Woman In You – 10

1987

Disco 45

John McClean If I Give My Heart To You - Ariwa

Maxi Priest - Crazy Love – 10

The Administrators - Hand Clapping Foot Stomping Music - Groove and A Quarter

Debbie Glasgow - Your My Sugar – UK Bubblers

Winsome and Nerious Joseph - Rock With Me Baby - Fine Style

The Natural Ites - Lately - Realistic

Debbie Glasgow - Knight In Shining Armour - UK Bubblers

Barry Boom - Come Follow Me - On Top

Peter Hunnigale - Fool For You - Street Vibes

Winsome - Homebreaker - Fine Style

Aswad - Hooked On You/Gimme The Dub - Simba

The Administrators - Hand Clapping Foot Stomping Music - Groove And A Quarter

Deborah Glasgow - When Somebody Loves You Back

Maxi Priest - Let Me Know/I Dream - 10

Winsome - Home Breaker - Fine Style

Nerious Joseph - No One Night Stand - Fine Style

Aswad - Hooked On You/Gimme The Dub - Simba

Senior Sandy - Public Enemy Number One - Saxon

Aisha - Prophecy (Vocal) - Ariwa

Joseph Cotton - No Touch The Style - Fashion

Maxi Priest - Let Me Know - Ten

Judy Boucher - Can't Be With You Tonight - Orbitone

Nerious Joseph - No One Night Stand - Fine Style

Janet Kenton - Don't Stay Away - High Power

Joseph Cotton - No Touch The Style - Fashion

Maxi Priest - Woman In You - 10

Lloyd Brown - Sharing The Night

Roger Robin - More Love -

Sweetie Irie & Joe 90 - New Talk

Peter Spence & Tippa Irie - Girl Of My Best Friend - GT's

Private Collection - Slow Down

Ciyo - Jazzy Mood For Love

Macka B - Proud of Mandella

Pure Silk - Do You Ever Think About Me

Barry Boom - Number One Girl

Junior Dan & General Levy - You Can't Hurry Love

Wendy Walker - Gone She Gone

Leroy Mafia - Finders Keepers

Peter Hunnigale - Falling

Peter Spence - Don't Leave Me Lonely - GT's

Anette B - Fairy Godmother

Kofi - Stand By

Nerious Joseph - I Need Your Loving

Sweetie Irie - Magga Man

John McLean - Never Risk Losing Your Love

Macka B & John McLean - Gone Home

Macka B & Kofi - Dread A Who She Love

Barry Boom - Hurry Over

Sandra Cross - Don't Leave Me Now -

Peter Spence - I Believe Love -

Vivian Jones - The Hurt

Private Collection - Direction

Albums

Maxi Priest - Intentions - 10

Sandra Cross - Country Living - Ariwa

Asher Senator - Born To Chat - Fashion

The Investigators - First Case - Inner City/Private Eye

Investigators - First Case - Private Eye

Testimonials

Keith Brown - Business Partner, Chair Wheeler Street Young Entertainers and Entrepreneurs in Action and Area Catering Manager - *"My name is Keith Brown, and I am one of Grantley Haynes's best friends. I've had the distinct pleasure of knowing Grantley Haynes for over 45 years and can say without hesitation that he embodies the qualities of a loyal friend and exceptional individual. Grantley's unwavering integrity, thoughtfulness and infectious enthusiasm make him a joy to be around and someone you can always count on.*

Grantley attended Lea Mason Secondary School, and I attended St Albans C of E Secondary School. Then, we had the Highgate Park situation between the two schools.

My first memory of Grantley was whilst playing in Highgate Park I would see him cut across the park from time to time, and he knew some of the friends I was out playing with. I was also aware that he was the boyfriend of one of my school friends, a sister who attended my school. Even though we did not speak, based on the small geographic district, I knew his face and no doubt he knew mine based on our neutral acquaintances and our attending the same social spaces in the area.

I recall Grantley having a disco set GT 600, played at a community centre just off Edward Road, Balsall Heath, and the Earl Grey pub in the same district. What was unique for me was Grantley. He was the first black man I knew who had such a neat, tidy-looking disco set like this. I'm sure he also had disco lights and played some softer music, which at the time was strictly reggae.

When I left school in the summer of 1979, my first job was working for Trust House Forte Group, which led to my going to Garretts Green Catering College (one-day release per week).

Towards the end of my 4-year course, Grantley started to attend the same college I'm sure he said he returned to complete his catering certificates as he had stopped doing to attend work the first time around. These days, I used to catch the number 17 bus into the city centre, and if Grantley saw me at the bus stop, he would give me a lift to the Highgate area in his van. Somehow, we hired Grantley and his van to move our local, small sound system, Celestial City Hi-Fi.

I went to a gig with Pato and his band, and I remember Grantley doing everything, including driving the van. I offered to help support him and take the van away from him. Grantley accepted, which was the beginning of our long-standing friendship and professional relationship.

It was Grantley who encouraged me and gave excellent advice to go into adult further education, pursue the NEBS Supervisor course and gain a supervisory qualification (I'm sure Grantley had already done these certificates) to progress out the kitchen and into *catering management and, significantly progress up the management ladder and earn more money. This led me to complete a 3-year HNC Catering Course and attain the necessary qualifications at the College of Food to enable me to move into catering management.*

After driving the van, I assumed the position of road manager for the artists Grantley worked with. We shared an ambition of making it big in the music industry, attaining financial success, and turning our passion into a full-time career with the ultimate goal of leaving behind the constraints of a regular nine-to-five job.

Over the forthcoming years working with Grantley, he has given me the grateful opportunity (which at the time lots of individuals would seek after) to share numerous enjoyable adventures and, more importantly, as a valued friend in the UK reggae music industry, which with gratitude has also personally taken me to USA, Africa & Europe. I gained various people skills, business acumen, and valuable knowledge from working with them, which has contributed to my being the person I am today.

Opposite to me, Grantley is outgoing, has a presence about him, is comfortable in any given setting, and can enter and light up any room or space. Grantley has an incredible ability to make those around him feel valued and appreciated. He listens intently, offers counsel, and never fails to bring a positive outlook, even in the most challenging situations. His empathy and kindness have touched the lives of everyone fortunate enough to know him.

Our journey together through the reggae scene has been filled with unforgettable moments, from late-night studio sessions to iconic performances. Still, I concentrate on Grantley's unwavering strength of character, which stands out most. Upon reflection, even I questioned Grantley's foresight and vision at the time, but now they have undeniably been proven to be critical works of greatness and have stood the test of time. I am honoured to call Grantley my friend, and I am grateful for the opportunities and countless ways he has enriched my life.

His enterprising spirit is driven by his deep understanding of the music industry and commitment to creating positive change. Throughout the years I have known him, Grantley has demonstrated a remarkable eye for an opportunity to develop innovative business ventures that, in some cases, still thrive today. These ventures offer opportunities and more fundamental life skills for me.

I am compounded by his undeniable love and dedication for his two sons. Grantley is an incredible father. He is always there for them, offering guidance and support or being a constant source of love and laughter. Grantley is a devoted, loving father to his children. His dedication extends beyond his sons. Grantley is equally committed to his grandchildren, sisters, and mother, always showing up with the same level of care, respect, and love. He's the kind of man who puts his family first, no matter what, and that speaks volumes of his loving, reliable character, which is truly inspiring.

Standing by Grantley as his best man for his wedding was both an honour and a privilege, one that reflects the deep bond we've built over the years of friendship and shared adventures in life. Grantley is not just a remarkable individual; he's my dependable, loving brother in every sense of the word, someone whose loyalty, kindness, and integrity have made a profound positive impact on my life.

Knowing Grantley's commitment to his projects, and naturally, I'm experienced or know of most experiences Grantley is about to tell, I am genuinely looking forward to this completed body of work. In my opinion, Grantley has consistently underplayed and underestimated his contribution to the UK reggae industry. Grantley's passion for the subject is evident, and I can say with confidence in his book that he will capture the essence of a vibrant and influential music scene when at its peak. Grantley has lived and breathed the very stories he will so eloquently captures, offering readers an insider's perspective that is as authentic at it is insightful. His story will educate and immerse the reader in the unique riddims and stories of reggae in the UK.

For me, he's just Grantley, or "G," as I like to call him, and consequently, despite his well-earned celebrity status, I treat him as such.

I'm so pleased Grantley is taking this opportunity to record his valued version of his significant role in the UK reggae industry.

Grantley is a person of immense musical talent and dedication. He approaches every task with an elevated level of commitment and passion that is truly inspiring. His work ethic and cheerful outlook make him a standout in any endeavour he undertakes.

We still work on various projects together, including my favourite Wheeler Street Young Entertainers and Entrepreneurs, which we enjoy, get me away from work, and contribute to my personal well-being. Long may these business opportunities continue.

I could not ask for a better person to have by my side through life's journey." - **Pato Banton – Minister, Author, International Musical Artist and MC**

"I have known GT since I was 16 years old. He was not

like the other youths in my community. He was friendly but mostly thoughtful, disciplined and focused. It didn't take me long to realise that he was an intellectual with a solid vision to achieve big things in every avenue of life.

Our shared love of music eventually united us as friends, and GT was always willing to offer a helping hand to anyone he thought worthy. He taught me not to waste too much time on "time wasters", to "think about the future", to "try and save something for a rainy day", and to "never stop learning!" He also helped me learn how to drive, set up a bank account and many other lessons relevant to my practical progress in life.

It was after a major concert in London hosted by David Rodigan when I was a new artist performing with many leading reggae acts, where GT strategically helped to "steal the show" when I was called back to do another song at the end of the night. I had to decide quickly on which song to perform, and GT told me to perform a song I had just written called "Allo Tosh Gotta Toshiba?" I was approached by two management companies and three labels who wanted to sign me immediately! On the drive home, I asked GT what I should do, and he said, "I'll manage you." I laughed so hard at first, but when I realised, he was serious about taking responsibility for my career, I agreed, and together, we made history.

I could go on and on and on, but I will say that GT helped Tippa Irie and me establish our names and tour around the world. He negotiated significant record deals for me and helped produce my most successful album (Never Give In). He deserves the title "Manager, Brother & Friend" because he was always concerned about my life, not just "the business."

I don't know a lot, but I do know that whatever GT puts his mind to, he succeeds.

One Love Always" - **Tippa Irie – Author, International Musical Artist and MC**

"Well, what can I say about Grantley Haynes?

Grantley is a very hard-working, ambitious, and great manager. He has been a friend of mine for over 30 years. GT knows how to take care of and appreciate his clients. He's very reliable, trusting, hard-working, and thorough in everything he does about his clients.

GT knows how to get the best out of his clients by pushing them, encouraging them & appreciating their opinions.

Grantley is an excellent negotiator & I rate him highly. 10/10.

When it comes to strategies & creativity, I also have a 10/10.

He is ice-cool when operating under pressure and very good at handling situations when most people are flustered. Grantley is excellent at dealing with the matter. On many occasions, Grantley has gone above and beyond his duties & delivered beyond all expectations. I highly recommend GT, as he is excellent at what he does.

Much Respect!"

Peter Spence – Professional Vocalist – *"My name is Peter Spence. I have known Grantly Haynes for 30 years, serving as a Manager, Mentor, and Friend.*

Grantley managed the beginning of my music career from 1984 to 1996 and then 2014 to 2016, in between he left the music business to carve out a very successful career with the NHS, rolling out new initiatives across the city and nationally. This, in turn, has led to him creating "The Wheeler Street Project", where he and his team work with and engage with young people who may be affected by drug abuse, gangs and problems within the education system.

During my early years in the music business, Grantley mentored, encouraged and supported me. Gaining me great signing deals with, for example, Island Records. Plus, supporting me through the nurturing of my children, as I was a young father with difficulties that created.

Having returned to the music business and managing my career again, he is now multi-faceted with a considerable knowledge base. I am now privy to Grantly's extensive work with young people through music projects (GTs Records) and One-to-one mentoring (Wheeler Street Project).

While still maintaining projects with other agencies, e.g. West Midlands Police, Local Authority, etc., Grantley manages a successful Record & Management Company where he nurtures new talent. As well as managing my career, he has encouraged me to create my charity where we can work in partnership to create more opportunities for our young people in the community.

Like his father before him, Grantley Haynes is integral to our community. He maintains and encourages high standards and integrity and is an excellent example of Pro-Social Modelling to all who come into contact with him through his work and personal life.

Have a Blessed Day"

Sandra Cross – Professional Vocal Coach and Vocalist – *"I've known Grantley for over 30 years.*

I can only describe him as a rock in desolation and despair. I had ups and downs throughout my career, especially with the industry's business side. Grantley seemed to 'pop' in and out more or less at the correct times, always ready to give meaningful and valuable advice. He has a high level of understanding, interest and concern for artists. He can develop and improve any situation. He has always been a part of my journey – in every way.

His return to the music industry is a must and a blessing, especially for me. I count myself extremely lucky to be a member of his camp. Each day I rise, I feel his tremendous trust and belief in me, which, in turn, gives me the encouragement and courage to excel in this harsh and unpredictable industry.

I will always be grateful…..Thank you, Grantley..x"

King Zukie – Master Blaster – Luv Injection Music – *"I first met Grantley with my best friend, Corporal Billy, when we were part of the tremendous young sound system of the 1980s. We called ourselves MastaBlasta. I'm sure this was about 1984. At this point, MastaBlasta played out at various events seven nights a week. Grantley was looking for new local talent, and he had heard MastaBlasta had a young, raw set of talented individuals he was looking for.*

Later, we had a meeting at his flat, which was his office in Lea Bank, Birmingham. From the get-go, the team and I warmed to Grantley he understood our aims and goals, which matched his own. After the meeting, Billy and I agreed that this was an excellent opportunity for our team to be part of. From that day forward, it was agreed that Grantley would manage and inspire our sound system, "MastaBlasta."

Grantley orchestrated numerous events with other promoters and ensured we were on premier events around the UK. Grantley is a great motivator and got the best out of MastaBlasta as a team, including Corporal Billy, Stylee, Bongo D, Junior Dan, and Judah Lickshot. Grantley always ensured that Mechech, Beaver Militant, the selectors and I always had the latest releases.

One of the critical aspects of MastaBlasta was our unwavering commitment to sound quality. The microphone stage had to be crystal clear with various singers and DJs. This dedication to quality allowed us to provide sound for renowned artists such as Sophia George, Nitty Gritty, and many more, cementing our reputation as a top-tier sound system.

One of our most memorable events was the DJ clash at Maximilian Night in Birmingham. Under Grantley's management, the entire team delivered a performance that left the crowd buzzing. The sound was impeccable, and the event was a resounding success, solidifying MastaBlasta's status as a champion sound of the 80s.

Grantley, who also managed Pato Banton and Tippa Irie, saw them both have their hit singles

Pato Banton with "Allo Tosh, and Tippa Irie with "Hello Darling," this made them both household names, which left Grantley with less time with us and more time with them.

However, he still found time to release various albums and singles with Corporal Billy and others from Birmingham. He had an eye for talent and knew when a young artist had what it took to progress to be an international artist.

I have a great deal of respect for him and his team, who showed me a lot of behind-the-scenes information and how to be the best version of myself."

Don Kilbury – Former Road Manager and Territory Sales Manager USA – *"I first met Grantley Haynes in May 1, 1987, at a Reggae Festival on the campus of California State University, Northridge. He was managing Tippa Irie and Pato Banton, the show headliners.*

I was the Concert Coordinator and a member of the Student Productions and Campus Entertainment (aka SPACE) committee, the show promoters. We had a sellout crowd that night, and the performance was terrific!

From this first encounter, I took notice of GT's abilities and skill sets in managing all the logistical aspects of a live concert event, including stage, sound, lights, and talent. Soon after this first show together, he offered me the opportunity to work with him as a Road Manager and a part of his management team.

Over the years, our working relationship has grown into a life-long friendship. GT and I have been blessed to share many beautiful weddings and family gatherings together. Although we are separated by over 5300 miles between Southern California, USA and Birmingham, UK, I've always viewed my friendship with GT as a gift.

Grantley Haynes, in a word...Brilliant.

GT has the extraordinary ability to see the potential greatness in a person, regardless of how that individual may view themselves.

His Strengths:

- *A strong sense of organisation and planning.*
- *Vision for long-term project development.*
- *A natural aptitude to coach and mentor.*

These are his critical attributes for producing and managing talent with maximum potential for long-term growth and successful outcomes."

Rankin Bev – Teacher and Personal Assistant – "I have known Grantley for 40 years; we first met around 1985 when I was a DJ on a local radio station in Birmingham called PCRL. We became firm friends. At *the time, he managed internationally known reggae artists like Pato Banton, Peter Spence, Tippa Irie, and others. I became his assistant, helping to run his office while he was overseas managing tour dates for his artists.*

Grantley's management skills are on point; he has an eye for spotting talent and putting it on the right track for success. I would say there is nothing he does not know about this industry. From working with Grantley and knowing him personally as a friend, I have found him to be a very hardworking, determined, and no-nonsense professional who always aims high. We have maintained a warm friendship over the years. He has always been encouraging and has imparted good advice.

In 2018, my children participated in his theatre production, 'Mirrors and Makeup,' where he used his skills to empower youth through music. He later became my daughter's and niece's vocal coach when they decided they wanted to sing, giving them an insight into what a music career would look like.

As someone who has had the privilege of knowing Grantley professionally and personally for so long, I can confidently say that this book reflects his deep industry expertise and his genuine passion for nurturing talent and fostering creativity. With a formal yet accessible approach, Grantley offers readers a rare glimpse into the challenges and triumphs of managing artists, making this an essential read for aspiring music professionals and seasoned veterans. I have nothing but the utmost respect for him.

But one thing to add—he does not like to lose, so don't take him on in a dance battle. If you win, he'll try to take you on again to gain that victory for the next 35 years!"

Joycelyn St Juste – Personal Assistant and Senior Collage Tutor – "*Grantley Haynes, aka GT in the music industry, is a man who came from a humble background but aspired to do great things in his life. Grantley is well known in the music business as a record producer and manager of reggae artists such as Pato Banton, Tippa Irie, and Peter Spence. His love for reggae music was demonstrated in the recording studios time and time again. Through his determination, hard work and commitment to what he loved doing, Grantley made household names of reggae artists like Pato Banton and Tippa Irie, to name just a few.*

During my time working with Grantley as his personal assistant (PA), I found Grantley to be inspiring and encouraging, always willing to allow someone to be the best that they could be. Grantley did not suffer fools kindly and always operated with a kind heart and a mindset of being excellent in whatever he put his hand to. Not only did Grantley become one of my closest friends, but he was also a great mentor, showing me the management aspects of the music business (putting together contracts and riders for performances both local and abroad, dealing with the requirements of the artists and keeping track of the finances).

Grantley's success in the reggae music industry has been attributed to his passion, drive, and 100% commitment to something he loves, which is inherently a part of who he is."

Sue Brown - Poet & Broadcaster – "Although I have known Grantley for several years, it is only recently, while working together on his latest {books}, that I have come to appreciate his vast but sometimes understated experiences of identifying strengths, talents, challenges, and personal support needs in others.

Grantley also loves his work and his engagement with others, which is evident through the competent, genuine strategies and care he presents, enabling others to gravitate naturally toward him because they see authenticity in his actions, a collection of experience, and a quest for personal development which constantly strives for the best outcomes.

The Reggae industry, especially the British Reggae industry, has significantly benefitted from Grantly's contributions, collaborations, dedication, and commitment, adding to the great wealth and richness of the music and culture.

I feel that Grantly has honed these trusted skills, including a sense of self, patience, and empathy, from the guidance he'd experienced growing up around his loving, practical, and caring family and from the creative, dynamic, vibrant attributes of his Caribbean heritage and community. Gwan, Grantley... continue to share your reality and overstandings while documenting and contributing to the story and the Bigger Picture! Respect..."

Little Ritchie – Professional DJ - *"Grantley Haynes, aka GT,*

1st met GT back in the 80s when he was working with Tippa Irie, Pato Banton, Peter Spence & many other great artists,

GT would call me up & we would go around to his recording studio & he would ask my advice (being a radio presenter & DJ) on the tracks he was producing. Hopefully, I gave him the right advice lol,

I knew from then GT had a real passion for his work & valued other people's opinions; not only did GT take advice, but he would also offer sound advice.

GT & I lost touch for a few years while he went on to achieve many different things while I stayed in the music business. I am pleased to announce that GT has now returned to his rightful place in the music industry, producing some excellent music with My Boyz Production Team also doing

& creating tremendous opportunities for young people to get involved in music recording & performance as his management skills come in to play like a true professional.

I had an idea to set up a youth urban internet radio station in Birmingham, UK. I was pleased that GT and The Wheeler Street Young Entertainers in Action agreed to work alongside me to support young people with meaningful opportunities with training in broadcasting and radio.

GT is a person who will always talk his mind, he doesn't leave any grey areas, he is serious about his business & takes care of it & the people who are around it,

GT has always had time for me, even when I was just a teenager 1st starting in my radio career; he has always treated me equally with respect & manners,

GT is not just a business colleague; he is a real friend whom I believe I could trust with the most sensitive information or situations,

GT is a genuine man who will always have time for you; he is very caring and emotional & has a BIG heart; he truly understands & cares,

GT Is like a big brother to me & I wish him all the best in life & may God bless him with all the blessings he deserves."

Major Popular MVP – Professional Promoter, Host and MC – *"Another Top-Class studio session and production with Grantley GT Haynes. Although GT felt unwell, he still managed to record excellent vocal delivery before admitting himself to the hospital. When asked why you didn't stop and cancel the studio session, he replied that you sounded "great," so I had to get the vocals recorded first.*

Thanks, G! For your time, guidance, vision & dedication. Always getting that little bit more out of everyone when we think there's nothing left to give!

Truly professional, looking forward to working on the next project!

Positive Vibrations"

Jasonia Johnson – Vocalist and Teacher – *"If music is the food of love, play on! - William Shakespeare*

My discovery of art was found on the 25th of July 2010 at approximately 00:52. I know this is accurate, but it's true. I wouldn't even call it a discovery because my love for art has existed since childhood. However, that date and time were when I realised I would begin to express my art for all to see, hear, listen, and feel. It was then when Grantley Haynes joined me on this journey, with his hand reaching out and guiding me toward many more realisations. Lucky for me, I've had him in my life since 1994. The beauty of being family! He was very impressed with my writing skills and began helping me to further them. He introduced me to his studio, which at the time was in a small box room within his home; we would record many of the poems I had written, and he would give me pointers on delivery and maximise my mind even more, to enable me to write even more! This was a huge confidence builder for me as it helped me pluck up the courage to approach him and supply him with the information that I was not a writer but a singer, too.

I remember this memory from yesterday; my father and Grantley sat in my auntie's living room. I remember before approaching him, I turned to my father and asked for his approval on whether he genuinely thought I could sing, to which he said "yes" with that Grantley Haynes told me to sing something, there and then, on the spot! I was very shy to do so, but he explained to me how he would he or anyone else know I could sing if I didn't show anybody. With that, I began singing, and he told me I had a "voice", but this voice needed some work!

Growing up, he would always be on the scene introducing different types of music to my ears, from Jagged Edge to Michael Jackson to many,

many more other artists. The list goes on…

I have been working with Grantley since the age of 15. He has many, many vital strengths. One that sticks out for me is the ability to peel an onion! I say this because no matter how complex or closed an individual is, Grantley can always look into that human being. Unleashing their qualities that they may not have even acknowledged they had. He doesn't start anything he can't finish, and he believes in change; he's a man who believes in second chances. There have been many times when I have doubted myself and have found it hard to face some of the life experiences I have been forced to go through, but he never withdrew himself from being by my side, speaking to me with great depth and helping me to understand the bigger picture; with the world and most of all myself.

He has helped towards the gain of my wisdom and the improvement of my music. I have to hand it to Grantley; regardless of how busy he is, he will do his best to keep everyone from noticing. He believes in balance and harmony, which allows him to work well under pressure. For instance, when doing my studio sessions, I never felt rushed. However, this does not mean that targets are not met. Whatever targets have been discussed to meet beforehand, I assure you they will be achieved by the end of the process.

In all, this guy is what you call 10/10. He thinks outside the box, going far and beyond his duty.

He is the bigger picture; If you see 50, he sees 5000 a true investor."

Michael Jordan—Friend – *"I have known Grantley for a very long time. We have been childhood friends. Our respective parents were friends when they arrived in England from Barbados in the late 1950s. They are now known as the Windrush Generation.*

Grantley has always been ambitious and focused on his ambitions. As friends, we grew up with a keen interest in music, mainly reggae, dub, soul R&B, etc. Grantley would travel to various places in the UK to source music of multiple genres. We were both attached to a sound system growing up in Balsall Heath. The sound system, namely Duke Wally, became very popular in Birmingham and surrounding areas, mainly due to sound clashes in the Midlands area. This was when he started being a mobile DJ named 'GT 600 Roadshow.'

Aside from his music interests, Grantley also attached himself to various youth centres, doing voluntary work with young people. This is where I knew Grantley to be a very influential and hard-working person who would earn great respect for his voluntary work, which would become his passion. Grantley later became a highly qualified professional in this industry, so he now shares his experience through the books above.

Grantley became a promoter of various dancehall events and continued to manage well-known Reggae Artists such as Tippa Irie, Peter Spence and other prominent local artists. Grantley is a very well respected, talented, and experienced producer of some extraordinary young artists travelling to various parts of the world."

Dennis Hamilton - School Friend and Retail Entrepreneur HAT MAN Birmingham *"The first time I met Grantley was in a technical drawing lesson at Lee Mason Secondary School on my first day in the mid-70s. I was fourteen years old at the time, new to the school, and trying to settle into the new environment.*

When I first saw Grantley, he was a very smartly dressed young man with well-polished shoes and a big smile. The pen in his top pocket was the first thing I remembered when I saw Grantley.

Grantley came right over to me and introduced himself! From that day over 50 years ago, we developed a friendship that continues today. Grantley is a man of order and comes straight to the point with his opinions, but he is very funny, honest, and genuine. Grantley was an excellent impersonator of teachers and would have a room in fits of laughter.

Our interest in music stemmed from our early days at school. We would spend time pretending the tables were our drums and playing the reggae songs of that time on them. This led us to build a small sound system with Tony Bailey, Patrick Walker, and Winston Hales.

Enjoy reading Grantley's new book; bless up, my friend!"

Matt Flint – Digital Marketing Consultant - *Grantley "GT" Haynes is the epitome of professionalism and warmth, a rare combination that sets him apart in both his professional and personal endeavors. I had the privilege of working with GT for a decade in what started as a standard collaboration but soon blossomed into a friendship that I cherish deeply. From the very beginning, his passion for his work was evident. He brings not only extensive knowledge to the table but also a kindness that makes everyone feel valued and understood.*

GT has an uncanny ability to simplify the most complex concepts, guiding clients, colleagues and friends alike with patience and genuine care. His attention to detail is remarkable, and he approaches everything with the same level of dedication and enthusiasm, whether it's a routine project or a major life challenge. It's no wonder that he's become such an inspirational figure to so many.

Beyond his professional prowess, what truly sets GT apart is his commitment to the community. He's always finding ways to give back, using his expertise and resources to support local initiatives and empower others. His work in the community is a reflection of his generous spirit, and he never hesitates to lend a helping hand, whether it's mentoring young talent or contributing to causes close to his heart.

GT's warmth and positivity are infectious. Working

with him is a joy because he not only elevates the project but also the people around him. I am proud to call him both a colleague and a friend for life. His impact on my professional and personal life has been profound, and I am constantly inspired by his drive, compassion, and unwavering support for those around him.

Grantley Haynes, or GT as we know him, is truly a gem—an inspiration and a friend in the truest sense.

Purdy Bogal – Professional Sound Engineer – "Grantley Haynes significantly impacted my early experiences in the music industry, especially when recording Pato Banton's first album, "Never Give In", in Birmingham in 1985.

Remarkably, GT's professionalism and attention to detail during the recording sessions were at the highest level; we also consistently worked at building relationships with musicians and collaborators to improve the product constantly.

GT went on to manage artists like Tippa Irie and Peter Spence, showcasing GT's versatility and skills in the music business.

GT's reliability and trustworthiness speak volumes about his character and capabilities in handling various aspects of the music industry, from dealing with promoters and venue managers to interacting with record company executives.

It's invaluable to have someone like GT who can navigate such a complex and competitive industry with ease.

It's clear that Grantley Haynes has left a lasting impression on me, and it's wonderful to hear about his positive impact on younger artists' careers and the music industry as a whole.

I recommend Grantley Haynes to handle your music business management."

Miss Aliyah – Student and Vocalist – *"I have been given a chance to be myself and to do something challenging, but at the same time, it gives me so much joy. It all started in November last year when I was first introduced to Grantley. I was so shy as I was told who he manages and had seen some of his artists.*

I met Grantley again in the New Year; this time, he asked me to sing, which started my incredible journey.

The first lesson I had with Grantley, I remember feeling so shy and nervous because I didn't want to blow my chance with him, and I didn't want him to think that I couldn't learn a song, so I sang the lyrics, and he gave me some feedback. Each lesson thereafter, we did the same kind of thing, and not only did my knowledge of music grow, but my confidence did, too. Over time, I accomplished things I never even thought possible with my voice and the performing side. We even went to his studio a few times, and there, we wrote songs and recorded them. When I listened back, I was taken aback at the fact that it was me, but I soon came to my senses and started looking for areas for improvement. So, above all, I would like to thank Grantley for all that he has done because it matters, and he genuinely cares. Thank you."

Mr and Mrs Large (Parents of Lucy Tennyson) – *"During the past three years, we have had the pleasure of watching our daughter Lucy develop her dreams and talents under the guidance of Grantley Haynes.*

Their first meeting occurred on the Wheeler Street Bus, where Lucy expressed a desire to sing but admitted to a lack of confidence. This lack of confidence was immediately overcome when Grantley coached Lucy to perform on the spot in front of all present.

Lucy developed an early belief in Grantley due to his honest, intelligent and polite approach. We quickly mirrored this view despite early natural parental concerns.

At our first meeting, Grantley explained his various professional positions and offered to coach Lucy to perform at an upcoming Ball by Wheeler Street. After conducting some research, it was clear that Lucy was in a privileged position to work with someone who had selflessly achieved such extraordinary things.

Grantley's sincerity was evident to us at an early stage, which allowed both parties to communicate easily and honestly.

Not only has Grantley identified with Lucy's ability and potential, but he has also coached and managed her to the point where today, Lucy is recognised and respected as both a Singer and Songwriter.

The ranges of skills which have been formed and enhanced include:

vocals, studio performance and education, ability to perform live, song-writing, social media marketing and interview techniques.

Today, Lucy and Grantley enjoy a professional relationship that has taken them to the point where their regular interviews on Radio Stations in all major cities are coupled with consistent airplay. As Lucy's parents, we remain grateful and supportive of the proud position they have both put us in."

Lucy Tennyson – Radiographer and Vocalist –
"Three years ago, I returned to my friend's house after going to the local shop and passed a bus parked in the street.

We were approached by a man I now know as Grantley Haynes, who was running a youth bus in the community. After talking to Grantley, we discussed my ambition of becoming a singer. Grantley is my manager, an excellent friend, and a confidant.

He has opened up opportunities and introduced me to my chosen career choice.

Grantley is teaching me that the music industry is challenging, demanding and rewarding.

After hearing my song being played on the radio for the first time, I felt excited but also very surreal. But natural. At this point, I realised it was what I wanted to do. Once the song started getting airplay, I was asked to do radio interviews, where I met people like Little Richie, who has been a massive support, along with many outstanding people I've worked with, such as Tippa Irie.

Grantley has shown and still shows that anything is possible with determination and that the only person to stop you from fulfilling your dreams is yourself. I would only be starting this journey with Grantley's drive, determination and work ethic.

I feel blessed and privileged to have met him and to be working with Grantley Haynes."

With love, Modern Minds – Alternative Rock Band – "Matt Flint from Yogurt Top contacted us in early 2014, asking if we could arrange a meeting with GT. We immediately hit it off! We were recording our debut EP at the studio a couple of wheeks later and making a plan for the coming year. We all know we have *a great friendship and business partnership with GT.*

GT has often surprised us by doing things we did not expect as a manager. We booked gigs that we thought we could never get, and we went the extra mile when recording the EP to ensure we got the "perfect sound"! The great thing about GT is that if he states we can achieve something, it immediately materialises. He does not say things for the sake of it!

When it comes to making deals, GT's your man. The man is a genius when it comes down to sorting something out. Not only did GT help the band, but he also helped us become great musicians, letting us lay things down for other bands and working with different artists from the industry. GT has excellent knowledge of the music industry but doesn't keep it to himself; he often shares it with us and helps us understand how and why things work.

We have worked together for just under a year now, and it has been nothing less than extraordinary; 2015 is a big year for us, and we are chuffed to be doing something special, not just as a five-piece Indie band but as a close group of friends and family trying to take on the world."